ALLEGORY

Indispensable to an understanding of medieval and Renaissance texts and a topic of controversy for the Romantic poets, allegory remains a site for debate in the twenty-first century.

In this useful guide, Jeremy Tambling:

- presents a concise history of allegory, providing numerous examples from medieval forms to the present day
- considers the relationship between allegory and symbolism
- analyses the use of allegory in modernist debate and deconstruction, looking at critics such as Walter Benjamin and Paul de Man
- provides a full glossary of technical terms.

Allegory offers an accessible, clear introduction to the history and use of this complex literary device. It is the ideal tool for all those seeking a greater understanding of texts that make use of allegory and of the significance of allegorical thinking to literature.

Jeremy Tambling is Professor of Literature at the University of Manchester, and author of several books on literature and literary and cultural theory. His most recent books include *RE:Verse: Turning towards Poetry* (2007) and *Going Astray: Dickens and London* (2008).

THE NEW CRITICAL IDIOM

SERIES EDITOR: JOHN DRAKAKIS, UNIVERSITY OF STIRLING

The New Critical Idiom is an invaluable series of introductory guides to today's critical terminology. Each book:

- provides a handy, explanatory guide to the use (and abuse) of the term
- offers an original and distinctive overview by a leading literary and cultural critic
- relates the term to the larger field of cultural representation.

With a strong emphasis on clarity, lively debate and the widest possible breadth of examples, *The New Critical Idiom* is an indispensable approach to key topics in literary studies.

Also available in this series:

ALLEGORY

Jeremy Tambling

Routledge
Taylor & Francis Group

LONDON AND NEW YORK

First published 2010 by Routledge
2 Park Square, Milton Park, Abingdon, OX14 4RN

Simultaneously published in the USA and Canada by Routledge
270 Madison Ave, New York, NY 10016

Routledge is an imprint of the Taylor & Francis Group, an informa business

Typeset in Garamond by Taylor & Francis Books
Printed and bound in Great Britain by TJ International Ltd, Padstow,
Cornwall

British Library Cataloguing in Publication Data
A catalogue record for this book is available from the British Library

Library of Congress Cataloging in Publication Data
Tambling, Jeremy.
   Allegory / Jeremy Tambling. – 1st ed.
      p. cm. – (The new critical idiom)
   Includes bibliographical references and index.
   1. Allegory. I. Title.
   PN56.A5T36 2009
   895.6'1008–dc22
   809.915   2009005278

ISBN10: 0-415-34005-5 (hbk)
ISBN10: 0-415-34006-3 (pbk)
ISBN10: 0-203-46212-2 (ebk)

ISBN13: 978-0-415-34005-2 (hbk)
ISBN13: 978-0-415-34006-9 (pbk)
ISBN13: 978-0-203-46212-6 (ebk)

Contents

SERIES EDITOR'S PREFACE

The New Critical Idiom is a series of introductory books which seeks to extend the lexicon of literary terms, in order to address the radical changes which have taken place in the study of literature during the last decades of the twentieth century. The aim is to provide clear, well-illustrated accounts of the full range of terminology currently in use, and to evolve histories of its changing usage.

The current state of the discipline of literary studies is one where there is considerable debate concerning basic questions of terminology. This involves, among other things, the boundaries which distinguish the literary from the non-literary; the position of literature within the larger sphere of culture; the relationship between literatures of different cultures; and questions concerning the relation of literary to other cultural forms within the context of interdisciplinary studies.

It is clear that the field of literary criticism and theory is a dynamic and heterogeneous one. The present need is for individual volumes on terms which combine clarity of exposition with an adventurousness of perspective and a breadth of application. Each volume will contain as part of its apparatus some indication of the direction in which the definition of particular terms is likely to move, as well as expanding the disciplinary boundaries within which some of these terms have been traditionally contained. This will involve some re-situation of terms within the larger field of cultural representation, and will introduce examples from the area of film and the modern media in addition to examples from a variety of literary texts.

Acknowledgements

Many of the ideas in this book have been tried out on students, first in Comparative Literature at the University of Hong Kong, where the first draft was completed, and again in Manchester. Thanks are due to all those who have listened, and contributed, and who have helped with this book by reading either parts of it, or the whole of it, or who have suggested examples, or ideas: Ackbar Abbas, Jonathan Hall, Ian Fong, Paul Fung, Samuel Jenkins, Paul Kong, Pam Morris, Robert Spencer and Alfie Brown have all taken a hand at this. My family have looked on with interest and helpfulness and with a nice sense of irony. Particular thanks are due to John Drakakis, the series editor, first for accepting the project, and second for making substantial improvements at various stages with very rigorous, informed and useful comments. This book is for Louis Lo.

INTRODUCTION

I could never understand allegories. The two words in the language I most respect are yes and no.

(Henry James, 1995: 235)

Until recently, modern study of literature paid little attention to allegory, unless specialist work was being done on a religious, 'serious' writer like Spenser, or Langland, or Bunyan. Reading for allegory was regarded as getting in the way of an immediate response to a text, missing out on its vital, literal sense. The attitude of Mrs Touchett, the commonsensical American in Henry James's *The Portrait of a Lady* (1881), was typical, and still is with some: it likes a plain 'yes' or 'no'. Even medievalists played down the presence of allegory in medieval texts, where its presence could be expected. Allegorical implications in later texts, such as Daniel Defoe's *Robinson Crusoe* (1719) and Swift's *Gulliver's Travels* (1726) or George Orwell's *Animal Farm* (1945) were regarded as special cases. The old prejudice against allegory was both that it insisted on putting one thing in the place of another, saying that A meant B, and that this connection was rigidly, and rather abstractly, coded.

The situation is different now. Realism as a literary technique no longer seems so much to be a 'natural' form of writing, but has come under intense scrutiny as something artificial in its own way. Allegory has been reclaimed as a term within recent debates in literary and cultural studies. The assumption that it is an artificial device no longer seems so problematic, so that the word is now more prominent in literary use than it has been for some time. 'Allegory' has a broad set of meanings, but, since these have shifted in the last thirty years or so, there is now no consensus on how to approach it. Newer approaches, for example those associated with Walter Benjamin and Paul de Man, threaten to unsettle older senses of allegory altogether.

This book begins with examples of allegory, and then defines it abstractly, while definitions of technical terms used throughout appear in the glossary. The introduction considers some of the problems of allegory, before I look at its history in subsequent chapters; here I consider how allegory, though it exploits a punning and deceptive aspect of language, nevertheless is associated with great seriousness, and embodies abstract ideas. The introduction concludes with the question of the difference between reading for the literal sense and reading allegorically. Perhaps giving a definition of allegory may be misleading: perhaps there is no definite thing called 'allegory', only forms of writing more or less 'allegorical'. What is meant by 'allegory' within the discourses included in the 'new critical idiom' ranges, perhaps, from defining certain specific texts or types of texts, to claiming that all literature, and all writing, is allegorical.

The first example of allegory is taken from the opening of one of the most famous allegories of all:

> Nel mezzo del cammin di nostra vita
> mi ritrovai per una selva oscura
> che la diritta via era smarrita.
> (In the middle of the journey of our life I came to myself in a dark wood where the straight way was lost.)
>
> (Sinclair, 1948a: 22–23)

The speaker begins in the middle of a wood where he is lost, and since he does not explain how he came there, the poem also starts in the middle. The first line indicates a time: when he was thirty-five, having journeyed halfway through the seventy years of the Bible's specification of the life of man (Psalm 90.10). Life as a journey means that a temporal process is being explained as a movement from place to place. That is allegorical: putting one thing (time) in terms of another (space), and it appears at the beginning of another allegory, where life is explained by another term, a journey, drawing to the reader's attention the movement from one stage of life to the next (he has been young, he will be old). The text begins not at the beginning, but in the middle of this. The 'I' is already inside a wood full of shadows, caused by the loss of light, and has begun to realize it. The second line identifies a physical location and emphasizes the speaker's own self-reflective stance: 'I found myself, I came to myself'. The third line extends the metaphor of the journey in recognizing that 'life' is no longer a straight road, and that what was once perceived to be direct and right is now not so; this carries with it a series of moral implications (the light which is lost is good, desirable, and no longer attainable). The dark wood expresses an inner turmoil: if the road is lost, so is the 'I', with regard to his inner life which is portrayed in the figure of the wood.

This allegory, the opening of Dante's *Inferno*, and so the beginning of the entire *Commedia* (*c.*1310–21) begins 'in the middle' and moves sequentially from there. It seems that in saying 'mi ritrovai' – 'I found myself' – the middle of his life turns out to mean all his life; there is no sense of any origin of life, so that the origin is no more than a dark forest. Dante (1265–1321) writes about the year 1300 in the first line, and looks back to that date. The writing develops as a narrative through time, putting everything into a *metonymic* sequence, where one thing follows another in time, displacing what has gone before. Before leaving Dante for a further example, it should also be said that he is not only a very complex allegorist but a theorist of allegory; how this impacts on the *Commedia* appears in chapter 1.

The following quotation provides an example of another form of allegory, from the opening of *The Nether World* (1889), a novel about working-class London life, by George Gissing (1857–1903). An old man walks through Clerkenwell Green, past a burial-ground, and comes to an 'arched gateway closed with black doors':

> He looked at the gateway, then fixed his gaze upon something that stood just above – something which the dusk half concealed, and by so doing, made more impressive. It was the sculptured counterfeit of a human face, that of a man distraught with agony. The eyes stared wildly from their sockets, the hair struggled in maniac disorder, the forehead was wrung with torture, the cheeks sunken, the throat fearsomely wasted, and from the wide lips there seemed to be issuing a horrible cry. Above this hideous effigy was carved the legend: 'MIDDLESEX HOUSE OF CORRECTION'.
>
> (Gissing, 1992: 2)

The man stands in front of a prison. The face sculpted above the doorway can be interpreted in several ways: as a figure of judgement, like a figure of the damned, as a mirror of the man looking at it, or as his other self. The face is an image of the madness the prison produces, on top of torture and pain, and shows what mental torment awaits inside. It shows the need of the society to supplement the prison with a visual representation of its horrors. The face personifies the prison, in such a way that the words which name the prison can be placed above it, and because no cry of horror issues from the lips of the statue it seems to be also a figure of death. The imagined cry makes a joke out of the epigraph, 'Middlesex House of Correction': it is ironic for correction to produce horror. The contorted face shows what correction in this society really means.

Gissing places this sculpted head at the beginning of his book with as much deliberateness as the prison architects. The image indicates what awaits in *The Nether World*, both for its inhabitants, who, though outside, are like the people in prison, and for the reader, who is like the man 'reading' the sculpture. The title of the book is also allegorical, suggesting that conditions in nineteenth-century working-class London are like those in Dante's Hell, so that the allegorical, Laocoon-like face supplements another allegory. This allegorical image is *metaphorical* in character: it creates a sense of a resemblance which is not consciously remarked on, nor is it developed later by association with anything else. It does not work metonymically, linking one idea to another, so it is unlike Dante's allegory.

The face supplements the message the prison's physical existence conveys by providing a particularized, horrific image of it. And 'image' suggests that the head, because it stands for it, symbolizes the prison, while a prison is both a real structure of bricks and mortar to contain people and an abstraction, a state of confinement, which does not necessarily imply that the person feeling such confinement must be physically imprisoned. Gissing, like Dickens before him, makes prison-existence allegorical of the conditions of modern urban, industrial, life in the conditions of nineteenth-century capitalism. The face, as an expressive mask, allegorizes both the actual, real prison and the allegorical one. While the disembodied, contorted face functions as a deterrent to wrong-doers, it also personifies everything the prison stands for. The connection between wrongdoing, incarceration, and the suffering that punishment produces, is seen in the mask as a simple personification of what the prison means. A series of several, but causally connected, meanings are unified in one image, one personification. Personification is a particular type of allegory, so particular that some critics question whether it should be thought of as allegory at all (Maresca, 1993: 21–40). While taking up that argument later, I will, in order to present personification, assume throughout that it is an allegorical mode, providing concrete forms for complex, abstract ideas which it makes recognizable. This 'counterfeit of a human face' is artificial but it stands for everything the prison represents, from the abstract idea of justice to the concrete effects of its operation upon human inmates.

A third example gives a definition of allegory. In the comedy *The Rivals* (1775), by Richard Brinsley Sheridan (1751–1816), Mrs Malaprop says of another character, 'She's as headstrong as an allegory on the banks of the Nile.' Mrs Malaprop's name, derived from the adjective 'malapropos' ('inopportune, inappropriate' – *OED*) has created a neologism: a 'malapropism', 'the ludicrous misuse of words, especially in mistaking a word for one like it' (*OED*). Her name declares her character, her linguistic mistake having several layers of meaning. She intends to say alligator, but says allegory; but she means crocodile, since alligators do not live in the Nile. The comparison she formulates for someone who is headstrong is inappropriate, and the result is an example of catachresis. These displacements of language provide a definition of what happens in allegory, for at its simplest, allegory is a way of saying one thing and meaning another; however, her observation fulfils a function of allegory in that she tries to establish a connection between human stubbornness ('headstrong') and a reptile noted for its fierce self-interest. She performs the process of allegory by eliding 'allegory' and 'alligator' and 'crocodile' as the bearers of a universal human characteristic. Her choice of words, born out of geographical ignorance, inadvertently indicates what allegory does. 'Allegory' derives from the Greek word *allegoreo*, formed from *allos* (other) and *agoreuo*, (to speak in a place of assembly, the *agora*, the marketplace). The 'other meaning' of allegory may conceal a secret significance, in that it may persuade readers to probe for another meaning, it may enrich the meaning that has been given, or it may draw attention to a split between the surface meaning and what is underneath.

In the words 'she's as headstrong as an allegory', the conjunction 'as' introduces a *simile*. If the words indicating that a comparison is being made are discarded, that is a *metaphor*. A metaphor sustained, and developed, is *allegory*. Allegory describes one thing under the image of another, or speaks one thing while implying something else. A simile keeps the two terms of the comparison apart: the headstrong woman / the alligator. In metaphor, the word has been transferred from its literal signification. The slash-line marking a difference between the two sides of the comparison has disappeared. The words are interchangeable, or an exchange takes place whereby one word replaces the other. A textbook simile comes from Robert Burns (1759–96):

> O my Luve's like a red, red rose
> That's newly sprung in June:
> O my Luve's like the melodie
> That's sweetly play'd in tune ...

The simile is transformed into a metaphor, in William Blake's 'The Sick Rose':

> O Rose thou art sick!

That Blake (1757–1827) does not mean a literal rose is apparent from the apostrophe 'O Rose'. The rose may be a woman, but it is not certain, for the poem is too open-ended for definition, although the pronoun 'thou' suggests a personification of the 'rose', the poem's addressee.

An example of an allegory with a 'rose' theme is the French medieval poem *The Romance of the Rose*, begun by Guillaume de Lorris (*c.*1212–37) and finished by Jean de Meun (*c.*1237–1305). In its 21,780 lines, a Lover narrates his existence in the Garden of Delight, attempting to reach the Rose, who is the desired woman. Everyone in the Garden exists as a personification of qualities that either help or resist the Lover (Amant). For instance, the character of Fair Welcome (Bel Aceuil) stands for the spirit in the woman who is ready to yield to him, but Jealousy and Shame and Fear are also present, and Jealousy builds a castle to lock up Fair Welcome and the Rose. The meaning here is that the Lady's jealousy over her lover's faithfulness prevents her from being susceptible to him. The sustained nature of the personifications is sufficient to make this an allegory, but also, the reader is always being invited by the text to read it for secret, other meanings. *The Romance of the Rose* was immensely influential: on Dante, and on Chaucer (*c.*1340–1400), who translated it, and used it, especially in his dream-poetry. It also contributed to works of allegory central to literature of the sixteenth century, such as Spenser's *The Faerie Quene*, to be discussed in chapter 3. Paul de Man, whose theories of allegory will be discussed in chapter 6, claims its influence on Rousseau in the eighteenth century (de Man 1983: 202–5).

The narrative of *The Romance of the Rose* appears in the form of a dream. This raises questions about the relation of the allegorical figures who are also dream-figures to the truth which can be perceived in waking reality. It is as if the dream gives freedom to writers of allegory, and as if dreams have a fluidity which yields a special form of allegory. This relation of dream to allegory, also present in Bunyan's *The Pilgrim's Progress* (discussed in chapter 3), extends to Freud's *The Interpretation of Dreams* (1900), which interprets dreaming allegorically, since the images which persist through the extended action of the dream stand for other psychic agencies, which, repressed in the unconscious, can only appear in a figurative mode. The critic Hayden White, discussing utterance in language in terms of its tropes (figures of speech), supplements this intuition about the displacement, within a dream, of one figure by another by saying that 'all dreams are ironical – saying one thing but meaning another – in the way that poetic allegories are ironical' (White, 1999: 107). Since allegory says one thing and means another, it seems to be on the side of hidden meanings, riddles, and enigmas. Both allegory and irony trade in concealed meanings, suggesting that there is something within language itself, which when it is used, involves forms of deception, doubleness and punning.

ALLEGORY AND MEANING

Maureen Quilligan associates allegory with wordplay and punning, beginning with the point that in personification, such as with a name like Mrs Malaprop, words are already being wrested out of their normal grammatical uses (Quilligan, 1979: 33–51). Allegory becomes a form of self-conscious play within language generally, which Quilligan aligns with the verbal reflexivity of comedy (Quilligan: 282–84). This view of allegory as play may explain some of the hostility directed against it as being non-serious, merely fictitious. For example, Plato (427–348 BCE) expresses hostility to allegory through Socrates, in the *Republic* (*c*.380 BCE). Socrates talks specifically about the education that children should have; he does not want them to have to listen to stories about the gods, saying that 'Children cannot distinguish between what is allegory [*hyponoia*: "undersense", "undermeaning"] and what isn't' (Plato 378D, 1955: 116). This comment implies a split between literature and philosophy. Socrates, in Plato's writing, fears that literature, because it carries double senses, at the level of meaning and at the level of the language in which those meanings are contained, may be destabilizing, offering dangerous meanings inadmissible to adult common sense which expects language to convey a single truth. Socrates rejects the claims of 'literature' in favour of the 'truth' of philosophy and initiates a still continuing hostility between philosophy and literature. His fear is that poetry deploys language in such a way that it invites a variety of interpretations; and his dislike of *hyponoia* signals that literature may encourage a proliferation of meanings that could be regarded as a danger to the political stability of the ideal republic: hence Socrates' hostility towards both allegory and poetry in Plato's *Republic*.

Yet allegory is often associated with thoroughly 'serious' or 'moral' or nationalistic images. The figure of Justice above the Old Bailey in London, blindfolded and with scales and a sword, is an allegorical representation of the processes of the law as impartial, scrupulously weighing evidence, and possessed of the power to punish. The Statue of Liberty's uplifted torch shows that America is a beacon to other nations, providing the light of freedom. Cupid stands in London's Piccadilly Circus, at the end of Shaftesbury Avenue, as the God of love, though the sculptor, Albert Gilbert, intended him for serious purpose, to symbolize Christian charity, as a memorial to the Victorian Lord Shaftesbury (Gombrich, 1972: 1–5). Since to personify requires making a genderchoice, the feminine nature of Justice or Liberty supplements the ideological effect that these statues have, for no detail about an allegorical figure has been chosen innocently or accidentally. Sir Joshua Reynolds (1723–1892), the first president of the Royal Academy, painted the actress Sarah Siddons (1755–1831) as *The Tragic Muse* (1784) (Penny, 1986: 324–26). This depiction of the Muse has a history behind it, for stage acting often represents 'the passions': hence Hamlet speaks of bad actors who 'tear a passion to tatters' (3.2.10), while Thisbe's suicide over the body of Pyramus in *A Midsummer Night's Dream* is called a 'passion' (5.1.303). In Dickens's *Great Expectations* (1861), Mr Wopsle, wanting to become an actor, gives public readings of William Collins (1721–59)'s 'Ode on the Passions' (1746). Pip, the narrator, says

> I particularly venerated Mr Wopsle as Revenge, throwing his blood-stained sword in thunder down, and taking the War-denouncing trumpet with a withering look.
>
> (Dickens, 1965: 74)

The Penguin editor, Angus Calder, quotes the passage from Collins, where the 'Passions' contest each other:

Revenge impatient rose,
He threw his blood-stain'd Sword in Thunder down,
And with a with'ring Look,
The War-denouncing Trumpet took,
Were ne'er Prophetic Sounds so full of Woe ...

(Dickens, 1965: 501)

Capitalization of the names associates the passions with allegory. Mr Wopsle's acting personifies the passions, as does Mrs Siddons's. If such passions as Anger, Envy and Revenge are considered, it seems that all passions or emotional states are to be thought of as personifications, and therefore as allegorical. The capitalization serves to personify an emotion, and it is the process of expansion here that gives their personification its allegorical significance. Revenge has been gendered as masculine and war-like through personification.

Reynolds paints Mrs Siddons seated on a classical throne resting upon clouds, in the manner of a deity. The picture is recognizably baroque in its ornate depiction of a divine force. Indeed, the baroque, as an artistic, architectural and literary movement associated with seventeenth-century Europe, is distinguished by its frequent use of allegory. Baroque churches in Italy and Spain displayed painted heavens on their ceilings showing kings being raised up in apotheosis, attended by goddesses, or Fame, or the Spirit of Empire. The baroque ceiling plays on the difference between the natural and the spiritual world, trying, through a trick of architecture and perspective (i.e. through *trompe l'oeil*: 'deceive the eye'), to pretend that the roof does not exist. This enables the spectator to progress, to rise up in vision from the solid, quotidian world of architecture to the reality of the heavens as they exist to the spiritual eye (Harbison, 2000: 24). One historian of the baroque writes that 'of all the uses of allegory, the most spectacular was the glorification of the earthly ruler' (Martin, 1971: 140).

Mrs Siddons's pose follows the design of Michelangelo's Isaiah in the Sistine Chapel. A figure behind her, on the right of the picture, holds a cup; he is modelled on the allegorical representation of Fear, as shown in the 1734 translation by John Williams of the treatise on the passions written by the painter Charles Le Brun

(1619–90). Another figure, to the left, holding a dagger, is modelled on a similarly placed companion of Jeremiah in the Sistine Chapel. The cup and the dagger were traditional components that accompanied Melpomene, the Muse of Tragedy, and were so used in Renaissance emblem books (these are discussed in chapter 3). These flanking figures stand for Pity and Terror, the two passions that according to Aristotle were inspired by tragedy. The tragic muse – Mrs Siddons – arouses tragic passions as much as she acts them out. The atmosphere of awe is emphasized by the Rembrandt-inspired darkness in the picture.

The allegorical representation of Mrs Siddons points to a seriousness associated with tragedy as a dramatic and literary form, but in *Hard Times* (1854) Dickens, witty about allegory as he was in *Great Expectations*, draws upon its baroque associations in creating his own allegorical image. The plot involves Mrs Sparsit's jealousy of Louisa, who has been married off to Mr Bounderby, whom she herself was engineering to marry. Louisa's marriage is obviously loveless, and Mrs Sparsit gives way to her imagination, hoping that she will commit adultery with the upper-class James Harthouse:

> Mrs Sparsit was not a poetical woman; but she took an idea, in the nature of an allegorical fancy, into her head. Much watching of Louisa, and much consequent observation of her impenetrable demeanour, which keenly whetted and sharpened Mrs Sparsit's edge, must have given her as it were a lift, in the way of inspiration. She erected in her mind a mighty Staircase, with a dark pit of shame and ruin at the bottom; and down those stairs, from day to day and hour to hour, she saw Louisa coming.
>
> (Dickens, 1969: 226–27)

This picture which Mrs Sparsit's prurience summons up, of a staircase going down towards the netherworld of Victorian sinful sexuality, so turning Louisa into a social outcast, inverts the baroque idea of going up to Heaven in an apotheosis. But the architecture of the staircase is equally baroque. Dickens not only makes fun of Mrs Sparsit, who wants Louisa to go down the staircase, but implies, by referring to the 'allegorical fancy', that he may be writing allegory himself, while critiquing the 'serious' and 'educative' pretensions that allegory normally possesses. Dickens the allegorist will be discussed in chapter 4. Playful about the passions as Collins or Reynolds conceptualized them, he makes Mrs Sparsit a representative of passions herself: Envy, Malice and Sexual Frustration.

ALLEGORY AND ABSTRACTION

'Serious' uses of allegory come about because allegory makes abstract ideas appear real, forceful. An example of this appears in the personification drawn on by Macbeth in a speech remembering what happened when he murdered the sleeping king, Duncan:

> Methought I heard a voice cry 'Sleep no more;
> Macbeth does murder sleep, the innocent sleep,
> Sleep that knits up the ravelled sleeve of care,
> The death of each day's life, sore labour's bath,
> Balm of hurt minds, great nature's second course,
> Chief nourisher in life's feast ... '   (2.2.34–39)

Macbeth's speech, and the 'voice' which is part of his conscience, and which he hallucinates, shows his appalled realization that in killing Duncan while he was sleeping he has effectively murdered 'sleep' itself. Duncan himself, whether alive or dead, has become an allegory of Sleep. The speech first uses sleep as a verb, but its next three uses, as a noun, transform the abstract quality 'sleep' into a person. Nouns, we know, are *proper*, naming one person, or *common*, where, subdivided into *concrete* and *abstract*, they refer either to what is tangible or to qualities not accessed through the senses. If sleep is 'innocent', the adjective says something more about it. If it knits up a ravelled sleeve it is an active subject, an agency; this goes further than saying it is innocent. If it knits up 'the ravelled sleeve of care', that includes another allegorization: an allegorical figure of Sleep repairs the entangled 'sleave' (silk) of another allegorical figure, that of Care. This personification is always, in Renaissance emblematic pictures (see chapter 3), shown leaning on his elbow, so creating a hole in the sleeve. If sleep is 'the death of each day's life', death in the abstract becomes concrete in the form of the temporal movement from day to night. It also becomes a regenerative 'bath' that refreshes and cleanses. Macbeth's regicide cuts him off from sleep's beneficent qualities, condemning him to a living death.

Shakespeare's text at this point is allegorical, in the service of wholly intense, serious language. But abstractions can be played with, as in Lewis Carroll (1832–98)'s *Alice's Adventures in Wonderland* (1865), which parodies Shakespeare while bringing out some of the duplicities involved in language which relies on abstraction. It records a dream, in which Alice's attempts to get into the garden may be compared with the plot of *The Romance of the Rose*. In chapter 6, 'A Mad Tea-Party', Alice says that the March Hare 'might do something better with the time than waste it in asking riddles that have no answer'.

> 'If you knew Time as well as I do,' said the Hatter, 'you wouldn't talk about wasting *it*. It's *him*.'
>
> 'I don't know what you mean,' said Alice.
>
> 'Of course you don't!' the Hatter said. 'I dare say you never even spoke to Time.'
>
> 'Perhaps not,' Alice cautiously replied, 'but I know I have to beat time when I learn music.'

The Hatter says that 'Time won't stand beating' and tells how he was singing at a concert given by the Queen of Hearts:

> 'Well, I'd hardly finished the first verse,' said the Hatter, 'when the Queen bawled out "He's murdering the time! Off with his head!"'
>
> 'How dreadfully savage!' exclaimed Alice.
>
> 'And ever since that,' the Hatter went on in a mournful voice, 'he won't do a thing I ask! It's always six o'clock now.'
>
> (Gardner, 1970: 97–99)

To 'murder time' is a technical phrase meaning 'to mangle the metre of a song', and the allusion recalls Macbeth murdering sleep. If we follow Maureen Quilligan's argument, we see how allegory works linguistically, since virtually any abstract word can be turned into a proper noun (time becomes Time), so that, as a proper name, it can participate in a narrative. Macbeth's speech transfers what he has murdered from the person of Duncan to the abstract quality of sleep. Lewis Carroll shows how ordinary verbs have no narrowly fixed sense, but play their part in a world where everything, including abstract nouns, is equally tangible. What happens when an abstract idea becomes allegorical, which happens all the time in English? For example, is 'common sense' an allegorical expression? If something is 'opposed to common sense', the grammar makes 'common sense' a sentient force, an agency. If a politician tells the electorate that 'Common sense tells me that this is the way we should go,' he is drawing on personification allegory: Common Sense has become the subject, independent of the speaker, thinking, acting independently. Just how deceptive that allegorization may be is illustrated by the politician's language, which draws on an abstract concept to obscure his real motivations. It seems impossible to think outside such allegorizing when allegorical constructions form part of normal grammar: 'History teaches us ... ' or 'Love inspires me ... '. All types of language use incline towards allegory, whose existence indicates the impossibility of keeping an abstract conception, or construction, abstract. Thinking, which happens within figures of speech, becomes allegorical, giving a visual or linguistic shape to the abstract, which is perceived as personified and personifying, allegorical, creating allegory, and effacing the difference between the abstract and its embodiment as a figure.

LITERAL AND ALLEGORICAL READINGS

The dialogue between Alice and the Mad Hatter, and the intervention by the Queen, show different forms of understanding Time, or time, whether taking it as an abstract idea or as a personification. The Queen's interruption has created Time as a person or agency who must be taken literally, and not allegorically. Alice repeats the Mad Hatter's muddle, which confuses the issue of Time as real, as a person, or a signifier, a word in a sentence, that causes the Queen's intervention. This prompts the question: are literal readings and allegorical readings opposite to each other? Here, the division between literal and allegorical readings is not clear cut, because the Mad Hatter insists upon a strictly literal meaning in his use of the signifier, 'time' as it appears in language use, as a personification. Perhaps that is why he is mad: he lives with language itself as real, completely material, as a thing in itself, rather than passing to what it signifies conceptually. If this argument is followed through, to live and to talk in the language of allegory, making and taking abstractions as real – 'time' becoming 'Time', a real 'he' for the Hatter – may be to live in a mad language, which is not recognized as such when the literature of allegory operates within definite conventions.

We can say that reading involves choices, deciding, perhaps unconsciously, what should be taken literally, at face value, and what should be taken allegorically. In the history of reading, the hegemonic reading of the Bible was established to be allegorical, following St Paul, who in the New Testament gives priority to allegory. In the letter to the Christians at Galatia, he attacks those who believe that Christians should obey the Law of Moses, and uses an illustration derived from Genesis (chapters 16 and 21) in the Old Testament:

> Tell me, ye that desire to be under the law, do ye not hear the law? For it is written that Abraham had two sons, the one by a bondmaid, the other by a freewoman. But he who was of the bondwoman was born after the flesh, but he of the freewoman was by promise. Which things are an allegory, for these are the two covenants, the one from the Mount Sinai, which gendereth to bondage, which is Hagar. For this Hagar is mount Sinai in Arabia, and answereth to Jersualem which now is and is in bondage with her children. But Jersualem which is above is free, which is the mother of us all.
>
> (Galatians 4.21–26)

St Paul contrasts the patriarch Abraham and his relationship with Hagar and their son Ishmael with his relationship to his wife Sarah and their son Isaac. Hagar was the slave (bondmaid) from whom Abraham had a child, Ishmael, while Sarah is the wife, from whom Abraham had Isaac, the genuine heir, promised by God. The two sons cannot coexist in the same house and Sarah causes Hagar and Ishmael to be driven out by Abraham. St Paul interprets the Old Testament to show that its events are intelligible when they are read for their inner, hidden, meaning. The historical Hagar and her son Ishmael are compared to the Israelites seen as being under the bondage of the Law of Moses, given at Sinai (in Arabia), and the Jews are said to be in bondage because they are held under the domination of the letter of the law. In contrast, Sarah and Isaac are compared to the church whose spiritual mother is 'the Jerusalem which is above', which is heavenly. The logic of St Paul's argument is that in the time of Abraham these events could only have been understood literally, but now they can be freshly interpreted by Christians who read the Old Testament allegorically.

Allegory interprets events, or reinterprets them in such a way that exceeds their literal meaning. St Paul created the tradition by which the Church Fathers, such as St Augustine (354–430 CE), felt free to generate interpretations of the Old Testament which distinguished between the *letter* and the *spirit*. Reading according to the letter is reading literally, as the Law must be interpreted literally. Reading spiritually may mean reading allegorically, realizing that the Law cannot, or can no longer, since the time of Christ, be taken as commanding in a literal sense. A spiritual reading says that the literal meaning is not as important as the allegorical message that can be derived from it. The word, the New Testament *logos*, replaces the literal Law, and can be read in a dual sense, both literally and spiritually, so that familiar everyday objects or incidents, such as those in the life of Abraham, represent a higher, invisible reality. Elsewhere (1 Corinthians 10.6), St Paul gives examples of what happened to the Israelites in the wilderness under the authority of Moses, and says that 'these things were our examples', or, more literally, 'in these things they became figures of us' (Revised Version). Indeed, the Vulgate, the Latin translation of the Bible by St Jerome (342–420 CE) turns St Paul's Greek into the words '*haec autem in figura facta sunt nostri*'. Here, the word *figura*, 'figure', renders the Greek *tupos*, from which the word 'type' derives. '*Tupos*' denotes a blow, and hence the impression, or mark of a blow, like the impress of a stamp on paper, which yields a pattern or design. Old Testament people are figures, types, patterns, and as used by St Paul, they yield typological or figural allegory, in that one event or person becomes a picture of another, with the Old Testament Israelites being pictures, or figures, or types, of New Testament Christians. Elsewhere, St Paul says that things in the Old Testament were a 'shadow' of things to come (Colossians 2.17). An earlier action becomes a pattern, or adumbration of another.

Choosing to read something allegorically begs the question of the legitimacy of that interpretation. What governs it and gives it weight, stops it from going into free fall, from becoming inter-pretation that corresponds simply to the whim of the interpreter? St Paul imposes an account on perfectly 'innocent' events which do not appear to have a logical connection with the meaning that he gives them. This freedom of interpretation within allegory has been claimed to be the marker of what distinguishes it from symbolism. Hagar and her son Ishmael can only in a very loose way be said to represent the Law of Moses; there seems to be no reason why they should do so, except that St Paul is comparing the wilderness into which they were thrown with the wilderness where the Israelites received God's law. In symbolism, it is usually argued that if one object stands in for, or resembles, another, there is some fittingness in the comparison. In the simile that a person is 'as bold as a lion', there seems to be a natural carry-over of some characteristic from the person being compared to the lion; it fits in its essential respects: that of boldness. But allegory makes no such claims; St Paul never explains why he allegorizes in the way he does. But the relationship between allegory and symbolism becomes a crux for romanticism, which made a firm distinction between the two, and this issue will be discussed further in chapter 3.

The example of reading encouraged by St Paul establishes allegory as a term with a history. That history is begun in chapter 1, which traces it up to Dante, and the English medieval poet William Langland. Chapter 2 gives a similar historical mapping of personification, as a specific and popular form of allegory. Most examples in chapters 1 and 2 come from classical and medieval literature, while later chapters, 3, 4 and 5, look at Renaissance and post-Renaissance English and American examples. There is no attempt here to look at the question of whether Chinese or Japanese literature, for instance, may be thought of as allegorical (see Plaks, 1976: 84–145). Chapter 3, moving from the Renaissance to romanticism, discusses the emblem as a form of allegory, and discusses allegory versus symbolism in romanticism. Chapter 4 looks at allegory's fate in the nineteenth century, in the age of realism, and of the modern city.

For these chapters, three studies are seminal. The first is Erich Auerbach (1892–1957)'s essay 'Figura' (1946), an essay principally on Dante, but also incorporating insights that appeared further in his book *Mimesis*. Figural readings have generated detailed studies of medieval and figural allegory in such writers as Henri de Lubac and Jean Pépin. The second study is by C. S. Lewis (1898–1963), in *The Allegory of Love* (1936), which has been influential in medieval studies that take *The Romance of the Rose* as a key text for medieval poetry. The third is Angus Fletcher's book *Allegory: The Theory of a Symbolic Mode* (1964), which extends C. S. Lewis's work by adding to it insights derived from Freud.

Chapter 5 looks at the theory of allegory advanced by Walter Benjamin (1892–1940) in *The Origin of German Tragic Drama* (*Ursprung des deutschen Trauerspiels*, 1927). Benjamin, a German-born Jewish and Marxist writer, who killed himself at the Franco-Spanish border in 1940 rather than fall into the hands of the Nazis, lived in Paris after 1927, and discussed allegory in relation to nineteenth-century Paris, specifically with reference to Charles Baudelaire's poetry, which we will encounter in chapter 4. Chapter 6 examines Paul de Man (1919–83), whose 'deconstructive' approach to allegory begins with the essay 'The Rhetoric of Temporality' (1969). This chapter will deal with the ways in which Benjamin and de Man relate to the theorists of allegory discussed in earlier chapters. Chapter 7 discusses allegory in modernism and post-modernism, and asks whether allegory may be regarded as a post-modern concept. The distinction between personification and allegory also appears here, rounding off discussion by considering what is gained, and lost, by writing in an allegorical mode, and returning to some psychoanalytic arguments proposed by Angus Fletcher.

But these questions, which involve consideration of allegory both as a formal mode of writing, and as a historical way of thinking, are implicit throughout, and they start with the allegories discussed in the next chapter. We begin with the Roman world, which produced St Paul's 'spiritualizing' of Old Testament narratives.

1

CLASSICAL AND MEDIEVAL ALLEGORY

This chapter does three things. First, it discusses the under-standing of allegory that existed in classical Roman writing, and which was passed on to the medieval world. It then discusses Dante, and the allegorical writing of the *Commedia*, looking at this in three ways: first, through the idea of fourfold allegory, which proposes that there are four ways to interpret each text; second, through the idea that allegory acts as a 'veil', and third, through a figural reading of the text. After seeing how these dif-ferent approaches offer three perspectives on Dante's allegory, it turns, finally, to another medieval allegory, *Piers Plowman*, and speculates on the reasons for, and significance of, the medieval world thinking so much in allegorical terms.

ALLEGORESIS

It was classical Roman writers who established definitions and uses of the term 'allegory'. They thought of it both as a mode of writing or speaking rhetoric, and as a form of interpretation.

Modern commentators, partly influenced by E. R. Curtius, have termed the latter *allegoresis* (Curtius, 204–5). We may gloss this term as 'interpreting a text in an allegorical manner'. It appears, then, that allegorical interpretation, as with St Paul's interpretation of the Old Testament for the Christians in Galatia, seems to be older than the conscious writing of allegory. Allegoresis predates the practice of consciously writing one thing and meaning another.

St Paul's example shows how allegorical interpretation was associated with the beginnings of Christianity in Roman times, but it goes further back: in Judaism to the commentaries on the early books of the Bible that were developed late in Old Testament times (the Midrash), and in Hellenism to Greeks such as Theagenes and Anaxagoras (500–428 BCE) who interpreted Homer (*c.* eighth century BCE) as though he had written veiled philosophy, the rational logic (*logos*) of which was perceptible underneath the story (*mythos*). That a text could be read in two ways, and that the *logos* might be more important than the *mythos*, suggests the existence of a tension between philosophy and literature. In these Greeks, in Plato, and in St Paul, much influenced by Platonism, a duality develops between literature, with its surface, or apparently 'natural', meaning, and the more 'philosophical', hidden meaning beneath. But although Plato identified allegory as a mode of reading, he was opposed to the process of allegorizing texts for specifically educational purposes.

In the first sense, as a Latin word taken over from Greek, 'allegoria' appears in Cicero (106–43 BCE) in *De Oratore* (III. xxxiv.46, xxvii.94). He defines it as continuous metaphors (*continuae tralationes*). Before Cicero, the term had appeared in the work of a near contemporary, Philodemus of Gadara (*c.*110–35 BCE) (Whitman, 1987: 264–65). Another early user of the term was Plutarch (46–120 CE), who observed that *hyponoai*, the word used by Plato, and referred to in the introduction, are now called *allegoriai*. Plutarch, looking at legends of gods such as Isis and Osiris, contended that myths should not be interpreted as though they were true accounts, but that 'we should adopt that which is appropriate in each legend in accordance with its verisimilitude' (*Moralia* 374E, quoted in Collinson, 1981: 6). This statement, when paraphrased, suggests that the truth that the legends convey is already known and that the task of interpretation is to read them so that these pre-existent truths will surface.

Cicero's primary concern in discussing allegory was to bring out ways of writing or speaking effectively and persuasively, as in oratory. He defined irony – which included sarcasm – as though it was a form of allegorical speech: as saying one thing and meaning another (*De Oratore* III.liii.203). Allegory, riddling, using allusions, and *permutatio* (alteration or substitution of terms; the word implies exchanging goods or bartering), were all identified and assembled as rhetorical devices. Cicero's successor Quintilian (*c.*35–100 CE), in his *Institutio Oratoria*, VIII.vi.44 ('The Training of an Orator'), defined allegory in such a way as to emphasize its two ways of being read; he defined it as 'a figure called inversion, where it is one in words and an other in sentence or meaning' (Fletcher, 1964: 2, quoting the translation of Thomas Elyot in his *Dictionarie* of 1559). This gap between latent and manifest meaning, between words as they appear, their lexical function, and what they may mean, their semantic function, is crucial to understanding allegory. These rhetoricians linked other tropes with allegory: 'irony', 'inversion', 'metaphor', 'translation' (Latin, translating the Greek 'metaphor'). For the medieval world, drawing on this Roman tradition, the definition of allegory that was taken over from this classical heritage was that of the seventh-century Spanish encyclopaedist, Isidore of Seville, 'Allegoria est alienoloqium, aliud enim sonat, aliud intelligutur' ('Allegory is other speech, for it occurs when one thing is said and another is understood' – *Etymologiae* 1.xxvii.22). Isidore made allegory a form of irony (Hollander, 2001: 97).

Allegorical interpretation was used, politically, to synthesize the various religions in the Roman world, Judaism and the polytheistic religions of Greece and Rome; its function was to allow for syncretism. Its exemplars include the Judaic-Hellenistic Philo of Alexandria (*c.*30 BCE–45 CE) who wrote commentaries on the Old Testament; the Christian Clement of Alexandria (*c.*150–215) and his pupil Origen (185–254); and, outstandingly, Augustine of Hippo (354–430). Philo interpreted the Old Testament both literally and figuratively, so that Abraham was made both a typical man of wisdom and, allegorically, the soul inclined to virtue and so searching for God (Collinson, 1981: 8). Where, however, the literal sense seemed puzzling or inadequate, Philo simply interpreted the text allegorically, not literally at all. As Collinson writes, 'literalists will be bothered by the eunuch Potiphar's having a wife [Genesis 39], but the passage is no problem for those, who, like Philo, read allegorically' (Collinson, 1981: 9).

Inspiration for Christian writers to interpret allegorically came from St Paul, who had written of his ministry that God 'hath made us able ministers of the new testament [or covenant], not of the letter but of the spirit, for the letter killeth, but the spirit giveth life' (2 Corinthians 3.6). This argument assumes that interpretation of the Old Testament could proceed either literally or spiritually. The Old Testament is the 'letter', which needs the supplement of another text which will interpret it allegorically and spiritually. If 'the letter kills', that is because literal interpretation, associated with Mosaic law, is death, and the text must be read outside the rigid constraints of the literal, outside the letter of the law. Thinking allegorically means escaping the material; so St Paul's successors in biblical interpretation disregarded the literal meaning of the Bible in their reading. This raises the question: what is required to guarantee the correctness of any interpretation? Augustine had an answer, in *On Christian Doctrine* (3.10,15): 'Scripture teaches nothing but charity, nor condemns anything except cupidity', therefore, 'whatever appears in the divine Word that does not literally pertain to virtuous behaviour or the truth of faith you must take to be figurative' (quoted in Robertson, 1962: 295). In other words, anything that cannot be read literally to promote the rule of charity is ironic: it must be read in a figurative manner in order to promote the overall meaning or significance of charity. This view, that any text, no matter how apparently unassimilable to Christianity, could be made to yield a Christian meaning, became influential in North America in the 1950s and 1960s, for the interpretation of medieval texts, such as *The Romance of the Rose*, or the works of Chaucer. For example, D. W. Robertson, Jr, and his followers such as J. V. Fleming, regarded medieval texts as always, secretly, if not openly, Christian, and the controversy that this occasioned

caused a reaction against allegory amongst those other medievalists who did not share such Robertson's omnivorous Christian
perspective. The source of the controversy was the claim, neither
provable nor disprovable, that a text could possess a particular
kind of secret meaning.

BEGINNING ALLEGORY

Allegory develops rapidly from a new approach to Latin classical
texts which took place during what some scholars, beginning
with Charles Homer Haskins writing in 1927, call the French
'twelfth-century Renaissance'. This included a new sense of the
importance of Plato, known directly only through the *Timaeus*,
which had been translated into Latin by Calcidius. A century
later, Greek philosophy, particularly Aristotle's works, began to
appear in translations derived from Arabic writers. The twelfth-
century writer William of Conches distinguished in a text
between the *fabula* (the fable: Latin writers had used it to translate
the Greek *mythos*) and the *integumentum*. The latter could mean the
text's hidden meaning; but the complexity of making this distinction
between the story and what clothes the story is apparent, because
the *integumentum* ('covering') could mean, as Peter Dronke has
suggested, 'both a fable that covers hidden meanings (especially
moral and cosmological ones), and the hidden meanings of the
fable themselves. The *integumentum* is primarily the covering, but
also what is covered by it – so closely are the two seen as related
in William's thought' (Dronke, 1971: 23–25).

An interest in distinguishing, and then uniting, the literal
sense and the allegorical sense appears in the writings of Bernard
Silvestris (*c.*1140). In his *Cosmographia*, 'interpretive and compo-
sitional allegory at last converge with full force, [and] decisively
transform the allegorical tradition as a whole' (Whitman, 2000:
219). In other words, the tradition of allegoresis created in its
turn a new form of writing, a text consciously written as allegory
with such concepts of interpretation in mind. Not much is
known of Bernard Silvestris, who was based in either Tours, or
Chartres. His commentary on Virgil's *Aeneid* (*c.*19 BCE) adopted
the interpretation of earlier Roman writers: Servius (late fourth

century), Prudentius (348–410), Macrobius (*c.*400), and Fulgentius (*c.*500–600) who wrote a commentary entitled, *The Exposition of the Content of Virgil According to Moral Philosophy*. Servius had allegorized Virgil according to four modes: (a) the historical, whereby the fictional poem represented real people and events; (b) the physical, where gods represented physical forces in nature; (c) the moral, where gods were identified with abstract qualities, and the text was read for ethical significance; (d), the euhemeristic, where gods were rationalized as being deified heroes, and mythological stories rationalized as historical occurrences (Jones, 1961: 217–26). For Bernard Silvestris, the first book of Virgil's *Aeneid* represented the state of infancy. The second dealt with childhood, and the third adolescence. Dante (1265–1321) takes this view over completely in his prose work the *Convivio* (*c.*1305), written before he began work on the *Commedia*. In book 4, chapter 26, Dante offers an allegorical interpretation of the *Aeneid* books 4 to 6. In this section Aeneas leaves Dido, who commits suicide, and journeys to Italy. His father, Anchises, dies, and Aeneas, before founding Rome, must descend to the underworld:

> Virgil, our greatest poet, describes Aeneas as acting in such an unbridled way [i.e. unbridled by reason] in the part of the *Aeneid* where this stage of life is symbolically portrayed [*si figura*], comprising books four through six. How Aeneas bridled himself when, after having received so much pleasure from Dido, and when experiencing delight with her, he tore himself away in order to follow an honourable, praiseworthy and beneficial course! What a spurring onward occurred when the same Aeneas had the courage to go alone with the Sibyl down into hell in quest of the soul of his father Anchises, exposing himself to so many dangers! It is clear, then, that in our maturity being perfect necessarily involves being 'temperate and strong'. A good nature produces and displays these qualities, as the text expressly says.
>
> (Dante, 1989: 190)

Dante reads Virgil's text as a charting of the ages of man, which, as a moral allegory, teaches virtue. In the quotation, the emphasis is on temperance, one of the four classical cardinal virtues. The text that Dante refers to in the words 'temperate and strong' is one of his own lyric poems, written to encourage the practice of virtue, and defining true nobility. He comments on his own poem, in order to show that it must be read allegorically.

Similarly, Bernard Silvestris wrote not only allegorical commentaries, but allegory. The *Cosmographia* is a creation myth, using allegorical figures: Natura (Nature), Noys, meaning the divine mind, or soul, and Hyle, primal matter. In the first book, the universe is formed out of primal matter into a complete order. In the second, Man, as the microcosm of the universe, comes into being through the agencies of Noys, Natura and Urania, who represents celestial knowledge. Here, the tradition of practising allegoresis offers Bernard Silvestris a particular freedom: that of being able to interpret non-Christian classical, pagan writings in such a way that they yield broadly Christian meanings. He felt no opposition between classical non-Christian texts and Christian texts, or between secular and spiritual wisdom, and although he was a Christian, he could write an allegory whose mode is syncretic, and whose personnel do not derive from Christianity. Because his mode of writing was allegorical, the disparity between the pagan and the Christian could be eliminated.

DANTE: FOURFOLD ALLEGORY

If the *Convivio* uses allegoresis to interpret Virgil's *Aeneid*, then such a reading would generate meanings that Virgil would never have suspected. The *Convivio* contains a meditation on the nature of allegory and allegoresis. For example, Dante quotes two love poems that he has written, and then interprets the woman in them as an allegory of philosophy: it is to be noted that when he quotes a poem whose subject is not love, he refrains from allegorizing his verse. There is a teasing implication in this, which is that allegory is associated with love, and this requires further exploration. But as things stand, it should be noted that Dante distinguishes two forms of allegory. The first is 'the allegory of poets', and the second 'the allegory of theologians'. He says that in the 'allegory of the poets', the quarry is the truth 'hidden under a beautiful fiction' (Dante: 1989, 43), and that there is no necessary truth in the literal story being told. But the Bible is characterized by the 'allegory of theologians', where both the literal level and the allegorical levels are true.

But both these forms of allegory are said to possess four distinct meanings within them. A fuller explanation of these four appears in a letter of perhaps around 1320, called *Epistle X*, written to the Veronese lord Can Grande della Scala, who gave Dante patronage in his exile. (The authenticity of this letter is questionable, but we will assume it for now for the sake of convenience.) *Epistle X* defines the allegory of theologians, by running through the four levels of meaning of scripture which had been argued for by such commentators as Thomas Aquinas (1225–74) in the *Summa Theologiae* 1a.q1.a.10 (Minnis in Whitman, 2000: 232–33). Dante discusses these different levels of meaning, and extends them to the interpretation of his own poem, the *Commedia*, which records a journey that Dante made through Hell, Purgatory and Paradise. Claiming that these different levels are to be found in the *Commedia*, he says that the work is therefore 'polysemous', that its meanings are multiple. These four levels comprise: the literal, the allegorical, the moral or tropological and the anagogical. Dante expounds them from Psalm 114:1,2, referring to the Old Testament narrative of the exodus of the Israelites from their captivity in Egypt:

> It must be understood that the meaning of this work is not of one kind only; rather the work may be described as 'polysemous', that is, having several meanings; for the first meaning is that which is conveyed by the letter, and the next is that which is conveyed by what the letter signifies; the former of which is called literal, while the latter is called allegorical or moral or anagogical. And for the better illustration of this method of exposition we may apply it to the following verses: 'When Israel went out of Egypt, the house of Jacob from a people of strange language, Judah was his sanctuary and Israel his dominion'. For if we consider the letter alone, the thing signified to us is the going out of the children of Israel from Egypt in the time of Moses; if the allegory, our redemption through Christ is signified; if the moral sense, the conversion of the soul from the sorrow and misery of sin to a state of grace is signified; if the anagogical, the passing of the

sanctified soul from the bondage of the corruption of this world to the liberty of everlasting glory is signified. And although these mystical meanings are called by various names, they may one and all in a general sense be termed allegorical, inasmuch as they are different from the literal or historical.

(Reynolds, 1962: 45–46)

Like other accounts we have discussed, this distinguishes first between the literal and the allegorical. The allegorical is then subdivided into three categories. The first of the three, also, confusingly, called the *allegorical*, states the spiritual meaning of the literal event, which means seeing how an Old Testament event, recorded in the Book of Exodus, prefigures a central New Testament event, i.e. the redemption of the world by Christ. The *tropological* meaning indicates what the effect should be on the reader, e.g. in terms of moral response. If the reader examines the text tropologically, s/he will know how to act and behave. The *anagogical* level of meaning implies how the things which are recorded prefigure what lies ahead for the Christian in eternal glory ('anagogy' means a 'going up'; ascending to the highest level of meaning, or destiny). These three spiritual / allegorical meanings can be further linked to teachings about the triad of spiritual qualities faith, hope and charity which comprise the theme of St Paul in 1 Corinthians 13.13. Faith appears in the allegorical meaning, which tells you what to believe, charity in the tropological, which tells you how to behave lovingly towards others, and hope in the anagogical, which tells you what you can expect in the future.

A first point to be noticed here is that allegory is no longer the 'A equals B' type which was discussed in the introduction in relation to St Paul's allegorizing in the Epistle to the Galatians. It has now become associated with diverse meanings, which may even be irreconcilable with each other. A second point is that it is difficult to limit the 'polysemous' nature of the text to the fourfold classification, or even to decide which classification fits which reading. For example, the Epistle states that the literal subject matter of the *Commedia* is the state of souls after death. Those critics who have contested its authorship point out that that is *not* the *Commedia*'s literal subject matter: literally, it is 'about' the journey that Dante takes through Hell and death's other kingdoms. And since allegory has several meanings it is even impossible to decide what 'reading literally' means. Is not a literal 'meaning' already an allegorical one, in the sense that to read about an event means to ascribe a meaning to it? The act of interpretation, because it moves outwards from the event, means taking the event allegorically. This would lead to speculation that there is no such thing as a literal reading. Indeed, since the fourfold level applies equally to the 'allegory of theologians' and the 'allegory of poets', and since the journey is – presumably – a fiction, we may ask what is going on when Dante claims to be writing not the allegory of poets but the allegory of theologians, as he does in *Epistle X*? Is he claiming that he really, literally, made the journey which is described? Those who contest Dante's authorship of the letter have exploited the issue that this question raises.

THE VEIL OF ALLEGORY

How does Dante describe the plainly allegorical moments in the *Commedia*? To answer this, I will first jump forward to one of his earliest commentators, Boccaccio (1313–75) to see what image was commonly used. Boccaccio's *Genealogia deorum gentilium* ('The Genealogy of the Gentile Gods') discusses the difference between poetry and philosophy, saying that poets, unlike philosophers, protected truth by using what he called the 'veil' of allegory. Such allegorical writing was different also from rhetorical oratory, for 'among the disguises of fiction, rhetoric has no part, for whatever is composed as under a veil, and thus exquisitely wrought, is poetry and poetry alone' (*GDG* 14.7, Murrin, 1969: 10). But why must truth be put under a veil? Boccaccio gives three answers.

First, Boccaccio believed, because the 'veil' of allegory keeps truth away from the multitude. Second, because in poetry the 'veil' that conceals truth is already in place; the burden of responsibility for locating the truth is placed upon the reader or the beholder; he notes 'when things perfectly clear seem obscure, it is the beholder's fault. To a half-blind man, even when the sun is shining its brightest, the sky looks cloudy. Some things are naturally so profound that not without difficulty can the most exceptional keenness in intellect sound their depths ... ' (*GDG* 14.12, Murrin, 1969: 11). A third function of the veil follows on from this, for poets veil the truth with fiction 'to make truths which would otherwise cheapen by exposure the object of strong intellectual effort and various interpretation, that in ultimate discovery they shall be more precious' (*GDG* 14.12, Murrin, 1969: 11).

This image of the 'veil' comes initially from St Paul, whose Second Letter to the Corinthians, already quoted from, says that he preaches in a way that is different from the Old Testament figure of Moses, with whom he compares himself. Instead:

> Seeing then that we have such hope, we use great plainness of speech: and not as Moses, which put a veil over his face, that the children of Israel could not steadfastly look to the end of that which is abolished. But their minds were blinded [or, hardened – Revised Version]: for until this day remaineth the same veil untaken away in the reading of the old testament, which veil is done away in Christ. But even unto this day, when Moses is read, the veil is upon their heart. Nevertheless, when it shall turn to the Lord, the veil shall be taken away.
>
> (2 Corinthians 3.13–16)

St Paul alludes to the story that after Moses had been speaking with God, his face shone so brightly that he had to speak to the Israelites with a veil over it (Exodus 34:29–35). Paul allegorizes this in the following manner: the Israelites needed the veil because they were unwilling to face the fact that the glory of the old law which Moses brought to the people (the Ten Command-ments) would come to an end when Christ came, and that law would fade away in the light of the New Covenant, or Testament. The veil was *literally* on Moses' face, but *figuratively* upon their hearts. When the heart of Israel (the 'it' of the last sentence of the quotation) converts to Christianity, that veil, says St Paul, will be taken away. It is the characteristic of Christianity and the New Testament that it does not need a veil because the unfading glory of Christ can be seen openly. It follows that the characteristic feature of the New Testament language is that it exists in plain speech without allegory. However, St Paul's formulation is paradoxical since allegorical interpretation is the necessary means by which plainness of speech is identified. His claim that allegory no longer operates in the New Testament, where the 'veil' is removed, is undermined by an allegorical reading of the Old Testament. In short, whatever the claim that is made for the transparency of language with regard to the New Testament, the act of interpretation still cannot be dispensed with.

Dante makes a distinctive use of the idea of the 'veil' in the *Commedia*, which, if it is allegory, is only very problematically associated with fourfold allegory. In addition, it maintains a high degree of 'realism' throughout. In its first part, the *Inferno*, canto 9, Dante, escorted by Virgil, has been denied access by the devils to the City of Dis, the interior part of Hell. Virgil in particular is embarrassed by his failure to get Dante inside the walls, and that the two of them have to wait for an angel to come down from Heaven to force a way in for them. The female Furies on the walls of the city of Dis call for Medusa to come and turn Dante into stone, and Virgil makes Dante turn round to prevent him from seeing the Gorgon, and covers Dante's hands, which are over his face, with his own hands. At this point Dante writes:

> Ye that are of good understanding, note the teaching that is hidden under the veil of the strange verses.
>
> (*Inferno* 9. 61–63, Sinclair, 1948b: 123)

This indicates that the text is split between surface or literal meaning and an allegorical meaning beneath the veil, and Dante emphasizes that the language is 'strange'. Some commentators connect the address to the reader, which is unusual in itself, and which breaks the mimetic flow of the text, to the point that an angel is about to appear. The Greek word *angelos* means 'messenger', and Dante's angel seems to be inherently related to communication, enlarging and expanding meanings, making the text 'polysemous'. The angel derives, in a literary sense, from Latin epic descriptions of Hermes; the word 'hermeneutics', meaning interpretation, particularly biblical interpretation, comes from Hermes as 'a messenger of the Gods, and the tutelary god of speech and writing' (*OED*). Other commentators point out that the threat of Medusa is to turn the onlooker into stone. The literal petrifaction can be read allegorically as a hardening of the self, as St Paul thought the minds of the Jews had been hardened; and the danger of being inwardly hardened is that it only permits literal reading. At this point, therefore, Dante signals his text as allegorical, and as needing to be read spiritually (Freccero, 1986: 119–31).

The image of the 'veil' recurs in *Purgatorio*, 8.19–21. Here, at the end of their first day climbing the mount of Purgatory, Dante and Virgil have been led by the then modern Italian poet Sordello into the Valley of Princes, all of whom were negligent during life, and are now confined in the valley before they can begin their purgation. All must rest for the night. In a moment which recalls the episode outside the City of Dis, two angels descend from heaven to give these souls protection, and Dante writes:

> Here, reader, sharpen well thine eye to the truth, for now, surely, the veil is so fine that to pass within is easy.
>
> (Sinclair, 1948b: 107)

The reference to the 'veil' indicates how the text works on at least two levels: a literal and an allegorical one. The souls of the penitential, whom Dante and Virgil see, have just sung the evening hymn and the angels descend with wings and garments of green, a colour which commentators say symbolizes hope, drawing on an earlier passage where it definitely has that meaning (*Purgatorio* 3.135). The angels have flaming swords, like the angel guarding the Garden of Eden (Genesis 3.24) and the swords' points are broken, which is a symbolic, or emblematic, detail, indicating that the angels do not bring vengeance, or destruction, but peace. They have come to protect the souls in the valley from the snake that enters it, winding its way through the grass and the flowers. One other allegorical detail in the setting can be pointed out: three stars have risen up in the sky, representing faith, hope and charity. These have replaced the four stars that were seen in the early morning, which stood for the four cardinal virtues: prudence, courage, temperance, fortitude (*Purgatorio* 1. 23,24, 8.85–91).

The broken sword illustrates another feature of allegory. Of course it is not a realistic detail, but in a pageant, or painting, it makes allegorical, or symbolic sense; indeed, in relation to art, it would be called 'iconographical'. Yet that meaning of the broken sword is specific only to the context, as is always the case with allegory. For example, a sixteenth-century portrait of Richard the Third, painted for the Tudors who replaced him, shows him with a broken sword, which implies broken kingship (Hepburn, 1986: 71–89). The sword there symbolizes regal power. Clearly, the meanings of allegory are dependent on cultural circumstances, and risk being seen as arbitrary when they are separated from them.

ALLEGORY AND '*FIGURA*'

Another allegorical detail from this same passage in *Purgatorio* provides an insight into how many different types of allegory are present here. The description of the Valley of the Princes (7.64–81) recalls the Garden of Delight (French: 'deduit') in *The Romance of the Rose* (lines 631–60, 1323–680). The mountainside has a hollow which is called a 'lap' ('grembo'), a word which implicitly denotes it as feminine. This hollow's concealedness is part of a protection which both implies femininity, and recalls the prized medieval enclosed garden (*hortus conclusus*), that is an aristocratic garden closed off by a wall. Inspiration for the idea of the enclosed garden comes from the Old Testament Song of Songs 4:11, where the Bridegroom praises the Bride: 'A garden inclosed is my sister, my spouse; a spring shut up, a fountain sealed'. This biblical garden of the Song of Songs symbolizes, perhaps, the woman's virginity. In the 'twelfth-century Renaissance', and in something of a reaction to its intellectualism, the Cistercian monk Bernard of Clairvaux (1090–1153) pronounced the garden as an allegorical representation, perhaps of the Virgin Mary, or of the church, or Paradise. The Bride of the Song of Songs, who is, in the particular verse, called a garden, was to be seen as the Virgin, while the Bridegroom was Christ.

Dante's hollowed-out space within the mountainside of Purgatory is therefore syncretic, since it fuses together *two* allegories. It borrows from the secular garden of *The Romance of the Rose* as well as from the spiritual garden of the Song of Songs, as interpreted by Bernard of Clairvaux (who appears in cantos 32 and 33 of Dante's *Paradiso*). This plurality, that the garden is both secular and religious, adds to the 'polysemous' nature of the allegory. Further, the space of the valley is described in terms of precious stones which are surpassed in colour by the grass and the flowers. It is a medieval *locus amoenus*, a 'delightful, or pleasant place', which derives from the account of Elysium in Virgil's *Aeneid*, 6:638 (Curtius, 1953: 192). This natural space is described not literally but in a 'literary' mode. And it is a shadow of what lies before, in the Earthly Paradise, which, in the form of a forest, appears later in *Purgatorio* (canto 28). A forest was another form of ideal landscape, deriving from Virgil's pastoral poems, the *Eclogues* (Curtius, 1953: 192). The ideal forest contrasts with the 'dark wood' already discussed in the Introduction, in which Dante is lost at the beginning of the *Inferno* (canto 1: 1–3). This dark wood, with the danger it represents, prefigures both the hollow of the Valley of the Princes, with its safety, and the forest of the Earthly Paradise. In a strange layering, one landscape gives way to another, foreshadowing it, and each landscape is described in more detail than the one before. This is a feature of the complexity of Dante's allegory, which cannot be contained either by the category of 'the allegory of poets' or 'the allegory of theologians', but for which another model must be sought. It involves a process of 'prefiguring', whereby particular events, incidents, and situations foreshadow and prefigure later details.

The idea of 'prefiguring' evokes the German critic Erich Auerbach, whose first work on Dante appeared in 1929 as *Dante: Poet of the Secular World* (1929). A later essay called 'Figura' (1944) discusses typology (discussed in the introduction), defined as 'the interpretation of one worldly event through another' so that 'the first signifies the second, the second fulfils the first' (Auerbach, 1959: 58). In a later work, *Mimesis* (1946), which contains a concentrated reading of a single episode of *Inferno* (canto 10), Auerbach argues that although all the souls Dante speaks to have died, there is no attenuation of their individuality in the afterlife. He illustrates this through discussion of the canto's dominant figure, Farinata, placed in Hell for his atheism. Farinata in Hell is more vivid, more proud, more concentrated in his politics and more aggressive than he ever was on Earth. Souls as presented in Dante are in the perfect form of their existence, realizing in their afterlife the existence which their historical lives prefigured.

Auerbach differentiates between the *typological*, or the *figural*, and the *allegorical*, and he prefers the first two over the third term. In typology, 'the figural structure preserves the historical event while interpreting it as revelation, and must preserve it, in order to interpret it' (Auerbach 1959: 68). For him, allegory is, in contrast, a mode which disregards the surface, literal meaning because it privileges the spiritual meaning. It stands free of the surface meaning, and is not premised on the validity of the literal event. With *figura*, a literal event's validity is eliminated or diminished; rather, one event figures another to come. The Old Testament prefigures the New, but events in the New Testament, however unveiled they may be in their presentation, are also figural, as is plentifully indicated by the last book of the New Testament, the Apocalypse (literally: 'the unveiling'), which is full of symbolism left unexplained, awaiting fulfilment. Auerbach's figuralism recalls the importance of Old Testament events, whereas Christian commentators had dispensed with their literal sense. *Mimesis* opens by contrasting an episode in Homer with a biblical narrative; and Auerbach argues that 'the Homeric poems conceal nothing, they contain no teaching and no secret second meaning. Homer can be analyzed ... but he cannot be interpreted' (Auerbach, 1957: 11). Homer makes no claim to being either historical or truthful; indeed 'he does not need to base his story on historical reality, his reality is powerful enough in itself'. Auerbach contrasts this with biblical narrative, which he sees as both historically grounded, and as 'orientated towards truth' which would permit a reading that is figural of a truth yet to be revealed.

Auerbach does not oppose realism and the allegory which appears in typology and figuralism against each other. Instead, the realism guarantees the figural meaning. Auerbach invokes Hegel, suggesting that figural writing followed a dialectical synthesis. There is the literal event, which is the thesis. After that comes the antithesis, which is the spiritual meaning of the event, which negates the literal meaning by declaring itself to be the essential meaning. But in Dante there then comes the synthesis, in the figure seen in the afterlife. In the *Commedia* he combines the historical truth of the person or the event and the spiritual meaning. Or, to put the matter differently, and drawing out the implications of Auerbach's work as expounded by Alan Charity in *Events and their Afterlife* (1966), the Old Testament, with its literal events, is the thesis; the New Testament, with its spiritualizing of the Old Testament, is the antithesis. Dante and his modern world, that which the New Testament's spirituality prefigures, represents a synthesis of what has gone before. The events of the *Commedia* are both realistic and literal, and also to be read as the fulfilment of allegorical meaning. As Dante gives an 'afterlife' to the characters he meets, dead as they are, so his text suggests that it will have another afterlife for his readers.

Auerbach's argument for the figural makes sense of the point that, save for particular passages, such as those cited already, Dante's *Commedia* does not often lend itself to an obvious allegorical reading; for example, it has virtually no personifications, no-one called Love, or Reason, or Nature, or Wisdom. In that way it is quite different from *The Romance of the Rose* or English allegorical works of the fourteenth century, such as *Piers Plowman*, which we shall discuss in the next section, or Chaucer's early poetry, such as *The Hous of Fame* and *The Parlement of Fowles*, poems which are obviously allegorical, like the anonymous English dream poem *Pearl* (*c.*1360–95). Each of these texts shows its artificial nature. Each leaves the world of everyday realism behind, by beginning with the narrator falling asleep and dreaming. In the dream world, all identities become allegorical. But there is nothing of that kind in the *Commedia*, which does not call itself the record of a dream. Dante insists on the historicity of the events of his text. This returns us to the question of the authenticity of *Epistle X*, the letter to Can Grande, which supports an allegorical, rather than a figural reading of the text. Auerbach's *figura*, because it speaks of 'the historicity both of the sign and what it signifies' (Auerbach, 'Figura', 1959: 54) is more suggestive than the fourfold 'allegory of the theologians', for one simple reason. It attempts to do away with the dualism of reading the text for 'the letter' and 'the spirit', as St Paul puts it. That dualism is also Platonic, in that it corresponds to the difference between the body and soul.

The body, for Plato, looks more real, and more literal, but is actually less meaningful than the soul, which is real, invisible, and only perceived spiritually.

Auerbach wants to make allegorical and literal meanings fuse so that they cannot be separated. Perhaps it is relevant to recall his Jewishness, which facilitates a means of interpretation which is not bound to the Platonic-Christian tradition of St Paul and Augustine; Auerbach developed theories of figuralism in the 1920s and 1930s, decades in which a distinctive Jewish history was being set aside in Europe by anti-Semitic interpretations of the Bible, which ignored the historicity of the Old Testament in favour of a spiritualized, non-historical version of the New Testament.

PIERS PLOWMAN AND MEDIEVAL INTEREST IN ALLEGORY

Medieval allegory exists in other writers than Dante, and in many modes of writing; this chapter will conclude with one other example, from the English poem by William Langland, *Piers Plowman* (*c.*1360–80). This poem is an inquiry into the possibility of salvation, while being at the same time a social criticism of England, and of its three 'estates': the church, the knighthood, and the common people. In an introduction to an edition of *Piers Plowman*, selecting passages from the poem's probable final version (usually called the C text), two medievalist critics, Elizabeth Salter and Derek Pearsall, inspired by Auerbach, identified in it a range of types of allegory, in addition to figuralism. These they enumerate as: personification allegory, the subject of the next chapter, and dramatic allegory, where a narrative of events becomes the basis of allegory, bringing together conceptual and mimetic elements. Another type, which they label 'diagrammatic allegory', takes the form of verbal description, characteristically drawing on the iconography of medieval art, and medieval stained glass. Examples of this are the Tree of True Love growing in man's heart, or other trees, familiar in medieval wall paintings, such as a Tree of the Vices, or a Tree of Life. They see this allegory as communicative, as stating doctrines rather than as being evocative in the rhetorical sense of seeking to persuade. They also find examples of 'non-visual allegory', drawing on the idea of an allegorical depiction which is primarily realizable verbally, not capable of being seen in visual terms. Finally, they speak about 'allegory through *exempla*' (i.e. medieval versions of brief, pointed stories with a moral) where there are short narratives within narratives, often occurring within the speeches of allegorical characters. And they add that each of these types of allegory merge into each other (Salter and Pearsall, 1967: 9–20).

The following is an example of the mixed nature of Langland's allegory. Here, the Lady Holy Church is speaking to the dreamer of the poem. He speaks as 'I' and is called 'Will'. She personifies an entity (the True Church), while he is both real (Will is, probably, his 'real' name) and a personification of a desirable virtue, since Will names a needed quality for salvation: the power of the will. Lady Holy Church speaks about Love, which is the allegorical name for Christ. Here is the text, first in medieval English verse, and then in translation:

> For Treuthe telleth that love ys triacle to abate synne
> And most soverayne salve for soule and for body.
> Love is plonte of pees, most precious of virtues,
> For hevene holde hit ne myghte, so hevy hit first semede,
> Til hit hadde of erthe ygoten hitsilve.
> Was never lef upon lynde lyhtere her-after,
> As when hit hade of the folde flesch and blode taken.
> Tho was hit portative and pursuant as the point of a nelde;
> May non armure hit lette ne non heye walles.
>
> (C.II.147–55, Salter and Pearsall, 73–74)

> (For Truth tells that Love is the healing remedy [specifically: the herbal medicine for a snakebite] to stop sin, and the most sovereign salve [medicine] for the soul and body. Love is the plant of peace, most precious of virtues [or, most precious in its healing powers], for heaven could not hold it, it seemed so heavy, until it had begotten itself of earth. There was no leaf on a linden-tree lighter after that, as when it had taken flesh and blood from the earth. Then was it portable and piercing as the point of a needle; no armour could hinder it, nor high walls.)

Glossing this: Truth and Love are both names of God, but they are distinguished here, and both have plural significances: e.g. Truth is also the Bible, and Love is both a quality as well as the name of Christ. Love, seen symbolically as a herbal remedy, produces the word 'plant', and another abstract name for Christ, 'peace'. There follows a literary 'conceit' where love is said to be too 'heavy' to stay in Heaven, but must come down to Earth. But when it has been incarnated (to use the language of John 1.14), and so made heavy with flesh and blood, it is so 'light' that it can return upwards to God. This refers to the Ascension of Christ, returning to Heaven, and it implies that redeemed souls go up to Heaven. The weightlessness of love produces the idea of a needle which is so sharp that it can pierce both armour and walls. The armour, by metonymy, also applies to the armour of the Roman soldiers who guarded the tomb of Christ, with its high walls surrounding it, which still could not prevent his resurrection from the dead.

The quotation activates several ideas which appear to have no logical connection with each other; the reader passes directly from the plant to the leaf to the point of a needle. There is no explanation given for any of the images (the serpent's bite, the heaviness of love and its lightness) and to read the passage at all depends on seeing that in line 151 there is a complex reference to the Incarnation, with the Virgin Mary described figuratively as 'erthe' in addition to the literal meaning of 'earth' as the place from whence come the elements that make up flesh and blood. The word 'lyghter' implies not just weightlessness, but also joy, as the previous heaviness implies lack of joy (we speak of being 'heavy' with grief), which is a way of thinking about the incompleteness of Christ before the incarnation. Christ in Heaven felt heavy, and the imperfect pun on 'heaven' and 'heavy' reinforces this opposition.

The freedom of writing here is unpredictable, associative, metonymic, and its validity lies in how it speaks of metaphysical issues: it is, in other words, a mode of writing which is outside secular realism. This may be why such allegory distinguishes Langland from his contemporary Chaucer, for whom poetry is more obviously secular; though it should be said that Langland, too is secular enough in his sense of the corruption of the political world. And Chaucer also leans on the religious; since allegory as a religious mode was so dominant within the medieval world, its presence is also to be found in his writing, and what he took also, in the form of personification, from *The Romance of the Rose*. Langland, whose text moves so freely between concepts, some literal, some completely non-literal, shows the absolute relevance of allegory to the medieval world. E. R. Curtius describes how that world saw creation as a book, alongside the Bible as book, and even God as book (Curtius, 1953: 321). A complete interchangeability between these three images means that every idea or concept can be found to have correspondences in the universe and in the Bible; everything can be described in terms of everything else. Something of that freedom can be seen in *Piers Plowman*, whereby everything is symbolic of another part of creation. Indeed the tradition of interpretation associated with Augustine seems to have made no distinction between a sign, a symbol, and allegory. As Gerhart B. Ladner puts it:

> it was one of the fundamental character traits of the early Christian and medieval mentalities that the signifying, symbolising, and allegorical function was anything but arbitary or subjective; symbols were believed to represent objectively and to express faithfully various aspects of a universe that was perceived as widely and deeply meaningful.
>
> (Ladner, 1979: 227)

That was the belief, but we have already seen, and it will become even clearer in the following chapter, that attribution of meaning presents more difficulties than Ladner suggests. But before passing on to these problems, it should be noted how the capacity to articulate the whole of creation in symbolic terms is at the heart of medieval allegory, and accounts for some of its attraction.

2

MEDIEVAL AND RENAISSANCE PERSONIFICATION

BRONZINO'S *ALLEGORY*

Personification was defined in the introduction, but we can approach it afresh by considering a picture: *Venus, Cupid, Time and Folly* (1545) by the Mannerist artist Agnolo Bronzino (1503–72). It hangs in London's National Gallery, and is there called *Allegory*. It shows a nude Venus, an apple in her right hand and an arrow in her left; if we say her body is seen in a snake-like zigzag across the picture, reference to the snake will suggest how interpreting one visual personification inevitably suggests others. Two doves, which often accompany Venus in classical literature, are seen to the left of the picture. Venus is being embraced by a nude, winged young man, Cupid, who kneels on a red cushion. There is a very full discussion of the imagery of this painting by the art critic Erwin Panofsky, who describes this embrace as an 'image of Luxury' (Panofsky, 1972: 16, 86–91). Panofsky's method of interpretation places special emphasis on the iconic value of these images, and iconology as a mode of reading will be further discussed in chapter 5.

On the left of Cupid an old woman is seen madly tearing her hair: and, according to the Renaissance historian Vasari, she represents Jealousy, which includes Envy and Despair. Behind Venus, another young Cupid (a '*putto*') throws roses. At his feet are two masks, one of a young woman, one of an old man, which together signify the contrast between beauty and ugliness. Behind the *putto* is a representation of Fraud, who holds out in her left hand – though it seems as if it is her right hand – a honeycomb, while with her right she hides what Panofsky calls 'a poisonous little animal'. Fraud's face is that of a girl, but she has a lion's paws and a serpent's tail. Behind her is the figure of Time, who is marked out by his wings, and behind him, an hour-glass, while Truth is on the left hand. These are the personified forces who are unveiling the figures already described.

Bronzino's allegorical picture illustrates an abstraction: the unmasking or unveiling of the deceptive figure of Luxury. But the explanation of the picture turns out to be allegorical; indeed, we have not left allegory behind when we say that the picture shows Luxury, for this is as much an allegorical personification as any of the figures in the picture. And the figures interpreting the allegory, the female Truth, and Time, are also allegories. If allegorical figures unveil allegory, by pulling a curtain back to reveal Venus and her son, then one allegory uncovers another. This is a problem which Panofsky's iconological study, reading the allegorical significances of Renaissance pictures, cannot quite cope with, because the assumption that a figure in the picture equals an abstraction assumes that there is a metalanguage with which it is possible to discuss allegorical images. But perhaps there is not. We can discuss an allegorical image of Love, but the word 'Love', as in the idea that 'love has taken hold of me', is already an allegory, a personification. We are always inside the field of allegory even when we are trying to talk about it.

But there is already an unveiling within the picture that Truth and Time wish to display: the revelation that sexual love turns into death. Indeed as part of the process of historicizing this abstraction, commentators have interpreted the figure of Jealousy as a representation of syphilis, which in 1545 was, in Europe, a new sexual disease (Parker, 2000: 130). This interpretation suggests that there are different forms of allegorical reality within the picture. To name a representation 'Syphilis' is to give it a different form of name from Jealousy, or Love, since one is a physical concept and the other abstract. If the meaning is that Love produces syphilis, then allegorical interpretation involves the viewer being aware of a temporal process; understanding can only be instantaneous if the causal connection between 'love' and 'syphilis' is acknowledged. And the figure who has been identified with Truth has been seen by one critic (Hope, 1982) as Oblivion; Panofsky, at one stage, personified her as Night. Time and Oblivion are covering over, or veiling, the scene with darkness. In which case, allegory here may be seen to obscure meaning. Another interpretation has identified 'Truth' with Fraud, and reads 'Time' as Saturn (Mendelsohn, 1992). This reading suggests that each personified figure is theatrical, posturing, not real but fraudulent. If the figure represented in an allegory personifies an abstraction, as in Bronzino's painting where the masks on the floor show that the characters are no more than theatrical impersonations, then allegory becomes a self-consciously deceptive mode. Personification implies that, as a physical manifestation of abstraction, it exists in its own right and is therefore 'real'. But if personification is nothing more than a representation, and its point of reference is an allegorical abstraction, then neither can claim to offer direct access to a reality beyond these representations. We are dealing here with traditional representations of virtues and vices in literature and art that comprise an established repertoire of images, which in turn helps establish ideological views that see such abstractions as substantial, real. Bronzino's painting, which may allow Truth and Fraud to coexist in one representation, derives its interest from the way it plays with these allegorical significances, not fixing them, as such a commentator as Panofsky was inclined to do. How it is impossible to fix a single meaning to an image, to say that A personifies B, is something which will emerge throughout this chapter, which moves from classical personifications of virtues and vices through to Giotto and Chaucer, and finally Spenser.

DEFINING PERSONIFICATION

'Personification', as described here, may be different from allegory, as has been suggested, or it may be the essence of allegory, as it was for John Ruskin (1819–1900). In *The Stones of Venice* he defines it as 'the bestowing of a human or living form upon an abstract idea' and finds it at its most advanced in Spenser (Ruskin, 10.377). It was an essential category for C. S. Lewis, whose work will be discussed later in this chapter. 'Personification' comes from the Latin 'persona', meaning the mask worn by actors in Roman drama: 'persona' is a translation of the Greek 'prosopon', a face or theatrical mask, or a person in a drama. 'Prosopopoeia' is a word associated with personification and was used in books of classical and Renaissance rhetoric, in which a fictitious, or absent, or dead person is endowed with the power of speech. The etymology of the term suggests that it is the theatrical mask that confers this power on the speaker. Cicero described prosopopoeia as 'the introduction of fictitious persons' into oratory (*De Oratore* III. liii.205). So also Quintilian used it (*Inst. Orat.* VI.i.25; Whitman, 2000: 269).

For William Blake in *The Marriage of Heaven and Hell* (1790):

> The ancient Poets animated all sensible objects with Gods or Geniuses, calling them by the names and adorning them with the properties of woods, rivers, mountains, lakes, cities, nations, and whatever their enlarged and numerous senses could perceive.

Blake gives an account of 'animism', where through the abounding energy of the poetry that was in the ancient poets, objects are thought to be alive. Wordsworth in *The Prelude* 5.383–84 (1850) similarly speaks of 'the voice of mountain torrents' (Wordsworth, 526). Here, animism is actually more specifically related to personification, which, like prosopopoeia, ascribes a mask, or face, and by implication a voice and personality, to an object or something in nature, or even to a man-made object, such as a statue. Two things have happened here. First, a quality has been singled out, constructed, isolated, and attributed to an object, and by being brought into visualization that quality has been personified. Second, an object has been thought to be the adequate embodiment, or impersonation, of an idea, or emotion. But for Blake the latter condition was unnecessary since the comparisons made were more improvisatory, spontaneous and poetic. However it is always possible for such improvisatory creations to become fixed over time, so that what was originally spontaneous becomes fixed, stable and authoritative, as the representation of an emotion.

Blake's view of animism may be compared with Freud writing about people 'projecting' their feelings onto the universe outside them, and making that the cause of their emotional, or affectual, states:

> a large part of the mythological view of the world, which extends a long way into the most modern religions, is nothing but psychology projected into the external world. The obscure recognition [...] of psychical factors and relations in the unconscious is mirrored – it is difficult to express it in other terms, and here the analogy with paranoia must come to our aid – in the construction of a supernatural reality. [...] When human beings began to think, they were, as is well known, forced to explain the external world anthropomorphically by means of a multitude of personalities in their own image; chance events, which they interpreted superstitiously, were thus actions and manifestations of persons. They behaved, therefore, just like paranoics, who draw conclusions from insignificant signs given by other people.
>
> (Freud, 1975: 321–22)

Freud here describes 'projection', where internal feelings are located, projected onto, another person or thing. Normal animism is part of the process whereby obscure feelings were identified with external forces which were supposed to have controlling powers. This form of projection was designed to forestall danger, and it is thought of by Freud as 'superstitious' in the sense he gives to superstition as entailing 'in large part the expectation of trouble' (Freud, 1975: 323). Blake's account of animism belongs to the world of spontaneous, poetic creativity; Freud's to the world of experience.

Other accounts of animism have asked whether the abstraction now personified as a god was considered to be actual or fictional. Does the object worshipped arise out of a desire by worshippers to endow a force of a god with 'human' attributes, or does it appear when the 'god' is no longer believed in? (Whitman, 2000: 271). These two aspects of personification may correspond to two different stages in religious belief. The first explanation suggests that there is either the attempt to raise an abstract conception, such as Love or War, to the level of a god with human characteristics, producing as a result the character of Aphrodite (Love) or Ares (War), or else to see the unique characteristic of the god as also a human quality. On that basis the god becomes the symbol of a human emotion, or state. This second view assumes that personification may continue after belief in the particular divinities has been abandoned. So, as with Bronzino, the Renaissance produced many statues and paintings of Aphrodite (Venus in her Roman form) after people had given up believing in Olympian deities. At both stages, the ambiguity within the word 'impersonates' should be recalled. To represent a god or emotion by a statue or painting, for instance, implies that the action of representing something by impersonating it is false. In such cases, allegory tends towards fiction, play, or deceptiveness.

It is not easy to determine, when an abstract noun is used, whether the writer means to suggest that there is some definite force behind it or not. The classical scholar E. R. Dodds discusses *ate* (Greek: 'ruin') as the destructive force in Greek heroes' lives, and says that it is 'allegorically described' by Agamemnon as Zeus's eldest daughter (*Iliad* 19.91), and so gives some idea of her power. But Dodds thinks that she is not thought of by Homer as a literal person, and goes back to Agamemnon's defence of his earlier tyrannous behaviour towards Achilles (*Iliad* 19.86), which he translates as follows:

> Not I, not I was the cause of this act, but Zeus, and my portion (*moira*) and the Erinyes (Fury: a feminine figure) who walks in darkness: they it was who in the assembly put wild *ate* in my understanding, on that day when I arbitrarily took Achilles' prize from him. So what could I do? Deity will always have his way.
>
> (Dodds, 1951: 3)

Dodds adds about the word *moira*, which scholars usually translate as 'fate', or 'necessity' or 'destiny', but which he renders as 'portion', that 'it is quite wrong to write *Moira* with a capital "M" here, as if it signified either a personal goddess who dictates to Zeus or a

Cosmic Destiny'. He adds that Agamemnon 'is taking a first step towards personification' in speaking about *moira* as the portion that has fallen, or been allotted to him (Dodds, 1951: 6–7). Without necessarily disagreeing with Dodds, we can see that the question of how much weight to put on the word *moira* is difficult to resolve. In the first instance we need to ask whether abstract nouns, Fate, or Love, possess a commanding force. Second, following Freud, whether such nouns refer to external agencies or are projections of the inner emotional states of individual speakers. Third, there is, especially for modern readers of texts of the past, the question of deciding whether such abstract nouns should be capitalized or not, where capitalization confers an allegorical status that transforms the abstraction into a 'real' figure, or person.

Certainly, if emotions are like the gods and goddesses presented in allegory, they may represent internal or external qualities. Agamemnon uses allegorical language in order to avoid blaming himself for what he has done. He has mentioned the Fury, which Dodds considers may be the minister of vengeance who enforces a person's *moira* (Dodds, 1951: 8). The Greeks associated the Furies with madness, while the Romans associated them with vices, as in Virgil's *Aeneid* 6.273–89, which describes what Aeneas sees as he enters the Underworld:

> Just before the entrance, even within the very jaws of Hell, Grief and avenging Cares have set their bed; there pale Diseases dwell, sad Age, and Fear, and Hunger, temptress to sin, and loathly Want, shapes terrible to view; and Death and Distress; next, Death's own brother, Sleep, and the soul's Guilty Joys, and, on the threshold opposite, the death-dealing War, and the Furies' iron cells, and maddening Strife, her snaky locks entwined with bloody ribbons.
>
> (Virgil, 1.551–53)

Vices are not only associated with the irrational and the mad; they are also, in Virgil, external to a person, so that their influence over human life cannot be explained. Moreover, allegorical emotions are also tendentially mad states of affect, or passion; indeed it has been argued that classical epic itself is based on the idea of irrational fury; for example, Homer's *Iliad* has as its principal subject the anger of Achilles, which takes him over. These affectual states, as they are named as attributes or tendencies of a person, construct allegory. In turn, allegorical interpretation of the classics, such as Virgil, as discussed in chapter 1, sees the text as needing to be interpreted allegorically, as a means of showing how to conquer passions.

ALLEGORIES, VIRTUES AND VICES

The Romans worshipped abstract virtues, such as the feminine Spes (Hope). In *The Allegory of Love*, C. S. Lewis traces a process whereby Roman poets after Virgil (70–19 BCE) become more allegorical: gods behave less as figures in their own right and become abstractions of qualities, a process developed in Statius (45–96), whose epic *Thebaid* influenced Dante in the *Commedia*. Lewis argues that a new perception of the 'divided will' had grown up, unknown to the Greeks, so that:

> to be conscious of the divided will is necessarily to turn the mind in upon itself. ... It is plain that to fight against 'Temptation' is also to explore the inner world; and ... to do so is to be already on the verge of allegory. We cannot speak ... of an 'inner conflict' without a metaphor; and every metaphor is an allegory in little.
>
> (Lewis, 1936: 60)

Lewis has been criticized for making allegory exclusively 'inward' in character, referring to a clash of emotions inside a person, as in the case of Jealousy fighting Love, for instance. However, what emerges here is a sense that the subject matter of allegory tends to be temptation, giving way to a particular state. If so, this puts allegory simultaneously on the side of both restraint and transgression. If evil qualities must be personified, allegory becomes a way of showing, or discussing, the forbidden, or the excessive: it shows the 'heterological', the other. This recalls the prefix *allos* in allegory: allegory is from, and to do with, 'the other'. Angus Fletcher, whose study of allegory applies psychoanalytic insights to it, develops Lewis's point, relating it to the asceticism of the monks in the desert, whose 'physical debility induces extremely varied, abundant fantasies' of fantastic animals personifying the passions (Fletcher, 1964: 36). The birth of allegorical visions, Fletcher argues, emerges from the spirit of asceticism. The imagination that wants a passionless state, *apatheia*, as recommended by the Stoics, showed itself with the Egyptian hermit Evagrius Ponticus (346–99), who dreamed up the figures that became the seven deadly sins (Pride, Envy, Anger, Sloth, Greed, Gluttony and Lust – all allegorical qualities).

Evagrius Ponticus's list of capital vices was adapted by Cassian (c.360–433/5), and applied to the figure of the monk in the communal monastery. Cassian produced a comparable list of sins: gluttony, lust, avarice, sadness ('tristitia'), wrath, sloth ('acedia'), vainglory, and pride. The progression goes from fleshly vices to the more serious spiritual ones (Bloomfield, 1952; Neuhauser, 2000). The order of sins was revised several times later on, for instance by Gregory the Great (c.540–604), and, as sins, these vices appear in Langland and are discussed by Chaucer's Parson in 'The Parson's Tale'. They structure John Gower's poem *Confessio Amantis*, they appear in Spenser's *The Faerie Queene* and in Marlowe's *Doctor Faustus*. In all these texts it seems that qualities in the self have been projected onto external figures. Or, reading the process through Freud's account of 'projection', qualities or feelings which the subject refuses to recognize in the self become aspects of another person or thing. This is the condition which Freud associates with paranoia, as a defence mechanism, where feelings the subject censors in the self are said to belong to another. An allegorical personification of the monstrous, or disgusting, may be a way of removing blame from the self, transferring it to another. In Marlowe, Faustus's viewing of the seven deadly sins keeps him from self-awareness.

One classic text for the idea of the human subject being internally divided between different forces is by Prudentius (348–410), a contemporary of Augustine, whose *Confessions* (397) classically describe the autobiographical subject as having a divided will. In Prudentius's poem, the *Psychomachia* (c.405), the word 'psyche' means both soul and life and the title either implies a struggle taking place on behalf of the soul, or by the soul, or else within the soul. The first part of the *Psychomachia* retells stories from the Old Testament. In the second, these are seen to prefigure the virtues and vices, which are personalized and shown to be at war with each other and to each have its separate opponent. Faith, an Amazonian figure, destroys Idolatry in the Roman arena; Chastity fights the courtesan Lust; Anger, who commits suicide, fights Patience; Pride opposes Humility and is destroyed by a trap that Dishonesty has dug on the battlefield. Self-indulgence (Luxuria) is overcome by Temperance; Avarice cannot be destroyed by Reason, only by Beneficence (Operatio – Charity and her works). Concordia (Peace) is attacked by Discord, or Heresy, and finally vanquished by Faith. One of Prudentius's sources was Tertullian (*c*.160–220), who had represented the virtues as warrior-maidens struggling with vices. Emile Mâle (1862–1954), the French art historian, quotes Tertullian's *De Spectaculis* xxix: 'See wantonness overthrown by chastity, perfidy killed by honesty, cruelty thrown down by pity, pride conquered by humility; these are the games in which we Christians receive our crown' (Mâle, 1913: 98). Mâle shows how virtues and vices appeared freely in Romanesque and Gothic churches. For example, at Chartres Cathedral, in the north porch (*c*.1280), Prudentius's seven virtues have become bas-reliefs of Prudence (opposed by Folly), Justice (by Injustice), Fortitude (Cowardice), Temperance (Intemperance), Faith (Infidelity), Hope (Despair), Charity (Avarice), Humility (Pride). The names combine the four classical cardinal virtues with the three theological virtues. Humility and Pride are added, because of the place given to Pride in theology (Mâle, 1913: 109–30). The allegorical forces which oppose Christianity are seen as integral to it and included in the complete statement of faith that the Gothic cathedral aspires to be.

The *Psychomachia* presupposes a Manichean universe, comprising a series of antitheses, whose tensions are repeated in the war waged in the individual psyche. But by the time Chartres was constructed, the virtues and vices are not in conflict, but exist side by side. Prudentius can be supplemented by Martianus Capella, author of *De nuptiis Philologiae et Mercurii* (The Wedding of Philology and Mercury, written *c*.420). Here the seven 'liberal arts' (Grammar, Rhetoric, Dialectic, Arithmetic, Geometry, Music and Astronomy) are given to Philologia as a wedding present. They are different

women, distinguished by their age, clothing and manner, and
they are represented on the facades of cathedrals such as Chartres.
There they are associated with the inventor, or chief exponent, of
each art, who is represented by being shown in a characteristic
position. So we see a progression from a series of martial antitheses to the beginning of a humanist division of the corpus of
human knowledge into categories, all of which admit of a particular allegorical personification.

ALLEGORY AND REALISM

One representation of abstract virtues and vices appears in the
work of the artist Giotto (1266–1337), who was a contemporary
of Dante, who refers to him in *Purgatorio* 11 in a context which
suggests that he could see that both were attempting something
new, in literature and in art. Giotto completed painting the
Scrovegni chapel in Padua in 1305. He covered the walls with
pictures of the life of Christ, with, beneath, monochrome allegorical paintings of virtues and vices. The absence of colour makes
the vices and virtues resemble statues in niches: it gives to these
allegorical abstractions a permanent character. There are seven
virtues and seven vices, for Giotto. Prudence looks across at Folly,
Fortitude at Inconstancy, Temperance at Anger, Justice at Injustice,
Faith at Infidelity, Charity at Envy and Hope at Despair.

An interesting commentary on these appears in Marcel Proust's
novel *A la recherche du temps perdu* (1913–27), where, in a passage
influenced by Ruskin's interest in Giotto's work in Padua,
Marcel, the narrator, remembers the pregnancy of the kitchen
maid. Her smock reminds him of 'Giotto's Charity', since he has
looked at photographs of these pictures given to him by M.
Swann. The girl resembles 'those strong, mannish virgins,
matrons really, in whom the virtues are personified in the Arena
[Chapel]'. He adds that the image of the girl was supplemented
by the added symbol she carried 'without appearing to understand
its meaning'. Thus the girl is the personification of 'Caritas':

> the powerful housewife who is represented in the Arena below the
> name 'Caritas' [Charity] ... embodies this virtue without seeming to

suspect it. ... She is trampling on the pleasures of the earth, but absolutely as if she were treading grapes to extract their juice or rather as she would have climbed on some sacks to raise herself up; and she holds out to God her flaming heart, or, to put it more exactly, she 'hands' it to him, as a cook hands a corkscrew through the skylight of her cellar to someone who is asking her for it at the groundfloor window.

The narrator continues with a description of the personified Envy:

the serpent hissing at the lips of Envy is so fat, it fills her wide-open mouth so completely, that the muscles of her face are distended to contain it, like those of a child swelling a balloon with its breath ... Envy's attention ... entirely concentrated as it is on the action of her lips, has scarcely any time for envious thoughts.

Marcel, thinking of the near-bourgeois character of these figures, says that later he understood that

the startling strangeness, the special beauty of these frescoes was due to the large place which the symbol occupied in them, and the fact that it was represented, not as a symbol, since the thought symbolized was not expressed, but as real, as actually experienced, or physically handled.

Here the allegorical figure is so vivid that it is experienced not as a representation but as something real, while the pregnant woman herself becomes a figure whose allegorical significance lies for Marcel in the 'non-participation of a person's soul in the virtue that is acting through her' (Proust, 2003: 1.83–84).

This passage, which anticipates the subject of symbolism, is suggestive for Proust no less than for Giotto. It indicates something also apparent in the statues of Chartres: that allegorical personifications cannot simply be expressive of their respective virtue or vice. A charitable person cannot say she is charitable without evoking the antithesis (here, Envy), making the listener think she is really envious (charitable people do not say they are charitable, but envious people might). Similarly, an envious person (the complement, in Giotto's scheme, to Caritas, because 'charity envieth not' according to St Paul in 1 Corinthians 13.4) may not be aware of their envy. If someone says she is charitable, she is more likely to be a secret figure of envy, while someone who says and thinks she is envious is more likely to be truly charitable. Proust hints at a way in which charity and envy are actually allegories of each other, each having the potential to be the other. The task of Giotto may be stated thus: to make real a quality, or an affectual state such as charity through art may mean that similarity to that state can only be achieved through dissimilarity, and through making the person unconscious of what they are supposed to be. Allegory is the art of dissimilarity, of impersonating not the virtue or the vice, in the form in which it might be expected to be, but of veering away from it, speaking, or painting 'other'.

Proust recasts a familiar argument about Giotto that sees him at the beginning of a movement of a new 'realism' in art, breaking away from the stylised Byzantine models of his master Cimabue (1240–1302), and also moving away from allegory. In so doing, as with Dante in the *Commedia*, it seems that Giotto's work redefines allegory. Seeing a person as a personification of an abstraction is an act of violence, of capture and confining of that person, as Gordon Teskey argues in his book *Allegory and Violence* (1998), but the emphasis in Proust is different, because he sees that personification must exceed the single quality it portrays if it is to be that quality at all. In drawing this out, Proust resembles Freud, in perceiving the unconscious foundation of human qualities. Freud's projection means seeing that what is consciously acknowledged as an emotion may involve projecting other qualities onto another person who then virtually allegorizes them. As with Proust, so with Giotto: neither Charity nor Envy have any awareness of themselves because they are busy in what they are doing. Their activity conceals a revelation of what they are which may perhaps be worked out by others, or – and this is a distinctive feature of Proust – perhaps not.

ALLEGORY AND CHAUCER

The discussion of Giotto by Proust has suggested that a personification cannot represent a single state; it will suggest or contain its 'other'. So, someone who looks like Envy may be Charity, and viceversa. This argument has the potential to make all conditions allegorical of each other; making representations of virtues and vices threaten to change places with each other. If a single state knew itself as such, that would make it cease to be single. In discussing Langland in chapter 1, we noted a mobility of allegorical forms, and that transformability may be compared to this sense of the difficulty of representing one single allegorical state in one figure. It is not quite, as the medievalist scholar John Burrow implies, that there is in Langland a move from allegory to literality (Burrow, 1971: 80–82). It has already been seen, in relation to the Bronzino picture, that it is not easy to get out of allegory, without continuing to be allegorical in another way. Rather, without leaving an allegorical mode behind, personification allegory turns out to support and suggest plural and highly realist meanings, as can be seen with Chaucer (c.1340–1400).

Chaucer's dream poetry uses openly allegorical figures, such as Fame, in *The House of Fame*, or Nature in *The Parliament of Fowls*. While C. S. Lewis does not regard Chaucer as a primarily allegorical poet, *The Canterbury Tales* has the frame of a pilgrimage to Canterbury, beginning at the Tabard Inn in Southwark, London. This offers a possibly allegorical perspective, located underneath the text's 'realism'. Canterbury, the desired end-place, becomes a figure of Heaven. The 'General Prologue' to *The Canterbury Tales* describes a disparate collection of pilgrims, some presented in ideal terms, and some, such as the Pardoner (who appears in lines 669–714), in literal, realist terms. The Pardoner possesses some of the attributes of allegorical personifications in *The Romance of the Rose*: specifically, he derives from False Seeming ('Faus Semblant'), but Chaucer takes away the allegorical name, thus transforming the hypocritical religious figure into a 'realistic' pardoner. In medieval times, a pardoner travelled round different parishes, holding a papal licence to sell pardons to people who felt they had sinned, and he frequently used fake relics as part of his sales talk. False Seeming is a mendicant preacher, i.e. a Franciscan or Dominican friar, who is forbidden by his religious order from owning property, and must therefore beg his way. He calls himself the son of Fraud and Hypocrisy, and makes a long confession to

Love, describing his hypocritical practices (lines 10931–2380). Chaucer transmutes this material into the Pardoner, who in the General Prologue is described in a way which brings both his gender and his sexuality into question: 'No berd hadde he, ne nevere sholde have; / As smothe it was as it were late shave, / I trowe he were a gelding or a mare' (689–91). The Riverside Chaucer annotates that last line as meaning 'a eunuch or a homosexual' (Benson, 1987: 34, 825); how that relates to the Pardoner's character is open to discussion. The Pardoner parallels the confession of False Seeming in the Prologue to his Tale, where he describes his hypocrisy and his skill as an actor in winning money from people when in church he is preaching a sermon against one of the seven deadly sins, Avarice, using the text from 1 Timothy 6.10: 'Radix malorum est cupiditas' – the love of money is the root of all evil' (C.334, Benson, 1987: 194).

Chaucer's Pardoner illustrates a biblical statement about avarice by embodying and personifying the allegory of that abstraction. At the same time, just as Jean de Meung's character, False Seeming, declares his hypocrisy openly in *The Romance of the Rose*, so the Pardoner reveals all his avarice in an outrageous confession, which is followed by a dramatically powerful tale against avarice, where three young men, all wastrels, go out on a boastful mission to kill Death and end up each murdering the other. This narrative is then followed by a disastrous attempt to get the Host, a secular figure in the pilgrimage if there ever was one, to buy some of his relics. The Host responds with obscenities which expose the Pardoner's sexuality as much has he has openly revealed his avariciousness.

Though there is no single critical consensus on how to read this material, it seems that in both Jean de Meung's contribution to *The Romance of the Rose* and in Chaucer, personified Avarice speaks, and delivers a monologue. But that is problematic, because if Avarice speaks he must become more than the personification of a single quality. And if he depends upon an audience, then the abstract quality he embodies requires another person, an 'other', to exist at all. Chaucer's text imagines what it means for the abstraction to speak, and shows that Avarice cannot exist as a single state. The Pardoner is split between a sexuality which his physical presence proclaims but which he disavows by his speech, and an avarice which he certainly possesses and openly proclaims. It is as if he is willing to have the greed brought into the open, to validate it, perhaps as a screen so that his sexuality may not be acknowledged. In that sense Chaucer shows awareness of the unconscious nature of the Pardoner's utterance, and that there can be no one-to-one relationship between an abstraction and its representation. Personification is enriched by realism, making the object of the critique in the text much more full, because what is personified is not a single state.

SPENSER

The fullest proof of this complexity within personification comes from Edmund Spenser, (*c.*1552–99), himself much in debt to Chaucer, and engaged in writing allegory in *The Faerie Queene*. This long poem, much of it written in Ireland, where Spenser worked in repressing Irish rebellion against the English crown, was left incomplete at his death. Spenser related his work to the episodic narratives of Italian epic/romance: Boiardo, Ariosto and, lastly, Tasso (1544–95) in *Gerusalemme Liberata* ('Jerusalem Liberated'). Tasso's work, completed in 1575, was accompanied in its 1581 unauthorized publication – unauthorized because Tasso had been confined as a madman – by a prose defence called 'The Allegory of the Poem'. This explains that the army of the crusaders who liberate Jerusalem represent 'mature man, who is compounded of body and soul – the soul considered not as simple, but divided into many and various faculties'. All the crusaders, then, add up collectively to symbolize one man. Jerusalem signifies 'civic felicity', as an ideal for the earthly life (Tasso, 1987: 470). As Angus Fletcher quotes Tasso: 'allegory ... observes passions and opinions and manners, not merely as they are in appearance, but principally in their intrinsic essence, and expresses them more obscurely through signs that are mysterious (so to speak), and only to be understood fully by those who comprehend the nature of things' (Tasso, 1987: 469; Fletcher, 1971: 55).

But Spenser wrote in a relatively non-allegorical moment, and one in which allegory could be seen as politically dangerous. The 1590 edition of the first three books of *The Faerie Queene*, dedicated to Elizabeth and aware of Tasso's work, includes a letter to Sir Walter Raleigh (1552–1618), beginning with Spenser's diffidence about his achievement, 'knowing how doubtfully all Allegories may be construed'. This can be put into the context of the new sophistication of language-use within Renaissance England. Though allegory was still popular, it had also come under attack, for instance by George Puttenham (d.1590), whose *The Art of English Poesie* must be mentioned here. Puttenham relegated allegory to the status of a mere rhetorical figure, while declaring a preference for clear, unambiguous speech. He saw figures of speech as rhetorical, deceptive, like the figure of False Seeming in *The Romance of the Rose*, or Chaucer's Pardoner. We can derive from this the idea that perhaps hypocrisy and falsity, examples of 'moral virtues', are at the heart of allegory: that allegory, in being the art of the mask, is the art of deception. Puttenham writes:

> For what else is your *Metaphore* but an inversion of sense by transport; your *allegorie* by a duplicity of meaning or dissimulation under covert and darke intendements: one while speaking obscurely and in riddle called *Aenigma*: another while by common proverb or adage called *Paremia*: then by merry scoffe called *Ironia*; then by bitter taunt called *Sarcasmus*: then by periphrase or circumlocution when all might be said in a word or two: then by incredible comparison giving credit, as by your *Hyperbole*; and many other ways seeking to inveigle and appassionate the mind.
>
> (Quoted in Fletcher, 1964: 329)

Puttenham had already called allegory the 'chief ringleader and captaine of all other figures, either in the Poeticall or oratorie science'. For Puttenham, metaphors, riddles, proverbs, irony and sarcasm, going round the subject (circumlocution), or jumping over it (hyperbole), are forms of saying one thing and meaning another: which is, of course, the meaning of allegory. Such a double-tongued use of language appears in Mark Antony's highly rhetorical irony in *Julius Caesar* (3.2.82), when he keeps repeating to the Roman crowd, who accept the fundamental honesty of Brutus, the murderer of Caesar: 'For Brutus is an honourable man'. By constantly returning to it as a refrain, while building up a case against Brutus, Mark Antony turns the simple statement into its opposite (see Jakobson, 1960: 375–76). Irony, for Puttenham, is one form of allegorical address, and he will not have it that allegory clarifies meaning by illustrating it; on the contrary, he emphasizes how allegory veils meaning, so emphasizing the difference between it and personification, where the personified object puts the emotion, or quality, on display.

While such a writer as Ben Jonson, Spenser's contemporary, implicitly opposed allegory, claiming that 'the chiefe virtue of a style is perspicuity, and [with] nothing so vitious in it, as to need an interpreter' (quoted in Murrin, 1969: 80), Spenser writes what he calls 'a continued Allegory, or darke conceit' whose 'generall end' is to 'fashion a gentleman or noble person in virtuous and gentle discipline'. While claiming Homer, Virgil, Ariosto and Tasso for precedents, Spenser acknowledges that to some 'this Methode will seeme displeasaunt, which had rather have good discipline delivered plainly in way of precepts, or sermoned at large, as they use, then thus clowdily enwrapped in Allegorical devises'. This recalls the image of allegory as a veil, while 'device' suggests emblem allegory, which is the subject of the next chapter. The plot is that King (or Prince) Arthur, the poem's hero, has seen the Faery Queen in a dream or vision, and has gone to seek her in Faery Land. And 'in that Faery Queene I meane glory in my general intention, but in my particular I conceive the most excellent and glorious person of our soveraine the Queene and her kingdom'.

For Spenser, Arthur represents Magnificence, his knights Holiness, Temperance and Chastity (Spenser, 1978: 15–17). As with Tasso, each knight allegorizes one quality which, along with the others, goes to form the complete man. There is also another form of allegory, where, especially in Book 5, 'Contayning the Legend of Artegall [equal to Arthur] or of Justice', Spenser deals with events in Ireland, in such a way that figures in the poem correspond to historical figures, such as Philip the Second, or Mary Stuart, or Henry the Fourth of France. Spenser calls himself a 'poet historical' rather than a 'historiographer', and distinguishes these two types through their different attitudes to chronology. The 'poet historical' has the freedom to start in the middle, 'recoursing to the thinges forepaste, and divining of things to come'. Allegory seems to be a historical mode, recording events in a narrative sequence – although it could be said that Spenserian allegory works contrary to narrative, insofar as narrative assumes that people develop and change through what happens to them, which does not really describe what takes place in Spenser, since allegorical personification presupposes that there can be neither change nor development in people. The opposite takes place: though the Redcross Knight expresses the fixed allegorical state of holiness (as the letter to Raleigh states), yet he must continue to learn the state of holiness, as when he is brought to the 'house of holinesse' in Book 1 canto 10.

The critic Rosamond Tuve sees Spenserian narrative as 'entre-lacement', depicting multiple action with multiple actors, all woven together, one incident being begun, unresolved and then followed by another. Tuve associates allegory with romance, not with the didactic form of the Renaissance epic. While Spenser may seem to be writing a didactic, moral work, Tuve implies that the entrelacement dissolves this rigidity of design (Tuve, 1964: 362–69). But perhaps 'entrelacement' implies something too organized and with too much clarity. The poem begins with the Redcross Knight and Una going into a wood, which bears a resemblance to Dante's narrative at the beginning of *Inferno*. This, as a labyrinth, as it is called (1.1.11.4), is 'the wandering wood, this Error's den' (1.1.13.6); so much so that the critic Anne Barton suggests that the poem's 'entire world consists of one vast, dangerous and complexly allegorized forest' (quoted in Burlinson, 2006: 173). The setting implies the danger of madness, and of monstrosity (Error is a monster): allegory is in the service of the irrational, perhaps that which cannot be given a form.

One specific example of Spenser's allegory may be given. In Book 2.1.51, Sir Guyon, whose name is that of a medieval romance hero, and who is the personification of Temperance, comes across Acrasia. She is a 'false enchaunteresse' who has already been figured twice in the poem: first in the false Duessa (1.2.34), who is the allegory of 'false' duplicity, and then in the enchanter Archimago (1.1.43). Acrasia's name derives from a Greek word meaning 'incontinence': she embodies intemperance. Her snaring of men recalls other literary women who have done the same: Circe (Homer's *Odyssey*, 10), Ariosto's Alcina, who seduces Ruggiero (*Orlando Furioso*, cantos 6 and 7), and Tasso's Armida with Rinaldo (*Gerusalemme Liberata*, cantos 14–16). Acrasia's sphere is the Bower of Bliss, whose literal veils, which surround and contain it, evoke allegory, while, as an enclosed garden (2.12.43), it recalls the *locus amoenus* of *The Romance of the Rose*.

The description of the Bower of Bliss in canto 12 is read by C. S. Lewis as allegorizing the dangerous triumph of art over nature, which, in *The Faerie Queene*, he argues, 'can symbolize God' (Lewis, 1936: 330–33). Spenser deploys material from Ariosto and Tasso to suggest that the Bower of Bliss is the image of the deceptiveness of the senses over the spirit. The episode therefore suits the Platonic dualism that produces allegory, because it sustains a division between the superficial, realistic, literal level of the poem, which includes the Bower of Bliss, and the 'real' spiritual level, which condemns that Bower; it indicates that the 'real' meaning is not to be found on the surface. Acrasia is not what she seems to be. Allegory must be discovered by getting below the poem's surface meaning, but because it seems to work by attracting readers to the attractiveness of the poem and its expression, allegory also threatens to become a false reality, covering over the real values of nature and spiritual reality.

The guardian of the Bower of Bliss is the figure of Genius. It is said that 'his looser garment to the ground did fall, / And flew about his heeles in wanton wize, / Not fit for speedy pace, or manly exercize' (2.12.46). Genius represents male genital ability, and sexual fertility, but he is the 'foe of life' (2.12.48) since he does not permit reproduction (a medieval complaint, appearing in *The Romance of the Rose*). He is effeminate, unmanly, aligned with the woman. Sir Guyon, when meeting him, breaks his staff 'with which he charmed semblants sly' [i.e. called up false appearances in a cunning manner] (2.12.49). What masculine power Genius has is soon broken, and Sir Guyon's action with regard to him makes it appropriate to ask what gender politics are played out here. Is Spenser's allegory, in supporting the destruction of the Bower of Bliss, antagonistic to the feminine (including Genius), which, through Acrasia, it aligns with deception, appearance, non-truth? But Spenserian allegory is, throughout, artificial too, not natural. Does that align it with Acrasia and her forces?

Spenser's poetry would not wish to be identified with the seductive figures of the Bower of Bliss, but because it is allegorical, that quality of allegory may be indeed what Puttenham calls it, 'false semblant, or dissimulation' (quoted in Watson, 91), and also feminine, which makes it in ideological terms more deceptive.

Acrasia, as a 'faire Witch', is associated with music and the singing of 'many faire Ladies, and lascivious boyes, / That ever mixt their song with light licentious toyes' (2.12.72). Feminine like the women, these boys assist in disarming the masculine male. The young man whom Acrasia has just seduced is called Verdant; but he has been prefigured in the poem by a young dead knight, Mordant (2.1.41), whose name Verdant echoes, and by yet another, Cymochles (2.5.34). Both these were victims of the results of debauchery, and the allegorical method makes Verdant a repetition of them. While Verdant sleeps, the moral didacticism of the poem appears, as it is said of him that:

> His warlike armes, the idle instruments
> Of sleeping praise, were hong upon a tree
> And his brave shield, full of old moniments, [monuments: inscriptions]
> Was fowly ras't [erased], that none the sights might see.
> Ne for them, ne for honour cared he,
> Ne ought, that did to his advauncement tend,
> But in lewed loves, in wastfull luxuree
> His dayes, his goodes, his bodie he did spend.

> (2.12.80.1–8)

The opening lines contain a complex pun, which fuses together Verdant's loss of sexual potency with (a) his abandoned armour, by which he should win fame for himself, and (b) an image of musical instruments, which should sound forth his fame, and which are referred to because the lines echo the captivity of the Jews in Psalm 137:

> By the waters of Babylon, there we sat down ... we hanged our harps upon the willows in the midst thereof. For there they that carried us away captive required of us a song ...

Spenser's reference makes the experience of the Old Testament Jews in captivity in Babylon figural of the state of England in the

1590s, as if England was in a state of virtual captivity to the forces of luxury. Spenser allegorizes the masculine 'arms' of Verdant as musical instruments which should also be used to praise God. The allegory implies that a feminized England is no longer the source of praise: it has wasted its days, its goods and its body: doubtless Spenser saw these things as having happened to him personally during his service in Ireland, which, if it is true, changes and widens the scope of the allegory: inadvertently, he shares the fate of Verdant. The episode ends with the destruction of the Bower of Bliss, duplicating the triumph of Redcrosse over the Dragon of the Apocalypse in book 1 (Fletcher, 1971: 84). The episode seems also an allegory of outraged masculinity taking its revenge upon the female, which has the power so to seduce men from honour and advancement. But the significance of the incident cannot be confined to such a 'literal' destruction of a single 'Bower of Bliss'. Stephen Greenblatt relates the episode to the destruction carried out by English soldiers in Ireland in the 1590s, which would make the experience doubly allegorical, possibly in a way that Spenser himself was not aware of (see Greenblatt, 1980: 183).

If we consider the gendering of the episode, as the allegory of the destruction of intemperance by Temperance, there is the possibility that Spenser inhabits both sides of the argument: he is in favour of allegorical enchantment and romance, which is why he writes it, and against it, as the masculine colonial Protestant. The conflict suggests that allegory may be aligned with the dangerous and unstable feminine, who may even personify how allegory has the power to disturb clear, natural meaning, like the destabilizing forest, the background for the work. Yet soldiers on the rampage, ravaging what they see, like the English troops in Ireland, are also a figure of intemperance. It is not possible to stop the allegory unfolding, to limit it to one meaning, as we have seen to be the case throughout this chapter. In respect of the Bower of Bliss, the text may be on the side of allegory and its destabilizations, and also willing the destruction of the same bower. It is not wholly possible to say that Spenser's allegory is fixed, and this may contribute to its abiding fascination, and that of allegorical writing itself.

3

FROM ALLEGORY TO SYMBOLISM

EMBLEMS AND ALLEGORY

This chapter moves chronologically from the sixteenth to the eighteenth century, first by exploring another form of allegory, the emblem, a mode of writing which led to accusations that allegory was arbitrary in the way it used images, and second by exploring the Romantic reaction against allegory, in favour of the symbol. The debate will be explored here as part of a historical shift in poetic discourse, which required the invention of symbolism as a stronger, more spiritual, and more vital form of expression. The main reason for the downplaying of allegory was that it was considered unable to yield a sufficient intensity of spiritual meaning.

We will begin with the allegorical emblem. What emblems are, can be illustrated from a poem full of images derived from the tradition of emblematic thinking. Written by the religious and 'metaphysical' poet George Herbert (1593–1633), it is called 'Hope':

> I gave to Hope a watch of mine: but he
> An anchor gave to me.
> Then an old prayer-book I did present:

And he an optick sent.
With this I gave a vial full of tears:
But he a few green eares.
Ah Loyterer! I'le no more, no more I'le bring:
I did expect a ring.

(Herbert, 1961: 112)

The title's personification of 'Hope' is followed by the listing of a
formidable number of symbols, as the poem proceeds to evoke a
courtly exchange of presents. It is as though the 'I' of the poem is
a courtier hoping for royal preferment, but enlisting the aid of a
wealthier agent or courtier. William Empson sees an irony in the
poem, arguing that the 'I' treats only with Hope, 'not with the
person or thing hoped for; he has no real contact with his ideal
but only with its porter' (Empson, 1966: 119). Hence the gifts
given in return become, for the speaker, more and more inadequate. Empson also says that the gifts have less meaning in
themselves than as symbols of an exchange, but we can add that if
such an interchange of emblems can be imagined, each is given
not as a present, but as something that requires to be interpreted
by the receiver: each gift is a riddle.

These gifts: watch, anchor, prayer book, optic and vial, the few
green ears and the ring, exist as complex images, which are both visual
and non-visual. The watch, for instance, denotes both the object, but
also the brevity of human life, and indicates the length of time
which has been spent waiting. As a sign of the passing of time, it
implies the need for action. The reciprocal gift of the anchor is a
visualization of an image in the Bible – 'which hope we have as
an anchor of the soul' (Hebrews 6.19) – so the picture of the
anchor also connotes hope. It also suggests the quality of endurance
that has already been learned from experience: an anchor must
remain firm and endure the buffets of the sea. The old prayer
book is a sign of dedication. Its age indicates calculation on the
part of the giver who thereby wishes to emphasize how long he
has been waiting for advancement. The optic (eyeglass) is another
sign, indicating that the soul can scan the heavens, though it also
suggests that the heavens are far away. The vial full of tears is a
marker of sorrow and faithfulness; the ears of corn given in reply

are a testimony to the possibility of future resurrection, but the colour indicates that there will be delay, since the harvest is not ripe, and the speaker must continue to hope. The soul admits that it has been hoping for a symbol of reciprocity: a ring. It is perhaps a wedding ring (Empson connects it with the prayer book containing the marriage service), so implying a consummation more real than these signs which defer fulfilment; hence the accusation that Hope is a loiterer, deferring, wasting time. But the 'real' loiterer is the speaker who only deals with the inter-mediary, Hope, the allegorical figure. The poem does not explain itself; it has no commentary. It stands as a riddling text, as much as any of the emblems which it shows going back and forth as gifts to be interpreted.

Empson analyses 'Hope' as part of his discussion of the third of 'seven types of ambiguity' in poetic writing. In this third type, 'what is said is valid in, refers to, several different topics, several universes of discourse, several modes of judgement or feeling'. And Empson links it with allegory, which rests on ambiguity when it 'describes two situations and leave[s] the reader to decide which can be said about both of them' (Empson, 1966: 111–12). Allegory, punning, ambiguity, and variety of feeling all work together, unfixing meaning. And meanings are equally unfixed with emblems, several fine examples of which have been passed to and fro in the poem. With these examples given, we can now turn to definitions.

EMBLEMS AND SIGNS

The *Oxford English Dictionary* cites the fifteenth-century poet John Lydgate, writing in 1430, as the first writer to use the term 'emblem'. It means a mosaic, or inlaid work, but it then meant a parable which was expressed visually in picture or in verse, and often in both. Mottoes (heraldic devices), which were to be interpreted by pictures, and so became 'emblems', were popular in late fifteenth-century France (Curtius, 1953: 345–46). The motto and the device (French *devise*) together, as a personal badge, was, in Italian, an *impresa*; English first records the word in 1589. Italian humanists, such as Marsilio Ficino (1433–99), whose

Neoplatonism gave them an interest in mythologies, were attracted to Egyptian hieroglyphics, pictures without words: in 1419, a Florentine priest, Cristoforo de' Buondelmonti, had brought back to Italy a Greek manuscript, the *Hieroglyphica* of Horapollo Niliacus, an Alexandrian (*c.* third century CE), a dictionary comprising 189 ancient Egyptian hieroglyphics, which were all, at that time, indecipherable. The *Hieroglyphica* prompted the move to invent some modern European equivalent. In 1531, a Milanese lawyer, Andrea Alciato (1492–1550), following Horapollo, produced the *Emblemata liber*. In 1556, Pierio Valeriano (1477–1558) followed with the *Hieroglyphica*, where the emblematic picture is a rebus, to be interpreted as a riddle. 1593 saw Cesare Ripa's *Iconologia*, a handbook of visual symbolic imagery. By now, emblems comprised three parts: a motto (*inscription*), a symbolic picture (*pictura*: this by itself was sometimes what was called the emblem) and an exposition (*subscriptio*). The word 'emblem' can be applied either to the sum of all these parts, or else to just the *pictura*. But though the latter may be the case, it can be seen that an emblem often implies the conjunction of word and image, as seems to be the case with Herbert's 'Hope'. It suggests that an allegory is a form in which either the picture needs supplementing by the text, or the word and image each modifies, pluralizes or contradicts the other's message. In emblem books, motto, picture and subscript do not necessarily unify in giving a single meaning.

Emblems suited the teaching purposes of both Catholics and Protestants, and so became popular throughout Europe. Emblematic images were of animals or plants or humans, or of gods. The last were an example of what Jean Seznec calls 'the survival of the pagan gods' into the Renaissance, as classical deities were turned into allegorical figures who were then used to teach moral lessons (Seznec, 1953). The emblem was both didactic and secret, riddling, like the emblems exchanged in 'Hope', and the context was needed to decide on the picture's meaning. A snake could represent evil, or, if sloughing off its skin, it could be a symbol of renewal. The emblem does not aspire towards a universal, unchanging meaning, although it was claimed that the ancient Egyptian hieroglyphics were God's writing, and also that such hieroglyphs were visible in nature itself, though only mystically perceived. In contrast, the emblem is artificial: uninterpretable out of context. It is a question in 'Hope' whether the emblems are interpretable only by context, or whether they resemble what they describe, like God's writing in nature. If they are to be read as God's writing, then the images would be more *symbolic* than emblematic. At the end of 'Hope', the disappointment is not having been given the ring, which has symbolic value, since its complete circle suggests eternity. The disappointment, in that case, is because the 'I' of the poem is made to tarry with the emblem, not with symbolic truth.

Books, emblematic paintings and objects, and emblematic architectural features, became part of the visual culture of the sixteenth and seventeenth centuries, providing a ready-made vocabulary. The erased 'moniment', or record, on the shield of Verdant in *The Faerie Queene*, as discussed in the last chapter, will stand as one example of a visual emblem. But more examples can be given. In Middleton's play *The Revenger's Tragedy* (*c.*1606), formerly ascribed to Cyril Tourneur, Vindice, who character-istically satirizes the condition of the world, says that he is plan-ning to produce a 'conceit' in the form of a picture which will set forth how things are; it will show, he says, 'A usuring father to be boiling in hell, and his son and heir with a whore dancing over him' (4.2.81–82; Tourneur, 1978: 137). Vindice is describing an emblem which could appear in a book; but the image deliberately satirizes, by its excess, the tradition of emblem books, and implies that they do not go far enough in characterizing the corruption of the world. The word 'emblem', meaning 'sign', became common, as in the opening of John Donne's 'A Hymne to Christ, at the Authors last going into Germany' (1619), written before embarking on the sea voyage:

> In what torne ship soever I embarke,
> That ship shall be my embleme of thy Arke;
> What sea soever swallow me, that flood
> Shall be to me an embleme of thy blood.

> (Donne, 1933: 321)

Donne's poem suggests that there is the potential to turn anything into an allegorical emblem: the ship may be torn apart by the elements (as the word 'whatsoever' is torn apart by 'torne ship'), or have its sails torn, or it may be a wreck like the ship Prospero was put into when he was exiled from Milan (in Shakespeare's *The Tempest*), but it will seem to Donne the emblem of another ship – the Ark, which itself, as part of an Old Testament story, was regarded as the *figura* of the New Testament idea of Christian redemption from Hell through Christ. The language brings out the pun: the word 'embark' becomes in the next line both 'emblem' and 'ark'. The sea, called a 'flood' in a recollection of Noah and his ark and the flood (Genesis 6–8), will be, even if it 'swallows' him, like the great fish swallowing Jonah, an event also figural of safety through the death and resurrection of Christ, emblematic of Christ's blood, which 'flood[ed]' out from his body, and through which Donne is redeemed. Through the rhyming, the word 'flood' seems to turn into 'blood'.

But the flood is only an emblem, not sacred in itself; the connection exists at the level of a 'conceit'; and even the blood may be for Donne more a sign of salvation than inherently sacred in itself, which means that one sign (ship, and ark, flood and blood) refers more to other signs than to ultimate reality. For it could be added that a Protestant, such as Donne was, at least in formal terms, and a Catholic would read these things differently. A Protestant would see the emblems as only pictorial signs, whereas a Catholic would be more inclined to regard the blood as 'real' and not the sign, or emblem, of something more abstract: salvation through Christ.

In his *Satyre II* (*c*.1594), Donne stages mock dialogues on the subject of which branch of Christianity to choose – Catholic or Protestant – and lines 79–82 advise his listener to 'doubt wisely':

> On a huge hill,
> Cragged and steep, Truth stands, and hee that will
> Reach her, about must, and about must goe;
> And what the hills suddenness resists, winne so ...
>
> (Donne, 1933: 139)

Truth stands, personified as a woman, or figured as a castle, on a hill; she is there to be won, whether as a woman or as a castle.

Here Donne's visual image, which produces this extraordinarily energetic poetry, may also have been derived from an emblem (Moseley, 1989: 24). Certainly the tradition persists beyond the early modern period. To give one Romantic example, Keats' 'Ode to Melancholy'(1819) concludes with a verse about 'she', meaning either the poet's mistress, or melancholy, or both:

> She dwells with Beauty – Beauty that must die;
> And Joy, whose hand is ever at his lips
> Bidding adieu ...

(Keats, 1970: 540)

The first line gives a simple personification, since if 'she' is Melancholy, the mistress has been personified as being that quality, and then has been linked with another personification, Beauty – but beauty which is death-marked, dying. The second line gives another personification in a form which implies something visual. The idea that joy disappears, or forces the person who approaches joy to depart, is conveyed in the picture of a figure with his hand to his lips, as if blowing a kiss. The tableau suggests that the source of this image may be the emblem books. In which case, part of the riddling quality characteristic of the emblem books has been carried over into the possible gender-shifting between 'she' and 'he'.

Perhaps Keats recalled Shakespeare's image, which is equally a combination of personification and the emblematic, in *Troilus and Cressida*:

> For Time is like a fashionable host
> That slightly shakes his parting guest by th' hand,
> And with his arms outstretched, as he would fly,
> Grasps in the comer. Welcome ever smiles,
> And Farewell goes out sighing.

(3.3.359–62.)

The passage opens with a simile, where the allegorical abstraction, Time, is compared to a host, whose gestures with his hand and open arms suggest that Shakespeare is thinking of how an actor playing a host would perform on stage; or else, he is considering the visual images in an emblem warning people how brief their welcome is on earth. The quotation closes with the new guest, the new arrival, personified as Welcome, and the departing person called Farewell (note the pun: *Wel*come /Fare*well*). Of course, it is the Host, not the visitor, who should say welcome, but through the device of a transferred epithet, the word applies not to the Host, but to the newcomer. The newcomer thinks he is welcome, and so lives in illusion: but that state of uncertainty and deception that allegorical modes of writing suggest is frequently the case.

BUNYAN

One of the most popular examples of the emblem book in England came from the Royalist Francis Quarles (1592–1644), who produced in 1635 *Emblemes, Divine and Morall* which were expanded as *Hieroglyphicks of the Life of Man* in 1638. Another was the satirist George Wither (1588–1667), whose *Collection of Emblemes* also appeared in London in 1635. Like the emblem books of the previous century, these may be, loosely, associated with 'the baroque'. The critic José Antonio Maravall discusses the Spanish form of the baroque in terms of the 'mass' production of images, suggesting that they had an important teaching role, shaping the thoughts and attitudes of people in what he calls a 'guided culture', one controlled by the power of the State and the Church. The point leads towards a consideration of John Bunyan (1628–88), whose classic use of the emblem book appears in *The Pilgrim's Progress From This World to That Which is To Come: Delivered under the Similitude of a Dream* (first part 1678, second part 1684).

A biblical quotation from Hosea 12.10 appears on the book's title page, justifying writing allegory: 'I have used similitudes'. *The Pilgrim's Progress* is a dream-vision, like the medieval texts discussed earlier, such as *Piers Plowman*. It uses personification allegory, while being also a narrative unfolding of scriptural figuralism, and an exposition of biblical allegories. Further, it makes the hero, Christian, in his journey to the Celestial City, a figure for the reader to follow and imitate. This is borne out in the second part, where Christian's experiences have become figural. Christiana (Christian's wife) and her family decide to follow Christian's example. They journey as a community – a church – to the Celestial City in a way that looks back to Christian's solitary journey.

The Pilgrim's Progress opens:

> As I walked through the wilderness of this world, I lighted on a certain place where was a den, and I laid me down to sleep: and as I slept I dreamed a dream.
>
> (Bunyan, 1965: 11)

The 'den' is usually seen as symbolizing the Bedford prison where Bunyan was confined in 1660 for twelve years. This historical allegorical location slips into another with Christian journeying from the City of Destruction to the Celestial City. On his way, he enters the House of the Interpreter, whose task, it might be assumed, would be to dismantle the allegory. The Interpreter takes him from room to room, showing him 'a very large parlour that was full of dust because never swept', and in another 'a place where there was a fire burning against a wall, and one standing by it always, casting much water upon it to quench it: yet did the fire burn higher and hotter'. These instances are designed to be read pictorially, like emblems embedded in an allegorical narrative. They do not interpret the journey, but must be followed by explanations, such as the following:

> 'This fire is the work of grace that is wrought in the heart; he that casts water upon it, to extinguish it and put it out, is the Devil, but in that thou seest the fire, notwithstanding, burn higher and hotter, thou shalt also see the reason of that'. So he had him about to the backside of the wall, where he saw a man with a vessel of oil in his hand, of the which he did continually cast, but secretly into the fire. Then said Christian, 'What means this?' The Interpreter anwered, 'This is Christ, who continually with the oil of his grace maintains the work already begun in the heart, by the means of which, notwithstanding what the Devil can do, the souls of his people prove gracious still. And in that thou sawest that the man stood behind the wall to maintain the fire,

this is to teach thee that it is hard for the tempted to see how this
work of grace is maintained in the soul.'

(Bunyan, 1965: 31)

Here the explanation, which 'is to teach thee', must be supplemented by another pictorial image, of the man with the vessel of
oil, and a further supplementary explanation. The earlier visual
image is not self-sufficient; just as the meaning of the emblem in
the emblem books was primarily contextual, needing to be supplemented by the script. In the Interpreter's terms, the most
important part of the explanation is another visual image: that of
the secret figure of Christ, whose presence and actions require
further explanation. It will be seen that the explanation and the
allegorical image are not separate: to explain the first image it is
necessary to give a second, more covert than the first.

This suggests the alliance of allegory with secrecy, as we saw in
discussing the 'veil of allegory' in chapter 1. Allegory aligns itself
with the hidden, and the teaching it gives does not just clarify,
but needs in its turn further explanation. It does not believe that
utterance can be plain and empirically understood. Bunyan, in
prison, knew the importance of things being hidden from general
view, and his form of Christianity is dependent on the power of
'similitudes' which are not apparent to everyone.

Roger Sharrock specifies of his Penguin edition of *The Pilgrim's
Progress* that he has restricted the use of capitals in previous edi-
tions, retaining them 'only in the case of personifications'
(Bunyan, 1965: xxiii), in the names of the various figures, such as
Mr Worldly Wiseman or Mr Facing Both Ways. But the editorial
assumption that personifications can be isolated misses the point
that everything here is personified, starting with the narratorial 'I'
who creates himself fictionally as a dreamer walking through the
wilderness of this world, much in the manner of Will in *Piers
Plowman*, who begins his literary dreams in a similar way. Everything in Bunyan could be written in capitals, for everything in
the text is personification allegory.

Nonetheless I want to stress a different point. Although the
quotation on the title page assumes that everything here is
'similitude', i.e. comparison, in Bunyan's autobiography, *Grace*

Abounding to the Chief of Sinners (1666), it is apparent that no distinction is made between the abstract and the real, since everything is equally real. A verse from the Bible follows him and sounds loud within him; a voice speaks to him while he is playing a game of 'cat' on a Sunday, saying 'Wilt thou leave thy sins and go to heaven, or have thy sins and go to hell?' and he sees 'with the eyes of my understanding' 'the Lord Jesus looking down upon me, as being very hotly displeased with me and as if he did severely threaten me … ' (Bunyan, 1966: 12). The writing assumes the reality of what appears as personification in *The Pilgrim's Progress*, when he says, in 'The Author's Apology for his Book': 'I, writing of the way / And race of saints in this our Gospel-day, / Fell suddenly into an allegory / About their journey, and the way to glory … ' (Bunyan, 1966: 3). He falls into allegory because his writing already assumes the reality of what, in a non-allegorical writer, would be seen as mere comparison, or image, or occasional metaphor.

Discussion of allegory cannot assume its existence as a literary device. It may, instead, be a way of seeing, which would align the allegorist / dreamer / pilgrim with madness, as Will in *Piers Plowman* is so aligned. In *The Pilgrim's Progress*, the pilgrim is certainly charged with madness, while his worst temptation is to fall into the hands of Giant Despair and his wife Diffidence [i.e. distrust: the opposite of Confidence], and to be imprisoned in Doubting Castle. The temptation to doubt and despair, which is part of Christian's psychomachia, produces the vice of acedia. This, as one of the seven deadly sins, was sloth and sadness combined, a melancholia that produces inaction. Such a state threatens to end the possibility of seeing visions altogether. We return to a point made in chapter 2: because allegory so often deals with emotions which have been personified, it may either be conventional, and general, non-specific, as with the emblem books, or it may show extremes of emotions, or even madness, as its subject matter. This becomes more evident in personification allegory because the narrative there is that of emotions conflicting with each other and with the self. Indeed, both as a mode of writing and through its tendency to transform the sensory world, allegory appears to have been produced during periods of emotional and/or religious crisis, whether personal or historical or both: certainly this is the case for Dante, Langland, Donne, Herbert, and Bunyan, and perhaps Spenser.

BLAKE

Eighteenth-century rationalism tended to oppose itself to allegory on the basis of an empirical desire to want literature to be realistic. The reaction against the Age of Reason, a reaction which characterizes Romanticism, also rejected allegory, but this time in the name of poetic immediacy, regarding allegory as something mechanical and predictable (A equals B), and therefore not marked by any dynamic life. The late-eighteenth-century response to allegory may be discussed through William Blake (1757–1827). He was aware of the emblem tradition from Bunyan, whose book of verses for children, *A Book for Boys and Girls* (1686), was called in its 1724 edition *Divine Emblems; Or, Temporal Things Spiritualised.* By then, Isaac Watts (1674–1748) had produced his illustrated *Divine Songs* for children (1715). Blake followed the tradition with an emblem book *For Children: The Gates of Paradise* (1793, revised in 1818). But Blake saw allegory as falsifying, reliant on memory, rather than being visionary; this formed part of his critique of Bunyan:

> Vision or Imagination is a representation of what Eternally Exists, Really and Unchangeably. Fable or Allegory is Form'd by the daughters of Memory. Imagination is surrounded by the daughters of Inspiration ... Fable is Allegory, but what Critics call The Fable, is Vision itself. The Hebrew Bible and the Gospel of Jesus are not Allegory, but Eternal Vision or Imagination of All that Exists. Note here that Fable is seldom without some Vision. Pilgrim's Progress is full of it, the Greek Poets the same; but Allegory and Vision ought to be known as Two Distinct Things, and so call'd for the Sake of Eternal Life
>
> (Blake, 1966: 604)

Blake regarded *The Pilgrim's Progress* as only a qualified success, because he thought Bunyan was content with the gulf between allegory and vision. Bunyan's highest state is Beulah (Bunyan,

1965: 134), which means 'married' (Isaiah 62.4). But for Blake, Beulah, which implies still a subservience to law, since marriage is a legal state, is below the state of Eternity (Damon, 1965; Brown, 2007: 42–45). Blake reads allegory principally as personifications of 'moral virtues' which are either constraining or chimerical:

> Allegories are things that Relate to Moral Virtues. Moral Virtues do not Exist; they are Allegories and Dissimulations.
>
> (Blake, 1966: 614)

Allegorization produces moral virtues, such as Pity, Mercy, Charity, abstract qualities which the eighteenth century had prized, because Deism, one principal form of religious belief in the century, regarded God as an abstraction. Allegorical techniques in writing or painting lead to representations of the 'passions' in a way that falsifies, making them no more than clichés which can be endlessly reproduced, lacking in individuality. An example here is an artist such as Charles Le Brun (1619–90), mentioned in the Introduction, who, in a lecture of 1668, 'Conférence sur l'expression des passions' given to the Paris Academy of Painting and Sculpture, formulated rules for the portrayal of passions in the human face. Le Brun claimed that 'a person affected by extreme terror will have eyebrows drawn up in the middle; the muscles controlling their movements will become very prominent, swollen and pressing against each other; descending towards the nose; the nose, as well as the nostrils, will appear drawn up. The eyes will appear fully open, the upper eyelid will be hidden beneath the brow ... ' (Gareau, 1992: 96). When an emotional state such as 'terror' can be so prescribed, becoming part of a fixed repertoire of the emotions, it is in danger of becoming imitation, so lending itself to dissimulation. For Blake, this is what the process of *allegoriz*ation entails.

The art and artistic theories of Sir Joshua Reynolds, discussed in the introduction, continued Le Brun's methods, and Blake was hostile to them. Hogarth (1697–1764) argued that art could not represent a hypocrite, indicating that whatever art represents must be an open passion (Hogarth, 1955: 126): in other words, the 'true' representation of a hypocrite involves a fundamental contradiction. However, we can add that no one passion can be isolated from the complex network of emotions that are in play at any one time. To reduce the representation of, say, hypocrisy by depicting it as a single passion is to exacerbate the process of dissimulation. So, for Blake, in the world of 'Experience', it seems that any emotional state that can be named allegorically, such as Love or Pity, will be hypocritical, dissimulating, exerting control. One of the *Songs of Experience* (1794) was first drafted under the allegorical title 'Christian Forbearance'. The meaning persists behind the later, more symbolic title 'A Poison Tree':

> I was angry with my friend:
> I told my wrath, my wrath did end.
> I was angry with my foe:
> I told it not, my wrath did grow.
>
> And I water'd it in fears.
> Night and morning with my tears;
> And I sunned it with smiles
> And with soft deceitful wiles.
>
> And it grew both day and night
> Till it bore an apple bright;
> And my foe beheld it shine,
> And he knew that it was mine,
>
> And into my garden stole
> When the night had veil'd the pole;
> In the morning glad I see
> My foe outstretch'd beneath the tree.   (Blake, 1966: 218)

The poem begins with a statement of emotion, emphasizing anger and 'wrath'. The speaker names 'wrath' as though it was an abstraction but then begins to create something more literal, as this affectual state becomes a seed that is nurtured until it grows into something else, a tree. The sustaining of the metaphor as part of a narrative has produced an allegory, and if we take seriously Blake's opposition to allegory, as 'dissimulation', the performing of a process, the poem turns into a commentary on the process of *allegorization*, even as it produces allegory. The allegorical tree further produces the apple 'bright', and at this stage the text moves beyond the dramatization of the speaker's obsession and 'my foe' is constructed as someone deceived by what is seen as central to allegory: its hypocrisy. By the end, the speaker not only has a tree with an apple, but a garden, and a foe outstretched at his feet. The poem demonstrates the lengths to which the speaker is prepared to go to deploy a range of social strategies to avoid articulating his anger. His foe is punished for the theft of an 'apple' that is much more than the literal object to which it nominally refers.

In Blake's longer prophetic poem, *The Four Zoas*, 8.169, the 'Tree of Mystery', which owes everything to this 'poison tree', 'unfolds in Allegoric fruit' (Blake, 1966: 345). Such a tree is associated with the 'tree of the knowledge of good and evil' from which Eve ate (Genesis 3:1–6). Blake would see 'good' and 'evil' as allegorical terms, because they are abstractions, not dependent on actual living examples to substantiate them. To have to name acts or people as 'good' or 'evil' is to kill them by allegory. 'A Poison Tree' becomes a commentary on the capacity of allegory to deceive. It is also the record of an anger which creates apparently 'real' shapes and enlists them in the pursuit of a deranged project. Not for the first time do we notice that there appears to be an alliance of allegorical thinking with madness.

'A Poison Tree' is an emblem poem, a riddling combination of word and picture. As it appears with its illustration in the *Songs of Innocence and Experience*, a tree runs up the right side of the page, its tendrils framing the title at the top. One tendril descends towards the ground on the left, as if it means to take root, like a banyan tree. Its ending integrates with the stem of the letter 'y' in 'My'. The branches are barren, and the foe, naked, lies on his back with arms outstretched, his head towards the viewer, his hair looking like roots that are about to go into the earth. Tendrils hang over him, completely overshadowing him. There is no apple visible, as if indicating, as the poem does not, that the apple was only an illusion. Where the picture differs from the text is in the way the foe's body seems to grow out of the trunk of the tree, which encloses his body; the 'my' and the foe are joined in the same tree, as if identities cannot be separated. The pictorial image, then, is both an emblem of the poem and a reading of it.

COLERIDGE AND GERMAN ROMANTICISM

Blake's hostility to allegory as abstraction is in part repeated by the Romantic theorist and poet S. T. Coleridge (1772–1834). Unlike Blake, he compares allegory not with vision or imagination, but with another literary form, symbolism:

> The Symbolical cannot, perhaps, be better defined in distinction from the Allegorical, than that it is always itself a part of that, of the whole of which it is a representative. – 'Here comes a sail' – that is, a ship, is a symbolical expression. 'Behold our lion!' when we speak of some gallant soldier, is allegorical. Of most importance to our present subject is this point, that the latter (the allegory) cannot be other than spoken consciously; – whereas in the former (the symbol) it is very possible that the general truth may be unconsciously in the writer's mind during the construction of the symbol; and it proves itself by being produced out of his own mind.
>
> (Honig, 1959: 46)

Honig points out that Coleridge's distinction is actually between *synecdoche*, linked here to symbol, and *metonymy*; nonetheless, the significant part is Coleridge's sense of symbolism emerging spontaneously out of the imagination, and allegory as an artificial conscious construction. In *Biographia Literaria* (1817), Coleridge discusses the primary and the secondary imagination, the first a mode of perception, the second of poetic creation, and contrasts both with the Fancy. Imagination, for Coleridge, struggles to 'idealise and to unify' and is 'essentially vital, even as all objects (as objects) are essentially fixed and dead'. In contrast, as we saw with Blake, 'fancy' works with existent 'fixities and definites' and is no more than a kind of memory, the opposite of imagination (Coleridge, 1965: 167). This, of course, would make allegory something predictable, mechanical. Using the same vocabulary, John Ruskin, a lifelong adherent to Romanticism, called symbolism 'the setting forth of a great truth by an imperfect and inferior sign ... and it is almost always employed by men in their most serious moods of faith, rarely in recreation'. But personification, in contrast, was for him 'a mere recreation of the fancy' (Ruskin, 10.377). The same language reappears in D. H. Lawrence (1885–1930):

> symbols are organic units of consciousness with a life of their own, and you can never explain them away, because their value is dynamic, emotional, belonging to the sense-consciousness of the body and soul, and not simply mental. An allegorical image has a *meaning*. Mr Facing-both-ways has a meaning. But I defy you to lay your finger on the full meaning of Janus, who is a symbol.
>
> (Lawrence, 1936: 295)

Coleridge makes a case against allegory in *The Statesman's Manual* (1816), calling it 'a translation of abstract notions into a picture language which is itself nothing but an abstraction from objects of the senses'. A symbol, however,

> is characterised by a translucence of the special in the individual, or of the general in the special, or of the universal in the general; above all by the translucence of the eternal through and in the temporal. It always partakes of the reality which it renders intelligible; and while it enunciates the whole, abides itself as a living part in that unity of which it is the representative. The other are but empty echoes which the fancy arbitrarily associates with apparitions of matter ...
>
> (Coleridge, 1972: 30)

This is part of a larger argument in which Coleridge contrasts 'Scriptural history' with 'histories of the highest note in the present age' in having 'freedom from the hollowness of abstractions'. He refers to David Hume (1711–76) and Edward Gibbon (1737–94) as authors of modern histories, but he also considers allegorical personifications, which he says are associated with 'mechanic philosophy' (Coleridge, 1972: 28). In the Bible, symbols are 'the living educts of the Imagination' (Coleridge, 1972: 28–29), and indeed symbols gain their importance for Coleridge as being related to divine truth, which he calls the 'idea': reality not perceptible by sensuous images. Hence, 'an idea, in the highest sense of the word, cannot be conveyed but by a symbol' (Coleridge, 1965: 57, 85).

Symbols involve an 'apparent contradiction' since they appear as sensory objects. A good example of a Coleridgean symbol appears in 'The Rime of the Ancient Mariner' (1798), when the albatross appears. It arrives, providentially, as the Mariner's ship sails south, it splits the ice as the ship reaches the South Pole, but the Ancient Mariner, quite arbitrarily, shoots it. It is not, in Coleridge's terms, an allegory, because that would imply that it had a single definite, explicable meaning. Coleridge would not want to think of the bird as representing any one thing, such as Nature, or Innocence, or Divine Grace or Christ coming to the aid of the mariners. Nor is it sufficient to call it 'the bird of good omen' or 'the bird of good luck' as Coleridge did when he wrote prose marginal glosses to the poem nearly twenty years later. Rather, the *lack of a single definite meaning* attached to the bird is the point. The poem refuses to interpret it. It is as if there is, in Romanticism, a new desire to see the universe as constituted by the unknown, and to write that 'unknown' quality into the poetry. The significance of the albatross is that it joins together the experience of the sailors and the outside world of Nature and of God, and that is exactly the function of the symbol; consequently, its death constitutes the loss of the symbolic.

Such loss produces the melancholia of a world without speech or creative breeze:

> Down dropt the breeze, the sails dropt down,
> 'Twas sad as sad could be;
> And we did speak only to break
> The silence of the sea.

(Coleridge, 1969: 190)

It should be noticed, in comparison, that Blake would not have called the animal in his poem 'The Tyger' a symbol. That would be too removed from reality, and it would still be dualistic, in that it would still separate the thing from its meaning. The 'tyger' is reality, and to see it requires 'Vision': it does not join different parts of reality together. The same point holds for 'A Poison Tree', where the tree is not a symbol of anything; rather, it just is, for those who have vision to see it. W. B. Yeats (1865–1939), however, in an essay called 'Symbolism in Painting' (1898), referred to Blake's 'Vision or Imagination' symbolism, seeing it, in contrast to allegory, as that which 'read a meaning ...

into something heard and seen, and loved less for the meaning than for its own sake' (Yeats, 1961: 146–47).

In Yeats, whose thinking is similar to the earlier Romantics on this issue, symbolism is that which gives an unlimited value to an object, because

> if you liberate a person or a landscape from the bonds of motives and their actions, causes and their effects, and from all bonds but the bonds of your love, it will change under your eyes, and become a symbol of an infinite emotion, a perfected emotion, a part of the Divine Essence; for we love nothing but the perfect, and our dreams make all things perfect ... symbols are the only things free enough from all bonds to speak of perfection.
>
> (Yeats, 1961: 148–49)

Coleridge's albatross exists outside all 'causes and their effects'; it just is, and in that way the Mariner's shooting it is an offence against symbolism, because he destroys that which gives value and which tends towards perfection.

Coleridge's allegory/symbol distinction also appears in the Jena-based German Romantic critics, such as August Wilhelm Schlegel (1767–1845), translator of Shakespeare, and Friedrich Schlegel (1772–1829), and their wives, Caroline (1763–1803), who later married Friedrich Schelling (1775–1854), and Dorothea (1765–1829). Other writers in this tradition include Novalis (1772–1801), Friedrich Schleiermacher (1768–1834) and the Shakespeare scholar Ludwig Tieck (1773–1853). Schelling's *Philosophy of Art* (1803) insisted that the symbol is not merely a sign for something, as allegory is; it both signifies and participates in the idea which it represents. As in Coleridge, the symbol is 'organically' linked to what it describes. These writers thought that the fixed quality of allegory associated it with the complete and determinate work of art, and preferred the idea of the fragment, because that suggests the infinite to which the work leads, and of which it is a part.

The 'Aphorisms' of Goethe (1749–1832) align allegory with clear meaning, with the 'concept', whereas symbolism has to do with the 'idea', which is ungraspable, ineffable:

> Allegory transforms the appearance into a concept, the concept into an image, but in such a way that the concept may be captured definite and complete in the image, and may be expressed by it.
>
> Symbolism transforms the appearance into an idea, the idea into an image, and in such a way that the idea remains infinitely powerful and unattainable in the image, and even if expressed in every language, would remain unattainable.
>
> (Wheeler, 1984: 229; see also 9–10, 128–35, 17–58)

The 'appearance' here is the phenomenon, what appears to the eyes. In allegory, the concept is always expressible through the image, but this is not so with the symbol. There, the 'idea' remains always open, always needing further interpretation. Allegory expresses what can be put into a concept, but symbolism expresses what cannot be conceptualized. But Goethe did not completely jettison allegory; indeed he used it in the second part of *Faust* (1825–31) (Brown, 2007: 219).

Karl Solger (1780–1819), professor of Philosophy in the then new University of Berlin, took a similar approach in *Erwin, or Four Dialogues on Beauty and Art* (1816). Here, art is the means of presenting a timeless and universal idea of things. Solger dismisses allegory as mere personification and sees the symbol as an expression of the universe in its completeness. The German Romantics were fascinated by the idea of nature as a hieroglyph that needed deciphering, like an aesthetic object; not coincidentally, Egyptian hieroglyphics were interpreted by Champollion (1790–1832) during this period. Solger distinguished the symbol from the image, sign or allegory. A symbol is the idea in its actuality, as distinct from its ideality which cannot be represented, hence a symbol is true, and not an image of truth. Allegory, on the other hand, is not connected to the universal idea; indeed all it can do is expose the differences between the individual gods within a polytheistic context. Such differences show that there are no 'general (i.e. universally valid) concepts' underlying allegorical figurations. But the symbol 'includes all tendencies in their universality', making it both individual and 'the Divine itself' (Wheeler, 1984: 134–35).

It has become apparent that symbolism, as it is deployed in Romanticism, is needed to rescue the idea of the divine: these

German Romantics felt the inadequacy of Christianity, but wanted to express a sense of the divine world for which allegory was thought inadequate. In correspondence with Tieck (3 August 1818), Solger enlarges on the allegory/symbolism distinction in a discussion of mysticism, which grasps reality in the form of revelation. However such mysticism is compromised by a tendency to 'draw it into our presence by means of *individual* symbols, or to lend it meaning by allegory' (Wheeler, 1984: 154). In a later letter (11 January 1819), Solger argues that allegory in art is based on a conscious mysticism, while symbolism rests on unconscious mysticism. The limits of these modes are reached when 'allegory becomes a mere game of the intellect and symbolism imitation of nature'. The danger with allegory is that it separates itself into different constituent parts, and Solger concludes with the example of Calderón (1600–681), the Spanish baroque dramatist much admired by Goethe, who was, Solger says, caught up in the 'dissipating effect of allegory, and that is exactly why he tends so much towards mannerism' (Wheeler, 1984: 157–58). Mannerism here is described as without unity of perception, an art that splits up reality into different constitutive parts.

Jean Paul Richter (1763–1825) offers another example of how German Romantics approached allegory. In his *School for Aesthetics* (1804), he discusses allegory in relation to wit, which Wheeler defines as the possibility of finding remote similarities between different entities (Wheeler, 1984: 197–98). Wit and humour form another aspect of German Romantic thought, which values irony highly, and, in Solger's case, extends it to include 'the entire nature of art' (Wheeler, 1984: 146). Irony is not a topic for Coleridge, but for the Germans it brings out the inadequacy of the writer's subjective vision to incorporate into itself the infinite; it becomes a form of self-criticism, 'at once self-creation and self-destruction', destructive of the writer's illusions (Schlegel, 1971: 145, 147, 167). But irony becomes apparent in writing which uses symbolism, since the symbol is a finite, sensuous expression of the 'idea', and therefore, imperfect. Irony enters into the argument because of the discovery that what is to be expressed is inadequately conveyed by the image. Irony, which we have already seen as part of allegory, has now, in the writings of Jean Paul Richter, been shown to compromise symbolism.

Thomas Carlyle (1795–1881), one of the few mediators of German Romantic thought in Britain, was aware of the differences between the emblem, the symbol and allegory. In *Sartor Resartus* (1834), the fictional editor cites the fictitious Professor Teufelsdröckh, who, in utter opposition to the materialist interpretation of reality, argues that:

> All visible things are emblems; what thou seest is not there on its own account ... matter exists only spiritually, and to represent some idea and *body* it forth ... what is Man himself, and his whole terrestrial life but an Emblem; a Clothing or visible Garment for that divine ME of his, cast hither, like a light-particle, down from Heaven?
>
> (Carlyle, 1959: 54)

A later chapter of *Sartor Resartus*, called 'Symbols', further extends the Romantic idea of the symbolic, arguing that:

> In the Symbol proper, what we can call a Symbol, there is ever, more or less distinctly and directly, some embodiment and revelation of the Infinite; the Infinite is made to blend itself with the Finite, to stand visible, and as it were, attainable there. By Symbols, accordingly, is man guided and commanded, made happy, made wretched. He everywhere finds himself encompassed with Symbols, recognized as such or not recognized: the Universe is but one vast Symbol of God; nay, if thou wilt have it, what is man himself but a Symbol of God?
>
> (Carlyle, 1959: 165)

Later, in 'On Heroes, Hero-Worship, and the Heroic in History' (1840), Carlyle follows the Romantic pattern of elevating symbolism above allegory, in seeing the symbol as giving an intuition of truth, preceding any revelation of truth, but leading towards it. Whereas, *'The Pilgrim's Progress* is an Allegory ... but consider whether Bunyan's Allegory could have *preceded* the Faith it symbolises!' Allegory is a *'sportful* shadow, a mere play of the Fancy' (Carlyle, 1959: 244) in relation to the faith which precedes it.

Here, in Carlyle, may be seen a nostalgia for the idea of some divine, but not Christian, spiritual force that writing gestures towards. It has been argued that interest in symbolism, as opposed to allegory, was a marker of the modern world. Romantic writers began looking back on past literature as forming a single unity, and a source of inspiration. So Gordon Teskey argues that 'the practice of literary history begins when the history of allegory ends', a practice of reading texts of the past which endowed past literature with a symbolic value. Teskey quotes from T. S. Eliot's essay 'Tradition and the Individual Talent' (1919), in which the past takes on the quality of 'monuments' attesting to an 'ideal order' which exists and is perceived in the mind, which becomes that which holds the whole of reality, past and present (Teskey, 1996: 150–51). Just as symbolism made the writer feel connected or at one with the whole world, so literature now becomes the symbol of an ideal order. And hence it also requires the downplaying of allegory, because this could never allow for belief in such a sublime unity, holding together 'the mind of Europe'. Literature itself has become the symbol of infinite value, and of an ideal history recorded in the tradition of great writing.

4

ALLEGORY IN THE AGE OF REALISM

Those who have read any Romance or Poetry antient or modern, must have been informed, that Love hath Wings, by which they are not to understand, as some young Ladies, by mistake have done, that a Lover can fly: the Writers, by this ingenious Allegory, intending to insinuate no more, than that Lovers do not march like Horse-Guards ...

(Fielding, 1999: 87)

A Man's life of any worth is a continual allegory – and very few eyes can see the Mystery of his life – a life like the scriptures, figurative – which such people can no more make out than they can the hebrew Bible. Lord Byron cuts a figure – but he is not figurative – Shakespeare lived a life of Allegory: his works are the comments on it.

(Keats, 1954: 241)

Two views of allegory are stated here. Fielding's joking with allegory illustrates what happens to it in the period of the realist novel, of which *Joseph Andrews* (1742) offers an early example. He mocks it in the name of common sense, and empirical logic, leaving open the question whether allegory can exist at all within the age of realism. Realism becomes a dominant nineteenth-century mode of writing, premised on the belief that speech should be direct, capable of being inspected empirically, and written about in language which purports to be a transparent window opening onto its subject matter.

Keats, however, uses 'allegory' to describe Shakespeare, against those tendencies in Romanticism which refused the term, and it relates to his conviction that the 'poetical character' is 'not itself – it has no self – it is everything and nothing – It has no character. ... It has as much delight in conceiving an Iago as an Imogen. ... A Poet is the most unpoetical of any thing in existence, because he has no identity' (letter of 27 October 1818, Keats, 1954: 172). Iago (in *Othello*) and Imogen (in *Cymbeline*) are opposites in gender, in good and evil, and in style: all that unites them is the letter 'I', which may make them figures of Shakespeare's auto-biography. Raised to the status of being characters, they become allegories. Byron keeps his identity whatever he writes, but a 'life of allegory' implies fluidity; there is nothing which the subject adheres to, no ego, 'no identity', and the only way to interpret allegory is by more writing.

This chapter looks at allegory in three ways. The first deals with two nineteenth-century American novelists, Nathaniel Hawthorne and Herman Melville, and one poet, Emily Dickinson; each of these, inspired by Carlyle, found excitement in the allegory/symbol distinction. They followed the New England writer Ralph Waldo Emerson (1803–82), a follower of Carlyle, saying that 'particular natural facts are symbols of particular spiritual facts. Nature is the symbol of spirit' (Matthiessen, 1941: 41–45, 57–58). Hawthorne and Melville show a resistance to realism in their novels, which they called 'romances', but unlike Emerson, they are not ready to discard allegory as inferior to the symbol, choosing rather to retain both.

The second way will follow Keats' hint: examining allegorical writing as contesting the fixing of identity that nineteenth-century modernity was so concerned to uphold. Allegory becomes a way of thinking about resistance to identity, or what remains monstrous. Since a life of allegory can only be explained by further 'commentary', it suggests its final uninterpretability. This is an issue which, developed through discussion of Courbet, will lead into the third approach to allegory: seeing it as a mode appropriate to the city, the place which baffles by its plurality of signs. Here I draw on Dickens, Marx and Baudelaire. Allegory, not symbolism, becomes identified with the text that cannot be read singly: like the modern city.

HAWTHORNE, MELVILLE, DICKINSON

Nathaniel Hawthorne (1804–64) and Herman Melville (1819–91) were admirers of Dante, Shakespeare and Spenser; they also emerged from the Puritan tradition within which Bunyan and emblem allegory appeared. Discussion of these two writers has sometimes, as in F. O. Matthiessen's pioneering study *American Renaissance* (1941), assumed a distinction between the symbol and allegory (Matthiessen, 1941: 242–315), but we may also see the distinction being questioned in their work. Hawthorne's short story 'The Maypole of Merry Mount' (in *Twice-Told Tales*, 1837), about the early Puritan settlers in New England, begins:

> In the slight sketch here attempted, the facts recorded on the grave pages of our New England annalists have wrought themselves, almost spontaneously into a sort of allegory.
>
> (Hawthorne, 1987: 133)

Here historical facts become allegory, and thus open to multiple interpretations. History, emerging in the nineteenth century as a modern discipline, cannot be approached for literal, unitary meanings, but only for that which is veiled, hidden. This section draws attention to Hawthorne's difference from Emerson, who asserted that 'every history should be written in a wisdom which ... looked at facts as symbols' (Emerson, 1981: 137). Emerson's 'symbols' may elevate facts, making them like divine truths, but if Hawthorne calls them 'allegories', after the influence of Romanticism with its stress on the symbol, that may involve questioning their 'divine' status.

In Hawthorne's short story 'Rappaccini's Daughter' (1844), the daughter is poisoned by her father, and is poisonous to anyone who comes in contact with her. Her name is Beatrice, the name of the woman who inspired Dante's *Commedia*. The name means 'blessed', and it is as if Hawthorne is trying to poison the name itself, as well as everything that it implies. It opens with an introduction, in which the writer – Hawthorne of course – comments negatively on the work of M. de l'Aubépine, the French version of 'Hawthorne', who is supposed to have written the story which he is translating:

> his writings, to do them justice, are not altogether destitute of fancy and originality; they might have won him greater reputation but for an inveterate love of allegory, which is apt to invest his plots and characters with the aspect of scenery and people in the clouds, and to steal away the human warmth out of his conceptions ... he generally contents himself with a very slight embroidery of outward manners – the faintest possible counterfeit of real life ... .
>
> (Hawthorne, 1987: 285)

By giving himself a French name, Hawthorne separates himself from the American Puritan tradition, and its commitment to truth. Hence, the word 'counterfeit', attached to allegory, aligns it with deceitfulness, and exoticism. In the same way, allegory becomes the topic of Hawthorne's novel *The Scarlet Letter* (1850), which opens with an autobiographical introduction, in which the author tells how he came across an embroidered letter (the letter 'A') in the Salem custom house where he is working amid old documents and letters:

> Certainly there was some deep meaning in it, most worthy of interpretation, and which, as it were, streamed forth from the mystic symbol, subtly communicating itself to my sensibilities, but evading the analysis of my mind.
>
> (Hawthorne, 1987: 62)

A few pages later, Hawthorne comments on the power of moonlight for a 'romance writer' to transform familiar things so that they 'lose their actual substance and become things of intellect'; everything becomes 'a neutral territory, somewhere between the real world and fairy-land, where the Actual and Imaginary may meet, and each imbue itself with the nature of the other' (Hawthorne, 1987: 66).

In the narrative of *The Scarlet Letter*, set in the seventeenth century, and taking as its subject the Puritan settlers in New England, Hester Prynne is punished for her adultery by having to wear the scarlet letter, 'A', presumably standing for Adultery. But this letter, it emerges, has multiple significations: including Arthur Dimmesdale (her lover), America, allegory, abolition, autobiography, and the letter 'A' itself, as an element of the alphabet. As a symbol, it ceases to refer to anything in particular, especially as Hester so embroiders it that it ceases to have a single meaning for her contemporaries, and frustrates the will to truth which is enforced within this society, with its demands for confession. 'Symbol' becomes allegory under the power of 'embroidery' which like allegory in 'Rappaccini's Daughter' 'counterfeits'. *The Scarlet Letter* is haunted by a past which it must read, though it is reluctant to do so, preferring to make New England history into an allegory. The past is laid open to reinterpretation, because its symbols are pronounced unreadable, as in the case of the decoration of the governor's hall, 'with strange and seemingly cabalistic figures and diagrams, suitable to the quaint taste of the age' (Hawthorne, 1970: 126). The word 'cabalistic' is deliberately anachronistic for the seventeenth century, as is the word 'hieroglyph' (van Leer, 1985: 58–59), and is part of an attempt to obscure the American past and read it allegorically. With 'Rappaccini's Daughter', the process is taken further, since the story is set in Renaissance Italy, which is made to serve as an allegory of America in the nineteenth century.

Herman Melville called Hawthorne an allegorist in an essay, 'Hawthorne and his Mosses' (1850), discussing his short story 'Young Goodman Brown' (1835). There, the titular hero, though married to Faith, walks out into the woods from Salem village one evening, after the witch trials of 1692, and has a visionary sense of all of the pious villagers being out there, in the place where Dante starts in the *Inferno*, and where Spenser's heroes go. The civilization of the village is meaningless, their real 'faith' being devil-worship. When the hero fantasizes the villagers in this 'other' way, as demonic, he becomes an allegorist. Matthiessen argues that Hawthorne knew how the Puritan theologian Cotton Mather (1663–1728) had claimed, in a work written in 1693 at the request of the judges of the witch trials, that 'the New Englanders are a people of God settled in those which were once the devil's territories' (Matthiessen, 1941: 282–83). This suggests that Hawthorne was responding to a reading of history by Mather which had itself allegorized New England's seventeenth-century settlements. Melville sees Hawthorne's response as a sign of his 'blackness', his diabolism (Melville, 1967: 541). 'Young Goodman Brown' is an allegory which de-allegorizes Mather; and plays with the symbol/allegory distinction so that, if Emerson thought facts were symbols, so potentially divine, allegory now becomes a diabolic truth which unveils the evil that respectable America has repressed.

Writing to Hawthorne on November 17, 1851, after the publication of his own novel *Moby-Dick*, Melville asks 'ever since Adam, who has got to the meaning of this great allegory – the world? Then we pygmies must be content to have our paper allegories but ill apprehended' (Melville, 1967: 566; see also letter to Sophia Hawthorne (January 8, 1852), 568). *Moby-Dick* may be read both as an allegory and as a meditation on allegory. Ahab, on his mad quest to kill the white whale, declares:

> all visible objects ... are but as pasteboard masks. But in each event –
> in the living act, the undoubted deed – there, some unknown but still
> reasoning thing puts forth the mouldings of its features from behind
> the unreasoning mask. If a man will strike, strike through the mask!
> (Melville, 1967: 144)

The language recalls Carlyle and Emerson. Because Ahab hates the 'mask', he may be said to react against allegory, wanting to reach towards a single truth, rejecting the idea that the world is a vast personification. In a later chapter, 'The Doubloon', Ahab pauses before the coin that he has nailed to the mast as a reward for whoever sights the whale first:

> newly attracted by the strange figures and inscriptions stamped on it,
> as though now for the first time beginning to interpret for himself in

some monomaniac way whatever significance might lurk in them. And some certain significance lurks in all things, else all things are little worth, and the round world itself but an empty cipher.

(Melville, 1967: 358)

Ahab may be a monomaniac, in which case allegorical interpretation, trying to read hieroglyphics, or making signs into meaningful hieroglyphics, appeals to an obsessiveness which comes close to madness. The comment that significance only 'lurks' in each object suggests such significance has faded in the age of realism; and the text cannot prove the validity of allegorical interpretation, save by asserting it, while retaining the tragic sense that 'else all things are little worth'.

Contemporary with Melville, Emily Dickinson (1830–86), from Amherst, Massachusetts, daughter of a lawyer and politician from the old Puritan tradition, did not write about allegory, but lived a 'life of allegory', as a recluse dressed in white who never published her verse in her lifetime. Her mode of existence may be compared with Hawthorne's clergyman in his short story 'The Minister's Black Veil'. The priest makes himself an allegory by walking around with his face covered with a black veil. Dickinson's poetry, which utilizes strict rhetorical devices (Cuddy, 1990: 92–102), evokes Puritan personifications through its capitalizations. In 'After great pain, a formal feeling comes' (poem no. 341), the body is divided up, in a manner which is characteristic of allegorical methods:

> The Nerves sit ceremonious, like Tombs –
> The stiff Heart questions was it He, that bore,
> And Yesterday, or Centuries before?

(Dickinson, 1970: 162)

The turn to allegory in Emily Dickinson comes from a sense of inner division caused by 'great pain' which then makes each part of the body act separately and independently. At a formal level, the poem moves in and out of allegory, while also using similes, as with the appearance of the word 'like'. Indeed the poem never moves from the figurative, while also suggesting that the allegory is part of an ongoing narrative, as indicated by the word 'yesterday'. It is structured by words which associate with each other: 'formal', 'ceremonious', 'stiff' (the machinery will not work easily – but the word also suggests the stiffness of death), and then, in the second verse, 'The Feet, mechanical go round'. The poem records both loss of identity and absence of feeling. It is not even possible to assign a single gender to the speaker, and there is no way in which the poem can be assigned a place in Dickinson's biography. In this 'life of allegory', life remembers allegorically: in the last of the poem's three verses, Dickinson declares 'This is the Hour of Lead', which personifies abstraction: emotional states have been turned into things, 'reified', deadened. A 'formal feeling' is 'stiff' and 'ceremonious', but it also suggests something only existing on the surface. It denies anything deeper, that there is any significance to be given to the 'great pain'. The poem suggests then a resistance to feeling, or affect, which happens by putting the affectual states into allegory, and it also suggests that an allegorical state – the formal feeling – means acceptance of death's stiffness. As with the near-despair in *Moby-Dick* that if allegory cannot be found 'all things are little worth', the poem is both allegorical and denies the power of allegory to change anything.

IDENTITY AND MONSTROSITY

Dickinson's poetry allows us to move from considering allegory as a preoccupation in nineteenth-century America to thinking about its relationship to identity. 'After great pain' gives a sense of all comparisons being odd, strange, not fitting naturally, or even 'formally', because the way the person feels cannot be turned into conventional imagery. It seems that allegory, which disrupts or undermines meaning, serves as a way to describe the indescribable, or the monstrous, like Beatrice in 'Rappaccini's Daughter' whose monstrosity, which is not seen formally on the surface, is that she is the incarnation of poison. We can consider Shakespeare's *Othello*, where Othello says to Iago, who is beginning to torment him by mockingly repeating his words:

> By heaven, thou echo'st me
> As if there were some monster in thy thought
> Too hideous to be shown ...

> (3.3.110–12)

Moments later, Iago says:

> O beware, my lord, of jealousy.
> It is the green-eyed monster which doth mock
> The meat it feeds on.

(3.3. 169–71)

Jealousy, as a familiar personification, turns into the 'monster', that which by conventional definition has no form, and cannot be represented: certainly whatever poisons Othello's mind is more than ordinary jealousy. But jealousy does have a form in this play – embodied in both Othello and Iago. Dickinson's poem resists monstrous possibilities, even what might be thought of as the temptation to see herself as monstrous, by insistence on the 'formal', the publicly presentable. But 'a formal feeling' is an odd phrase which defies a conventional meaning; formality is observable on the surface, but here the word is applied to an interior state, to feelings. 'A formal feeling' is an almost unnameable state. Perhaps allegory, not symbolism, is a way of considering what cannot be named. Mary Shelley (1797–1851), in the 1831 introduction to her novel of 1818, *Frankenstein, Or, the Modern Prometheus*, writes that she was often asked 'how I, then a young girl, came to think of, and to dilate upon, so very hideous an idea?' (Shelley, 1985: 5). The female writer has given birth, with *Frankenstein*, to a monster – as her protagonist, Victor Frankenstein, gave 'birth' to the 'monster'. *Frankenstein* is an allegorical and a monstrous text, not because the 'monster' symbolizes the energies of the French Revolution, or the British working class, or the rights of man or the wrongs of women, but because the monstrous cannot be given form, cannot be represented. When created, Frankenstein says of it, 'it became a thing such as even Dante could not have conceived' (Shelley, 1985: 57). Allegory has a place for monsters, but *Frankenstein*'s allegorical writing exceeds the bounds of traditional allegory. The concept revises Aristotle (384–322 BCE), who says in *The Poetics* (c.330 BCE) that 'the poet aims at the representation [*mimesis*] of life' (Aristotle, 1965: 69). Only that which can be assigned a discrete identity can be represented. The monster is brought together 'from bones of the charnel-houses' (Shelley, 1985: 53), as an assemblage, not organically put together, but as fragments. It points not to the idea of the symbol as a natural, organic whole, like Coleridge's albatross, but to allegory as artificial, incomplete, defying representation, like Blake's poison tree. The monster in *Frankenstein* breaks with the model of a figure of speech (simile or metaphor) being able to say what something is like.

Perhaps Mary Shelley and Emily Dickinson use allegory as a way of evoking what cannot be represented, or has no identity that can be publicly validated. Dickinson's reclusiveness evoked the confinement of Bertha Mason, shut up in the attic in *Jane Eyre* (1847) by Charlotte Brontë. She is Mr Rochester's Caribbean-born wife, whom he keeps secretly confined as mad, and Jane Eyre sees her as a 'figure' running backwards and forwards:

> What it was, whether beast or human being, one could not, at first sight, tell: it grovelled, seemingly, on all fours; it snatched and growled like some strange wild animal: but it was covered with clothing; and a quantity of dark, grizzled hair, wild as a mane, hid its head and face.
>
> (Brontë, 1996: 327–28)

A moment later, it is a 'clothed hyena', then a 'lunatic' described as a 'big woman' who showed 'virile force'. Whatever the reactionary nature of the politics of representation of the madwoman from the colonies here, the two women are in some ways mirror images of each other. If Jane Eyre cannot see her kinship with the 'other' woman, it is nonetheless signalled at some moments in the text where both figures are looking in the mirror in ways which align them with each other (Brontë, 1996: 21, 317). And even the madness which Bertha Mason suffers from may also be a quality in Jane Eyre's existence which she recognizes when she has been confined in the red room: she thinks of herself as 'a heterogeneous thing' (Brontë, 1996: 23). It may be argued that the monstrosity in Bertha Mason which makes her 'other', heterogeneous, has an allegorical function; it brings out the idea that there is something other, something monstrous, within Jane Eyre herself which her 'autobiography', as she calls it, suppresses.

After Jane Eyre has seen Bertha Mason, she chooses not to stay, certainly not to become Mr Rochester's mistress. The last meeting ends: "'Farewell!' was the cry of my heart as I left him. Despair added – "Farewell for ever!"'. The personification of the heart, and of despair, which recalls Bunyan, and the psychomachia of *The Pilgrim's Progress*, is followed by:

> That night I never thought to sleep: but a slumber fell on me as soon as I lay down in bed. I was transported in thought to the scenes of childhood: I dreamt I lay in the red-room at Gateshead; that the night was dark, and my mind impressed with strange fears. The light that long ago had struck me into syncope [unconsciousness], recalled in this vision, seemed glidingly to mount the wall, and tremblingly to pause in the centre of the obscured ceiling. I lifted up my head to look: the roof resolved to clouds, high and dim; the gleam was such as the moon imparts to vapours she is about to sever. I watched her come – watched with the strangest anticipation; as though some word of doom were to be written on her disk. She broke forth as never moon yet burst from cloud: a hand first penetrated the sable folds and waved them away; then, not a moon, but a white human form shone in the azure, inclining a glorious brow earthward. It gazed and gazed on me. It spoke, to my spirit: immeasurably distant was the tone, yet so near, it whispered in my heart –
> 'My daughter, flee temptation!'
> 'Mother, I will.'
>
> (Brontë, 1996: 358)

With slumber personified, and with the verb in the main clause, 'I was transported', which deprives the subject of agency, Brontë's realism turns into something else associated with medieval allegory: the record of a dream, which produces the image of the moon, which appears first as a portent, as though it was about to be the bearer of some strange message. It then resolves into a personification, of Jane Eyre's dead, never-seen mother, notably associated with the colour white, which makes her, contradictorily, virginal and a mother. Everything within this dream-vision, because it is associated with the red room, recalls that the self is 'heterogeneous'. It both externalizes and resolves allegorically the war of feelings going on in Jane Eyre, and is coded as feminine. Allegory cannot be seen as an exclusively feminine form, but certainly Mary Shelley, Brontë and Dickinson each use it in a way that suggests that it helps with non-communicable experience, giving expression to that which is singular, heterogeneous, lacking resemblance to anything else, and breaking with social modes of thinking about identity.

COURBET'S 'REAL ALLEGORY'

Allegory in the nineteenth century, as outside realism, and outside thinking which works with a sense of clear, single identity, ceases to be that which has one meaning only: allegory no longer means in the old A equals B mode. This can be seen in the openness to different interpretations – or to no interpretation at all – which is apparent in the work of the French artist Gustave Courbet (1819–77). In 1851, the year of Napoleon Bonaparte's *coup d'état* in France, which put the country on a reactionary course for the next twenty years, Courbet announced himself as 'not only a Socialist, but a democrat and a Republican as well: in a word, a lover of the whole Revolution, and above all, a Realist, that is to say a sincere lover of genuine truth' (Clark, 1973: 23). Courbet was famous for his anti-idealism in art and for his paintings of the French countryside and of peasants, which did not show the kinds of pleasant pastoral scenes whose idealized values the bourgeoisie could buy and feel thereby that they had appropriated them for themselves. Using huge canvases, whose monumental scale threatened the values of the middle classes, because they simply did not 'fit' with their world, he showed what T. J. Clark calls 'the invasion of the rural idyll by usury, class conflict, and expropriation' (Clark, 1973: 116). At the time they were called 'ugly paintings' (quoted in Herding, 1991: 53). In 1854–55, he produced a painting that is of direct relevance to allegory: *The Painter's Studio: Real Allegory, Summing Up a Phase of Seven Years in my Artistic Life* ('L'Atelier du peintre, allégorie réelle determinant une phase de sept années de ma vie artistique').

This was a huge canvas (359cm by 598cm) that was rejected by the selection committee of the World Exhibition in Paris in

1855, but became part of a one-man show put on by Courbet in a temporary pavilion during the time of the exhibition. The seven-year period dates back from 1855 to the defeat of the revolutionary impulse of 1848. The composition includes a self-portrait of Courbet seated in profile, but a little away from the viewer, working in his studio in Paris, painting a huge landscape. A naked woman is next to him, positioned behind his back, holding a long white cloth which cascades onto the floor towards the front of the picture. On Courbet's other side appears a peasant boy, his back to the viewer. Michael Fried points out that the painter is in such proximity to the canvas he is painting that he seems virtually inseparable from it (Fried, 1990: 100). There is a white cat between the boy and the woman.

On either side of this central group appear over thirty figures, including the poet Charles Baudelaire (1821–67), a friend of Courbet's, whose writing we will return to later in this chapter. He is seen reading on the picture's right-hand side. There are also seen other figures who supported Courbet: the socialist Proudhon (1809–65), Champfleury (1821–89), Max Buchon (1818–69) and Alfred Bruyas (1821–76), Courbet's patron at Montpellier. On the left-hand side of the picture are alternative figures; next to the canvas is an Irish woman crouching, suckling a baby. In a letter to Champfleury describing the picture (Touissant, 1978: 254–55) Courbet said that he drew her as he saw her in England: 'I saw her in a London street wearing nothing but a black straw hat, a torn green veil and a ragged black shawl and carrying a naked baby under her arm'. But we do not know if Courbet ever visited London, and this realist portrayal of the results of English rule in Ireland may be based on something entirely fictive. Other figures include a Jew, a priest, a Republican from the Revolution of 1789–94, a huntsman, an undertaker's mute, and, sitting, a male figure with two dogs.

In considering this picture, what is meant by the riddling phrase 'real allegory'? The art critic Linda Nochlin compares it with the allegorical title which Ford Madox Brown (1821–93) gave to his Pre-Raphaelite painting *Work* (1852–65), attempting to show the dignity of labour (Nochlin, 1971: 128). Nochlin argues that Courbet's painting shows the artist as the craftsman in a modern allegory illustrating the ideas of Fourier (1772–1837), who wanted to revolutionize work practices through setting up Associations of Capital, Labour and Talent. This interpretation takes 'allegory' in a specific sense, making the painting the illustration of an abstract idea, and the illustration of certain of Courbet's political commitments. Hélène Touissant draws on another sense of 'allegory', in arguing that Courbet's letter to Champfleury was 'a protective manoeuvre to conceal the true import of his work and that the letter was intended for others not for Champfleury' (Touissant, 1978: 259). She reads a deeper message into each of the persons represented; for example, the seated figure with dogs satirizes the Emperor, Napoleon III, a covert reference in the artist's attempt to avoid censorship (Touissant, 1978: 266). The 'allegory' then is a way of guarding a secret, of being able to say one thing while apparently saying another.

Michael Fried's interpretation, first formulated in 1981, offers a third possibility, concentrating on the figures in the centre, thus refusing the possibility of giving a single interpretation of all the details of the painting. He suggests that the self-representation is the point. Courbet paints a landscape without any model, or original image, to guide him. His landscape is not mimetic of a single place, but is an expression of himself, while the white cloth of the nude resembles a waterfall which, as it were, spills out of the landscape (it may be that the painted landscape includes a waterfall in it). Waterfalls are characteristic of Courbet's art, as in *The Source* (1868), in which a naked woman, with her back to the viewer, holds out her left hand under a waterfall, so that the water trickles through it. Her right hand holds a branch, which Fried compares to a brush, and her left hand is in a position in which it could hold a palette, as if she allegorizes a way in which Courbet as a male artist works. Nudity and fresh water suggest the new, the origin, and Fried records one early view which took the woman in *The Painter's Studio* to be a personification of truth (Fried, 1990: 158).

Two points follow from Fried's reading. The painter, the boy and the woman allegorize each other. For Fried, the woman, because she is actually standing behind Courbet, and because her figure cuts off the line of the edge of the canvas, is drawn into the landscape in the picture being painted. The conclusion from this would be that this lack of separation between those in front of the landscape and the picture itself shows the natural world as absorbed in self-representation, painter and landscape moving into and out of each other. By cutting out the painter as separate from his artwork, it is implied that in this realism nature speaks. That may be Courbet's provocation, his challenge to those who would resent his realism. It may also express a desire, giving the sense that that is how he wishes his art could be, and how he wishes it to be taken. His art can only be realistic inside an allegory, which means that allegory and realism are not opposites. Realism cannot be an objective view of reality, first, because there is a politics involved in wanting to represent reality in whichever way it is shown, and second, because the desire of the realist is the same as that which motivated those medieval artists, such as Giotto, who portrayed virtues and vices: it is didactic, to show people something, to educate them.

Courbet's 'allegory' makes clear that realism is figural, achieved through an act of representation, which, however much it assumes an ability to show fairly what is being represented, is an act of taking over. This may be illustrated by the woman's place in the picture: if she is part of what is being represented, the picture certainly objectifies her. The 'real allegory' reveals more than Courbet might be conscious of, since it illustrates a sexual politics. Allegory, then, differs from realism in that while the latter might think it delivers a single message, the former produces several, which may be 'other' than what is intended. *The Painter's Studio* asks what and who the work of art is for, and opens up the question of who represents, and what the work of representation involves.

In an interpretation which builds on this argument, Linda Nochlin returns to the painting in a reading which ignores Fried's, approaching Courbet as a woman who feels hostile to traditional allegory as being too directional in imposing interpretation, and that she feels thereby 'shut out of the house of meaning' (Faunce and Nochlin, 1988: 23). Taking hints from Walter Benjamin's conception of allegory as linked to the fragmentary and to periods of crises in meaning, the subject of the next chapter, she finds it an 'allegory of the unfinished, or the impossibility of ever finishing in the sense of imposing a single meaning'. She sees an example of this incompleteness in the Irish woman, a modern version of Dürer's engraving *Melencolia*. The woman allegorizes a melancholic state. This double reading – personification as well as realist image – makes the picture an allegory in a further sense. Nochlin notes a skull which is just to the left of the woman. It is a classic Renaissance emblem, linking the painting to the history of allegory, and it is oddly placed next to the woman who belongs, as Nochlin points out, to city-space, to the streets. This, of course, affirms the woman's place as part of an allegory of the nineteenth century (Faunce and Nochlin, 1988: 17–29).

URBAN ALLEGORY: DICKENS AND MARX

Through Courbet, we have arrived at a possible link between allegory and the city. Three different writers embody the idea that allegory may be the way to describe the city whose size and multifariousness otherwise defeats representation: Dickens, Marx and Baudelaire. Dickens' writing is throughout both realist and urban, yet in several places it evokes allegory, as, for example, when he quotes Bunyan, such as with the subtitle of *Oliver Twist* (1837), *The Parish Boy's Progress*. In doing so, Dickens is the successor to William Hogarth (1697–1764), whose series of pictures, such as *A Rake's Progress* (1735), present moral and allegorical subjects in a style that relates to personification, and which creates the conditions for urban caricature that we find in Thomas Rowlandson (1756–1827) and James Gillray (1757–1815). These sometimes work in an allegorical mode, showing one comic situation as a way of commenting on another. These artists' influence was felt on Dickens and his illustrators; his principal artist, K. Halbot Browne (1815–82), called himself Phiz, short for 'physiognomy'. This implies a fascination with what is in the face, and invites the question whether the face, or by extension the city, should be read scientifically, or allegorically. The nature of the city is not that it cannot be read, but rather that its signs are too many and plural, so that there is no adequate way of reducing it to a single meaning. Nor is the city, because it is a human construction and outside nature, the place for the Romantic symbol. Allegory becomes appropriate where the question of how to read, and the necessity of doing so, becomes prominent.

In *Bleak House* (1853–54) a baroque ceiling, decorated with the allegorical figure of a classical Roman, forms part of the decoration of the old house of the lawyer, Mr Tulkinghorn:

> [The house's] roomy staircases, passages, and ante-chambers still remain; and even its painted ceilings, where Allegory, in Roman helmet and celestial linen, sprawls among balustrades and pillars, flowers, clouds, and big-legged boys, and makes the head ache – as would seem to be Allegory's object always, more or less.
>
> (Dickens, 1971: 182)

The ceiling's painting is collapsed into the name of its principal figure and its genre. Mr Tulkinghorn seems, unconsciously, to be dominated by this Roman figure who points downwards as if he is a signifier, indicating the presence of a signified. When he is murdered in his room (chapter 48), Allegory points down at:

> an empty chair and at a stain upon the ground before it ... [and] an excited imagination might suppose there was something in them so terrific, as to drive the rest of the composition, not only the attendant big-legged boys, but the clouds and flowers and pillars too – in short, the very body and soul of Allegory, and all the brains it has – stark mad.
>
> (Dickens, 1971: 720)

Allegory's finger points not only at these traces, but down to the dead body, and Dickens, significantly, connects the 'body and soul' of the whole representation with madness. He had done so before, in his previous novel, *David Copperfield* (1849–50), in which the mad Mr Dick tries to write his life in the form of a 'memorial' to the Lord Chancellor, except that references to King Charles' head (Charles I) keep appearing in his text. Mr Dick cannot understand how the trouble that was in King Charles' head has been put into his. David Copperfield's aunt, who looks after Mr Dick and so keeps him out of the madhouse, replies:

that's his allegorical way of putting it. He connects his illness with great disturbance and agitation, necessarily, and that's the figure, or the simile, or whatever it's called, which he chooses to use.

(Dickens, 2004: 215)

The fragments, King *Charles*'s head in Mr *Dick*'s head, operate like a rebus, bringing Charles Dickens' name into the text. Fear of decapitation allegorizes the trauma of madness which Mr Dick has undergone, while the sense of the past as violent operates again, overflowing Mr Dick's memory and his memorial, and forcing him to displace his own agitation onto an external 'great disturbance'. The return in a city context of allegory and madness, conjoined with melancholia, implies that the finger-pointing is obsessional and that the condition of modern life is to be driven mad. Allegory seems to be arbitrary: nothing connects Mr Dick with King Charles, who was executed exactly 200 years before *David Copperfield* was begun in 1849. But there is a link, which is in the dual way in which the dead king has lost his head, and remains to haunt Mr Dick and make him 'lose his head' in a different sense.

Bleak House deals with a long-drawn-out lawsuit. One lawyer is called Mr Tangle, whose allegorical name recalls Dickens' enthusiasm for the city comedies of Ben Jonson (1572–1637). When, in *Bleak House*, 'eighteen of Mr Tangle's learned friends, each armed with a little summary of eighteen hundred sheets, bob up like eighteen hammers in a pianoforte, make eighteen bows, and drop into their eighteen places of obscurity' (Dickens, 1971: 54), the simile, which makes the human mechanical and the mechanical human, indicates that allegory now names not abstract ideas, but sees humanity as mechanical, dead. Dickens has literalized personification; so that, instead of the personified figure being full of life, as we saw earlier in the case of Chaucer's Pardoner (see chapter 2), the use of personification means that the people given personified names are now no more than their masks. The number eighteen, repeated, denies all power of individualization. In *Little Dorrit* (1855–57) Dickens gives his lawyer and the cleric the names Bar and Bishop; these are again personifications which produce abstractions, reversing the direction of medieval allegory which started with such abstractions as False Seeming and ended with the Pardoner. 'Realism' is replaced by allegory, whose anachronistic form seems, by being so developed by Dickens, to make realism anachronistic.

Dickens' use of personification suggests deadness, and we can establish a relation between his technique and that of Marx, writing about the 'commodity' (see Kelley, 1997: 217). For Marx, in the first volume of *Capital* (1873), though the 'commodity' in the shop appears an extremely obvious thing, it is not, because it abounds 'in metaphysical subtleties and theological niceties'. A table seems to be no longer just wood; it has become, in the world of the capitalist phantasmagoria, that magical thing, a 'commodity', and seems to assume a life of its own:

> It not only stands with its feet on the ground, but, in relation to all other commodities, it stands on its head, and evolves out of its wooden brain grotesque ideas, far more wonderful than if it were to begin dancing of its own free will.
>
> (Marx, 1976: 163–64)

An object such as a table represents a series of dynamic, social and economic relations. At one level, the table is a made object, but its meaning resides in the relations of production involved in its making as a commodity, which are obscured in the object's reified existence. Marx draws the universe of material objects into a narrative whose method is allegorical. The failure to recognize how and under what conditions goods are produced is at the heart of what Marx calls 'alienation', the sense of not belonging, not fitting, not relating, which characterizes capitalism:

> The definite social relation between men themselves ... assumes, for them, the fantastic form [*phantasmagorische Form*] of a relation between things. In order, then, to find an analogy, we must take flight into the misty realm of religion. There the products of the human brain appear as autonomous figures endowed with a life of their own, which enter into relations both with each other and with the human race. So it is in the world of commodities with the products of men's hands. I call this the fetishism which attaches itself to the products of labour as soon as they are produced as commodities, and is therefore inseparable from the production of commodities.
>
> (Marx, 1976: 165)

Marx explains the power of the commodity with reference to personification allegory, which, he says, gives a life to things. That this happens assumes that people are held under the power of the 'phantasmagoria', which was the 'name invented for an exhibition of optical illusions produced chiefly by means of the magic lantern, first exhibited in London in 1802' (*OED*). The fetishizing that invests commodities with life takes place under the power of the illusion, where the substitutional is valued over the real. Objects, treated as real and alive, personifications, become fetishes, like statues or relics which personify spiritual entities. The commodity, which W. J. T. Mitchell calls 'a figurative, allegorical entity, possessed of a mysterious life and aura, an object, which, if properly interpreted, would reveal the secret of human history' (Mitchell, 1986: 188), could not be produced without such fetishism. Marx makes the attraction of the commodity entirely dependent on allegory, as though it had the power of life and to control lives.

Kelley links Marx's sense of how things have become 'commodities' with the Victorian fascination with automatons. If capitalism turns people into things and things into people, this resembles a double operation of allegory that we find within Dickens' novels. Mr Tangle's colleagues, as piano hammers, and characters such as Bar and Bishop, are transformed into inert or dead objects. And objects, conversely, are imaged as people: 'Bar' in *Little Dorrit* means not a wooden stand in the courtroom but a live lawyer. In this animation of lifelessness, frequent in Dickens, there is a parallel with what Marx says happens to the table. It is as if the law has generated the person who now embodies it. And in calling the image on the ceiling in *Bleak House* 'Allegory', Dickens personifies allegory itself as part of a gallery of dead characters. 'Allegory' typifies a crazy baroque past, underneath which people walk and are eventually destroyed, and it will turn Mr Tulkinghorn into an allegorical figure. The lawyer was a depository of secrets, which he carried round with him and which could not be 'read' from looking at him; now he has been murdered and those secrets are for ever lost with him. A corpse is a strange allegory of the person, a likeness without the person being there in presence. But in the passage quoted above from *Bleak House*, where Allegory looks down at the murdered man, there is not even a corpse visible: the point is made clear in Phiz's picture which accompanies the text. Text and picture allude to the empty chair and the body replaced by mere bloodstains on the floor. Allegory's finger points down to nothingness, makes a gesture of signification but is signifying nothing.

BAUDELAIRE

Allegory in the nineteenth century can also be considered through the poet Charles Baudelaire (1819–67), whom Jauss called an 'allegorizer of modernity', and who depicts the 'view of the alienated' in nineteenth-century modernity (Jauss, 1982: 173). We may note here a possible connection between the ideas of 'allegory' and 'alienation'; the Latin root from which the word 'alien' comes means 'belonging to an other person or place', and relates to the Greek *allos* (other). Allegory is not 'natural' speech, and the alien is other to the place where he is found. In his sonnet 'Correspondances', Baudelaire suggests that material objects are symbols of ideal forms which can be glimpsed behind them, just as all images can be expressed through other images (as one sense can be expressed through another, as in synaesthesia). In this first stanza, temple pillars turn into trees, and although the statement that everything corresponds to everything else seems plain enough, there are signs that this is more complex than just a Romantic insight: the words that come from the pillars are 'confused', so that they do not give off a single meaning:

> La Nature est un temple où des vivants piliers
> Laissent parfois sortir de confuses paroles;
> L'homme y passe à travers des forêts de symboles
> Qui l'observent avec des regards familiers.
>
> (Baudelaire, 1982)

> (Nature is a temple where living pillars sometimes give out confused words; man passes it alongside forests of symbols which observe him with familiar looks.)

'Familiar looks', in Freud's sense, might be signs of the uncanny, of strangeness. Such confusion is intensified in the city, when

Baudelaire thinks in terms of alienation and allegory, particularly in 'The Swan' ('Le Cygne', 1859), one of a group called 'Tableaux Parisiens' ('Parisian pictures') in *Les Fleurs du mal* ('The Flowers of Evil'). (The word 'cygne' is a homophone of 'signe', sign.) The poem was dedicated to Victor Hugo, a political exile from Napoleon III's France, and written in the context of the modernizations of Paris carried out by Baron Haussmann (1809–91) under the authority of Napoleon III. The urban landscape becomes unrecognizable, generating images in the text which are strange and inexplicable: a memory of Andromache, the widow of Hector of Troy; a swan which has escaped from a menagerie in Paris and which Baudelaire says he saw in the dry Parisian streets. Andromache, now a political refugee, and the lost swan fuse in his mind as figures of exile, and these two images, placed side by side, are succeeded by the following stanza (lines 29–32):

> Paris change! mais rien dans ma mélancholie
> N'a bougé! Palais neufs, échafaudages, blocs,
> Vieux faubourgs, tout pour moi devient allégorie,
> Et mes chers souvenirs sont plus lourds que les rocs
>
> (Baudelaire, 1982: 269)

(Paris changes! But nothing in my melancholy has moved. New palaces, scaffolding, blocks, old neighbourhoods, all for me becomes allegory, and my dear memories are more heavy than rocks.)

Paris changes objectively, but the speaker's melancholy does not allow him to accept these changes. Everything has become de-realized because in his melancholy he still sees things that are gone as signs, while also seeing that every aspect of this new Paris is also to be read as an allegory, a commentary on what has been destroyed. Everything is seen in double vision: even the blueness of the sky is said to be ironic ('le ciel ironique', line 26). Not only are the new buildings now not seen as real, they speak of something else. Memories, which are attached to places no longer there, remain heavy, and allegorical since the memories are 'other' than the new places, built on land which has also been physically changed. While Paris 'changes', his memories do not, and this double consciousness creates the necessity to think allegorically: seeing one thing, but recalling a narrative whose traces have now been obscured.

If everything of Paris 'becomes allegory', this shows when images which have no organic connection with each other, or, even, necessarily with Paris, accumulate. The poem returns to Andromache, the swan, and, later on, to a black woman from the French colonies, lost amidst the fogs of the city, and to others who drink sorrow, which is called 'la Douleur' – an allegorical personification – 'from the breasts of a she-wolf'. There are other figures of exile, including marooned sailors. Describing Paris as a she-wolf recalls the city as the new Rome (an allegory of classical Rome), a point signalled too in the reference to 'ce Louvre' (this Louvre: note the contempt, line 33): the name evokes Rome, since it contains part of the word *loup*, wolf, and so recalls the wolf that suckled that city's mythical founders, Romulus and Remus. The poem ends with thoughts of 'captives, vanquished ... and many others' (line 52). It is as if the speaker's memories have become unbounded, uncontrolled, excessive, threatening to undo his powers of memory, and destroying the sense of a subjectivity which is both single, unified, and organized. One allegorical image generates another in an endless sequence, and each image takes him further away from a state of mind which he knows, as if exiling him from his own knowable experience, threatening his sanity (Holland, 1993: 157–61).

'The Swan' is absorbed by the modern city, with the sense of fixed identities and known states giving way to the uncertainties of allegory, whose function in modernity seems to be to remove a sense of reality. The city-dweller must read doubly, seeing the city signifying in differing ways, all of which must be held on to. Baudelaire's allegory, which has been related to the theories of Walter Benjamin (Jauss, 1982: 139–85; Chambers, 1993: 153–73; Blood, 1997: 15–28), differs from that of Courbet. Jauss argues that 'Baudelaire won back for the modern lyric a new means of rendering abstractions sensible, and he created the poetic model of a modern *psychomachia* that – as with Freud's psychoanalysis shortly thereafter – puts into question the supremacy of the self-conscious "I"' (Jauss, 1982: 175). While Courbet may have hoped to change reality by what he painted, the Baudelairean subject is overwhelmed by the power of capitalist modernity and what the French 'situationist' critic Guy Debord sees as its reduction of urban life to the spectacle, to commodities which are there for display. The 'society of the spectacle', argues Debord, gives '*capital accumulated until it becomes an image*' (quoted in Clark, 1973: 9). But not, it should be said, an image of one thing, or of anything which can be reduced to a fixed meaning. There are allegories to be read within the objects put on display behind the plate glass of the shopping arcades, things which do not seem to have fixed meanings, because in fashion, which controls what gets displayed, the meaning of things changes arbitrarily. When everything is open to constant reinterpretation, everything becomes allegory in the sense that it loses its identity. Symbolism tries to affirm the constancy of a spiritual meaning in objects, but allegory in this context is more modern and more sceptical about the ability of things to preserve their unchanging identity.

5

WALTER BENJAMIN: ALLEGORY VERSUS SYMBOLISM

We have traced historical moments where allegory in its different forms becomes particularly strong, and have given a tentative history of allegory in its classical, medieval and Renaissance forms. We have also discussed the reaction away from allegory in favour of symbolism and realism in Romanticism and beyond, while noting the continuation of allegory, sometimes in disguised forms, in the nineteenth century. This chapter changes direction, in beginning a theoretical consideration of allegory which will question some of the assumptions of the literary history which assumes there can be a 'history of allegory'. Specifically, it discusses the work of Walter Benjamin, the Jewish, Marxist writer, born in Berlin in 1892. Much of the chapter will be concerned with a reading of his work on allegory, but towards the end I will illustrate its use with a specific example from Milton and Milton criticism.

Benjamin was expected to become a university teacher in philosophy, and on completion of his doctorate on criticism in German Romanticism, worked on the *Habilitation* which he needed to pass to secure a university post. The attempt, in 1925, failed, but the dissertation was published in 1928 with the title *Ursprung des deutschen Trauerspiels* (1928), translated into English in 1977 as *The Origin of German Tragic Drama*. It is not an easy text, and it may be useful to summarize some of its propositions before starting. It argues:

1. That allegory corresponds to a perception of the world in ruins, and is therefore the art of the fragment, and the opposite of the symbol, which presupposes the value of 'Nature' preserving unchanging, complete, identities and values.
2. That melancholy is the medium through which allegory is discovered and becomes significant and readable.
3. That allegory does not work with the sense of an organic, natural relationship between things; but that it questions such a possibility.

The linking of melancholy and allegory, noticed already in Baudelaire's 'The Swan', suggests the material around which *The Origin of German Tragic Drama* is formed.

BAROQUE ALLEGORY

Benjamin's *Habilitation* dissertation concentrated on a specific period of German drama in the seventeenth century, during and after the Thirty Years' War (1618–48) which tore Germany apart in a struggle between Catholicism and Protestantism. Significant writers of this primarily Protestant drama include Martin Opitz (1597–1639), Andreas Gryphius (1616–64) and Daniel Lohenstein (1635–83), not easily available to English-speaking readers without German (examples are given in van Reijen, 1992: 1–26). But Benjamin also refers to the Spanish dramatist Calderón (mentioned in chapter 3) and makes references to Shakespeare, particularly to *Hamlet*. Benjamin's interest in the *Trauerspiel*, or German 'play of mourning', differentiates the genre from that of classical tragedy, because its topic is the fall of princes, the instability of fortune, the idea of life as a dream, life as a brief hour upon the stage, as a theatre only, an 'insubstantial pageant faded' (*The Tempest*

4.1.155), a stage only set up for mournful events. Shakespeare's *Richard II* dramatizes the theme of *Trauerspiel*, in a manner that is both theatrical and comments on life as theatre. At this point in the play, when his power has evaporated, Richard acts as an allegorist who produces a theatrical narrative of his own predicament:

> For God's sake, let us sit upon the ground,
> And tell sad stories of the death of kings –
> How some have been deposed, some slain in war,
> Some haunted by the ghosts they have deposed,
> Some poisoned by their wives, some sleeping killed,
> All murdered. For within the hollow crown
> That rounds the mortal temples of a king
> Keeps Death his court; and there the antic sits
> Scoffing his state and grinning at his pomp,
> Allowing him a breath, a little scene,
> To monarchize, be feared, and kill with looks,
> Infusing him with self and vain conceit,
> As if this flesh which walls about our life
> Were brass impregnable; and humoured thus,
> Comes at the last, and with a little pin
> Bores through his castle wall; and farewell, king.
>
> (3.2.151–66)

Richard begins by staging his grief, and the grief of kings, and the speech is richly hyperbolic, leading up to 'all murdered'. Its second half, beginning with 'For within the hollow crown … ', is influenced by the 'dance of the dead' tradition in late medieval visual art, for which many artists, including Holbein (1497– 1543), provided examples. In these illustrations, Death, as a skeleton and as a mirror of the living, dances with a living person, till he dances them into the grave. In Richard's use of personification, Death is king, but he is also the 'antic', i.e. the fool, the jester. This conjoining of the skull and the fool is par- alleled in another play: in the emblems contained in two of the three caskets which Portia's suitors in *The Merchant of Venice* must choose from. The lead casket contains her picture. The golden and silver caskets, when opened, like drawing aside the veil of allegory, contain respectively a death's head (the 'carrion death') and a fool's head (2.7.63, 2.9.58). Perhaps these are allegorical expressions of each other.

In *Richard II*, if Death keeps his court inside the 'hollow crown', which is either the literal crown, or the head, that which is 'king' over the rest of the body, then Death is inside the king, or part of him, which makes the king incomplete, a ruined figure. In allegorical terms Death adopts the role of the antic, mocking the pretentions of the kingly subject, and the ridicule of those pretentions derives from the certainty of death. Richard externalizes an inner drama, an anxiety which derives from a self-division. He is both a king and a 'subject'; in short, a 'split' subject. In containing Death, as well as being contained by death, the king has become an allegorical object. The figure of the skull, which is the king's only crown, and his only castle, as an emblem of what life is, becomes the dominant image in *Trauerspiel*: indeed Benjamin calls the corpse the pre-eminent emblematic property in the drama he discusses (Benjamin, 1977: 218). The use of Yorick's skull in *Hamlet* or Vindice's use of his dead lady's skull in Middleton's *The Revenger's Tragedy* (1606) are comparable instances. And so is T. S. Eliot's poem 'Whispers of Immortality' (1920), which says about the Jacobean dramatist John Webster (*c*.1580–*c*.1625) that 'Webster was much possessed by death / And saw the skull beneath the skin' (Eliot, 1969: 52). Eliot sees, in Shakespeare, Middleton, Webster and Donne, a de-idealizing, melancholic drive, which generates allegory, goes below the surface of the face, in a fascination with what is material and deathly. There seems to be in these Jacobeans a fascination to know 'what is beyond knowledge', and to be 'possessed by death' is to be obsessed with it, wanting to know everything that is in the grave (Empson, 1966: 78–79).

The Origin of German Tragic Drama comprises chapters on 'Trauerspiel and Tragedy' and 'Allegory and Trauerspiel'. Benjamin traces a history of melancholy which he reads in two ways: first, as a state akin to acedia, which was one of the seven capital vices, and second, as a basic psychological quality. Here he quotes from a pseudo-Aristotelian text, *Problemata XXX*, that creativity and genius are dependent upon the melancholic 'humour' (temperament) in the body. The latter view gains ascendancy in the Renaissance, but the earlier view returns in Luther's Reformation and Protestantism. Benjamin thinks Martin Luther (1483–1546) was a melancholic, and that his vision of the world saw its materiality as having no richness, no significance. A Lutheran sense of melancholy appears in his friend Albrecht Dürer (1471–1528), whose *Melencolia* (1514), mentioned in the last chapter in relation to Courbet, is an allegorical representation of melancholy. It is discussed in a book which, first appearing in 1923, influenced Benjamin: Panofsky, Saxl and Klibansky's *Saturn and Melancholy* (revised in 1964).

Melencolia shows a woman, who is also an angel, her head leaning on her left hand; her right hand holding, idly, a pair of compasses. Her wings are drooping; she portrays inactivity, while at her feet are numerous elements of the active life, such as instruments used for building. To her left a dog lies sleeping; beside her a *putto* sits scribbling on a mill wheel. In the distance, a bat flies, holding a banderole bearing the picture's title. Other elements in the picture, the magic square on the wall behind, the bell, the hourglass, the scales, the ladder, the polyhedron in the centre left of the picture and the comet in the heavens, are interpreted in *Saturn and Melancholy* as sixteenth-century emblems of the kind that were discussed in chapter 3. The picture has been interpreted as the representation of a mind incapacitated in the face of an insatiable and neurotic need for knowledge. For Benjamin, it implies a crisis of mourning:

> mourning [*Trauer*] is the state of mind in which feeling revives the empty world in the form of a mask, and derives an enigmatic satisfaction in contemplating it.

And in this state, which sees the empty world as no more than a mask, a personification of something which is without substance:

> the utensils of active life are lying around unused on the floor, as objects of contemplation.
>
> (Benjamin, 1977: 139)

This echoes stage directions for a play by Gryphius, *Catharine von Georgien*, where 'a whole collection of stage properties are lying scattered about the floor' (Benjamin, 1977: 124). The properties, like stage props generally, are emblematic, but with them, 'the most simple object appears to be a symbol of some enigmatic wisdom because it lacks any natural, creative relationship to us' (Benjamin, 1977: 139). This wisdom is lost; the property, with its emblematic character, is a shell, but the kernel of meaning has gone. That is the cause of melancholy. This empty or 'evacuated world' (Roberts, 1982: 140) Benjamin reads as fitting Lutheranism, devaluing everything earthly, material, a melancholic drive which negates the real world of time and sense. In such a state, mourning sees the world as no more than masks. There is no organic connection between the person who contemplates and the objects on the floor which should be put to active use. This break corresponds to a divide between the spiritually active and the spiritually contemplative life, the two forms of existence, which correspond to the lives of the Old Testament figures Leah and Rachel, discussed, by the medieval church, as types of Martha and Mary in the New Testament (Genesis chapter 30 and Luke 10.38–42). The objects lie on the floor, their meaning forgotten. The alienation between these two forms of existence is revealed in an allegorical picture. Such an alienation, which, we may recall, is the opposite of the symbol with its organic unity between object and spiritual meaning, was for Coleridge basic to allegory, which he called 'a translation of abstract notions into a picture language' which is 'an abstraction from objects of the senses'.

Though he does not refer to it, Benjamin works within the framework of Freud's speculative essay on the psychopathology of melancholy, 'Mourning [Trauer] and Melancholia' (1917), which makes this distinction: 'in mourning it is the world which has become poor and empty; in melancholia, it is the ego itself' (Freud, 1977: 254). Benjamin uses a perception akin to Freud's to think of melancholia as an alienated state, but the model that he works with is neither medieval acedia nor the Renaissance melancholia that produces works of genius. It is both and neither, in that, for Benjamin, part of the picture's complexity is to see how both are laid side by side, with neither being dominant. He connects the first form of melancholy with a negativity about the present which he sees as a kind of laziness (acedia). The second model gives too much weight to the Renaissance 'humanist' subject. Melancholia rather starts with alienation, including that of objects from each other.

Benjamin's view of the picture as illustrating disintegration, and as allegorical, contradicts Panofsky who worked with the symbol/allegory antithesis which was developed by the Romantics. It will be remembered that the symbol for the Romantics conjoined an object to a permanent truth, while allegory was seen as arbitrary in the way it linked an abstract concept to a thing. For Panofsky, Dürer's picture 'raised the allegorical figure of melancholy to the plane of a symbol'. He argued that it combined two things: first, it personified the woman as the type of geometry, which is the art especially related to Saturn and hence to melancholy, and second, it was a paradigmatic representation of a melancholic, as in medieval calendars. This ideal combination of two elements constituted, so Panofsky argued, a perfect 'symbolic form'. The term was first used in 1921 by the neo-Kantian philosopher Ernst Cassirer (1974–1945), who considered the distinct activity of humans to be that of producing symbolic forms derived from the human spirit which realizes itself in concrete, sensory signs and images; for Panofsky, in thinking of 'pure forms, motifs, images, stories and allegories [in Renaissance art] as manifestations of underlying principles, we interpret all these elements as what Ernst Cassirer has called "symbolical" values'. This allows the art historian to produce a 'history of cultural symptoms – or "symbols" in Ernst Cassirer's sense'. For Panofsky, the work of art becomes an index to history; everything unites in the picture to give 'insight into the manner in which, under varying historical conditions, essential tendencies of the human mind were expressed by specific themes and concepts' (Panofsky, 1970: 56, 65, 66; Panofsky 1972: 14–16). Art symbolizes permanent states of mind under differing conditions. Different elements have been condensed together to produce a single, symbolic state. This is obviously opposite to Benjamin's sense of Dürer's art as illustrating fragmentation. Benjamin, following Freud, would have found, in contrast, a contradiction, not a unity, in the way these differing elements are condensed together, and would see the work as displaying that contradiction. We will return to Panofsky, and other art critics who saw iconology as a complete pictorial symbolism, in chapter 7.

Benjamin discusses the Romantics' distinction between allegory and symbolism in the chapter 'Allegory and Trauerspiel', and he articulates the difference between symbolism and allegory:

> Whereas in the symbol destruction is idealized and the transfigured face of nature is fleetingly revealed in the light of redemption, in allegory the observer is confronted with the *facies hippocratica* [death's head] of history as a petrified primordial landscape. Everything about history that from the very beginning has been untimely, sorrowful, unsuccessful, is expressed in a face – or rather in a death's head.
>
> (Benjamin, 1977: 166)

This difficult passage is a critique of the Romantic valuation of the symbol. For Benjamin it is idealizing because it ignores history, claiming the absolute eternal value of nature, which supplies symbolism with its idea of unchanging, organic forms. Nature has been presented in ideal, not real, terms; indeed, it has been turned into an abstract but authoritative entity. Symbolism, because it implies unification, bringing things together, idealizes, and constructs a perfect transcendent world: these are ideas associated with Coleridge and Yeats. In this Romantic context, even suffering can be seen as redemptive. Romanticism celebrates nature, and symbolism, which draws on elements of nature, evokes timeless, beautiful, eternal truths. The result is that it seems that what the symbol describes is 'natural', making the danger of symbolism that it consecrates certain values as natural, permanent, and having an essential, unchanging existence. Hence its importance within any form of ideology, whether political or class- or gender-based, which makes much of saying that certain things are 'natural'. It may be said, following Benjamin, that ideology controls partly through the power of symbolism, but that allegory disrupts the rule of ideology.

In contrast to symbolism, allegory looks at history, which it reads as a 'landscape', using a term derived from looking at nature, and working with the idea of 'natural history'; a term which emphasizes that there is no distinction to be made between history as that which is specifically human, and the history of nature. Benjamin's specific terms 'petrified' and 'primordial' suggest that history is not marked by beauty, nor by spontaneous growth and movement towards progress. It is marked from the beginning by decay, not what Romantic symbolists dream of: immediacy and natural, organic growth. Allegory sanctions no idea of an originary Garden of Eden, or record of unity. Instead of timeless truths, there is the 'untimely', the history that stands outside the chronological narrative of progress that makes up 'official' history. 'Natural history' records sorrowful, or unachieved, states.

Symbolism offers as its characteristic image a 'face' – note the term from Benjamin here – so much so that Wordsworth can personify nature as 'the speaking face of earth and heaven' (*The Prelude* 5.13 (1850 version)). Allegory offers as image a death's head, as a mask; this is the second time that we have seen Benjamin use this image. He continues that:

> death digs most deeply the jagged line of demarcation between physical nature and significance. But if nature has always been subject to the power of death, it is also true that it has always been allegorical.
>
> (Benjamin, 1977: 166)

This argues that 'nature' becomes a concept which can be considered only when it is regarded as not immanent, or spontaneous, but marked by death. That is opposed to it being a tool of ideology, supporting arguments that there is such a thing as 'natural' behaviour. But to see it in relation to death is precisely how symbolism *cannot* regard nature, since it wants to assert the power of spontaneous life, growth and organic unity. Only when nature is not seen as immediate, alive, and having 'natural' significance, but as an entity that is shaped by the values of those who invest it with symbolic significance, can it be allowed to be seen as other. Then it becomes allegorical, different. The symbol, because it claims the power of nature, pretends to a kind of deathlessness. Allegory, in contrast, starts with the sense of dead fragments. To see death within nature means reading it allegorically, because for Benjamin allegory begins from death and the rejection of the organic power of nature and symbolism. Fragments displace the idea of a nature that creates natural connections or a live bond of nature that establishes a right, 'natural' way of seeing, or behaving. In allegory, there are no 'natural' comparisons; all terms of comparison are non-natural, ideological, non-proper, catachreses.

The image ceases to be an adequate representation of something. Because it is not part of an organic unity, it can be seen as 'a fragment, a rune' – that is, writing which is now partly indecipherable:

> The false appearance of totality is extinguished. For the *eidos* [idea] disappears, the simile ceases to exist, and the cosmos it contained shrivels up. The dry rebuses which remain conceal an insight which is still available to the confused investigator ... Classicism was not permitted to behold the lack of freedom ... the collapse of the beautiful, physical nature. But beneath its extravagant pomp, that is precisely what baroque allegory proclaims.
>
> (Benjamin, 1977: 176)

Again, this needs careful consideration. The term 'totality' derives from Hegel and implies the possibility of seeing knowledge as a whole, in terms of a Platonic idea, and it assumes that if knowledge can be seen as a single entity, as we speak of a 'body of knowledge', then it has its own organic unity, which can be expressed symbolically. Here we may note that Gordon Teskey (1996: 185–87) says that Hegel was important for C. S. Lewis, who found in Spenser:

> a sensation akin to that which Hegelians are said to get from Hegel – a feeling that we have before us not so much an image as a sublime instance of the universal process – that this is not so much a poet writing about the fundamental forms of life as those forms themselves spontaneously displaying their activities to us through the imagination of a poet ... his poetry has really tapped sources not easily accessible to discursive thought.
>
> (Lewis, 1936: 358)

Lewis's Romantic Hegelianism supports the primacy of symbolism which brings into focus life's 'universal processes'. Benjamin's reading undermines Hegel. Ideas of the 'totality' disappear when the allegorical image is only a fragment, or a rebus, which the melancholic 'investigator' probes. The idea of allegory as writing, implied in the 'rune', derives from Arthur Schopenhauer (1788–1860) in *The World as Will and Representation* (*Vorstellung*), who sees allegory, which he calls 'a work of art signifying something different from what it depicts', as, in plastic and pictorial art, 'nothing but hieroglyphics' which 'do not achieve more than an inscription' (Schopenhauer, 1969: 1.237). Classicism, with its interest in symmetry, Romantic thought of the 'totality', and symbolism, link through the concept of the beautiful, which Benjamin sees as an idealizing concept. In contrast, baroque allegory implies mere inscription, and the broken and discontinuous; 'Allegories are, in the realm of thoughts, what ruins are in the realm of things' (Benjamin, 1977: 178).

Susan Buck-Morss explains this last aphorism by comparing a Hellenic statue of Venus, as the 'divine symbol of love in the transitory form of natural beauty', with a picture of the three stages of life, illustrating the 'dance of the dead' theme, by Dürer's student Hans Baldung (*c*.1476–1545). In Baldung, death and the lady are seen dancing together; this allegorical image can be explained by saying that beauty is visible as a ruin in the very moment of its existence (Buck-Morss, 1989: 166–67). Baldung suggests that beautiful things become ruins, or that ruins take over in the realm of things. Similarly, allegories take over in the realm of thoughts. Allegories are ruins and they are the ruin of thoughts which think themselves whole and entire, with no gaps in them, self-existent, as what Nietzsche jokingly calls an 'immaculate perception'. Thoughts are never more than ruins; no thought can fully know itself, because it cannot know the unconscious that produces it. These gaps within thought suggest the presence of death, as splitting, internally, all thinking. The idea of thought as internally self-divided may help to explain further Benjamin's earlier aphorism, quoted above: 'if nature has always been subject to the power of death, it is also true that it has always been allegorical'. Like thought, nature cannot be considered as single or undivided; it contains death within it, and so, because of this contradiction, it is material for allegory, not for symbolism.

Another way of reading the statement 'allegories are, in the realm of thoughts, what ruins are in the realm of things' emanates from considering the skull. In the sphere of things, the skull suggests the 'ruin'; it is an empty fragment, telling of a significant life which has departed. What meaning it had has gone; nonetheless, the skull still has the power to speak to people, as has already been noticed. Benjamin's interest in ruins and the fragment opposes the Romantics' fascination with the fragment as an element of the 'totality'. The baroque writers of the *Trauerspiel* 'pile up fragments ceaselessly, without any strict thought of a goal' (Benjamin, 1977: 178). Similarly, and playing into the deepest fears of the Romantics, Benjamin quotes the art critic Karl Giehlow discussing Dürer in 1903, that 'one and the same object can just as easily signify a virtue as a vice, and therefore more or less anything' (Benjamin, 1977: 174), meaning that 'any person, any object, any relationship can mean absolutely anything else' (Benjamin, 1977: 175). The 'detail' is not of organic importance. This critiques the sense of a unique relationship existing between a thing and what symbolizes it. Symbolism encourages us to think of two things – the object, or the emotion, and its representation – as united in a perfect fusion. With the allegorical image, if any one thing can represent any other, no special, unique value can be given to either the object or its representation.

Benjamin's thesis contradicts Panofsky, whose views on iconology propose a natural conjunction between the object and the thing represented (Camille, 1986: 58–79). In Benjamin, the 'empty world' means that the object to be represented has gone, and is only present as an allegorical image (a mask or ruin or fragment). 'Piling up of fragments', which recalls the assorted objects lying on the floor in Dürer's print, suggests that no fragment can be other than partial, that it cannot deliver a complete truth, but must stand in a supplementary relationship to what has gone before, unable to complete it. This points towards surrealism, but even more to the montages of Sergei Eisenstein (1898–1948), whose film *Battleship Potemkin* (1925) created a shock effect by unexpected fusions, by the way it juxtaposed images alongside each other. Benjamin offers a theory of montage in his theory of allegory. Such linking together of disparate images becomes what

Benjamin calls a 'constellation' (Benjamin, 1977: 34–36), and the activity of the critical historian is to juxtapose, or to constellate, isolated images together, or re-constellate images already associated. As a constellation of stars forms a fictitious unity with a certain truth value (sailors successfully navigate ships by such an arrangement of stars), the constellation becomes an allegory; indeed, it is interesting that a familiar explanation of tropes in the Renaissance held that 'a simile is *like* a star, a metaphor *is* a star and an allegory is a *constellation*' (quoted in Watson, 1993: 89). The creation of a meaningful constellation is the same as the creation of allegory.

The piling up of fragments anticipates a particular passage of allegorical writing in Benjamin's 'Theses on the Philosophy of History' where the 'angel of history' is evoked, an allegorical image derived from a picture by Paul Klee which is like an emblem (Scholem, 1988: 51–89):

> His face is turned toward the past. Where we perceive a chain of events, he sees one single catastrophe which keeps piling wreckage upon wreckage and hurls it in front of his feet. The angel would like to stay, awaken the dead and make whole what has been smashed. But a storm is blowing from Paradise; it has got caught in his wings with such violence that the angel can no longer close them. This storm irresistibly propels him into the future to which his back is turned, while the pile of debris before him grows skyward. This storm is what we call progress.
>
> (Benjamin, 1970: 259–60)

Piles of wreckage, or debris, recall the fragments and ruins that comprise baroque allegory. Perceiving history as a 'chain of events' unifies them and threatens to produce an ideal narrative; it resembles the thinking which produces the symbol, seeing history as telling a narratable story. History as a 'single catastrophe' repeated again and again refuses the idea of progress, and leaves nothing but fragments. Perhaps it can be said that the angel is 'petrified'. Certainly it recalls the figure in Dürer's *Melencolia*, while the 'pile of debris' recalls the objects on the floor in that picture, objects which cannot be used. Reference to melancholy recalls the *Trauerspiel* study, where 'the object becomes allegorical under the gaze of melancholy' and 'melancholy causes life to flow out of it and it remains behind dead ... exposed to the allegorist ... unconditionally in his power' (Benjamin, 1977: 183). The melancholic's only pleasure is allegory (Benjamin, 1977: 185). Melancholy, starting from a perception of death, pierces surfaces, seeing 'the skull beneath the skin', undermining the power of ideology: Hamlet's melancholia means that he can see below the surface and is not fooled by anything in the court of Elsinore.

ALLEGORY AND THE SKULL

The medieval, and, even more, the Renaissance world, responded to the pagan classical world by interpreting its myths as Christian allegories. Benjamin calls this a form of 'mortification', making the pagan world both beautiful and dead by disregarding its difference, or otherness, or, in a word, its allegorical (i.e. 'speaking other') significance. In both the medieval and the Renaissance periods, the figure of Satan became the embodiment of both pagan energy and Christian evil. In his avatars, like the diabolic intriguer, such as Shakespeare's Richard the Third, whom Benjamin sees as an allegorical figure, Satan threatens because of the plurality of meanings that he generates. It is the character of Shakespeare's Richard to be always punning, joking with his opponents, trapping them into death through the power of his words. The diabolic reduces the world to mourning.

This leads Benjamin to his last point, that allegory always symbolizes its own transience, its own disappearance, its lack of definite existence. Baroque allegorical images signify

> death and damnation. For it is precisely visions of the frenzy of destruction, in which all things collapse into a heap of ruins, which reveal the limit set upon allegorical contemplation, rather than its ideal quality. The bleak confusion of Golgotha [*Schädelstatte*] which can be recognized as the schema underlying the allegorical figure in hundreds of the engravings and descriptions of the period, is not just a symbol of the desolation of human existence. In it transitoriness is ... displayed as allegory.
>
> (Benjamin, 1977: 232)

The reference to Golgotha – the place of the skull – recalls the earlier passage, which sees history imaged in a death's head. Both are encapsulated by Adorno (1903–69) discussing the Marxist Georg Lukács (1885–1971) on the phrase 'second nature'. This term refers to the world as alienated, reified, dead, dominated by commodity fetishism, as Marx discusses this (see chapter 4). According to Adorno, in Lukács 'the petrified life within nature is merely what history has developed into' (Buck-Morss, 1989: 160). The historical has become, in the modern world, frozen, petrified nature, where movement is impossible. For Lukács, this 'second nature' is 'not dumb, sensuous and yet senseless like the first'. While it seems to be alive, it is 'a complex of senses – meanings – which has become rigid and strange, and which no longer awakens interiority; it is a charnel house [*Schädelstatte*: literally, a place of skulls] of long-dead interiorities; this second nature could only be brought to life – if this were possible – by the metaphysical act of reawakening the souls which, in an early or ideal existence, created or preserved it' (Lukács, 1978: 64). The kinship between this and Benjamin's image of history as a 'petrified and primordial landscape' will be observed. The emblem of history cannot be a face, which would imply life, but a death's head, the sign of decay, of fragmentation after death.

The 'place of skulls' recalls the meaning of the Hebrew word 'Golgotha', 'the place of a skull', the place of Christ's crucifixion (Matthew 27:33). Medieval paintings of the crucifixion placed a skull at the foot of the cross; it was watered by Christ's blood. Medieval commentators, in an example of figural reading, argued that it was Adam's skull. But 'the place of skulls' refers also to the medieval urban charnel house, which was a novel late-fourteenth-century feature of European cities. It applies also to the Thirty Years' War (1618–48) fought throughout the German states, when, according to Benjamin, a *Trauerspiel* was enacted both in plays *and* in historical events. It also implies the First World War, which in propaganda and war protests produced its own pictorial images of hills of skulls (Buck-Morss, 1989: 169). These hills of skulls are what the Angel of History, at the beginning of the Second World War, sees in the wreckage that is piled in front of its feet.

The baroque allegorists worked with a dead landscape of this kind. They believed that allegory would one day be replaced by resurrection, which would invert all its hollowed-out values. They, however, thought not of resurrection, but gave their loyalty to dead things, making them subjects of their allegory.

BAROQUE ALLEGORY AND MILTON

Benjamin writes: 'Criticism is the mortification of the work' (Benjamin, 1977: 182). 'Central Park', a collection of aphorisms on allegory written in 1939, whose main topic is Baudelaire, supplements that with 'Majesty of the allegorical intention: to destroy the organic and the living' (Benjamin, 2003: 172). 'Mortification' is the secret 'truth' behind the impulse to symbolize, as when the power of the pagan world, so disturbing to Christians, was killed off by being made a symbolic form of Christianity. Benjamin sees allegory and the criticism that it performs as another 'mortification' which does not pretend otherwise; allegory does not bring the work of art close, so that it can be 'appreciated', nor act as if it could be seen in terms of a timeless beauty. Allegory rather foregrounds death, because it suggests that a text can only ever be incomplete, fragmented. It critiques any sense that there can be a complete canon, or a 'body' of literature, or of art. Piling up of fragments is a form of repetition which can never achieve completion, or transcendence.

This repetition is discussed by Herman Rapaport in *Milton and the Postmodern*, linking John Milton (1608–74)'s English epic poem *Paradise Lost* (1667) with the contemporary German *Trauerspiel*. The implications of Rapaport's argument are worth considering, and can be put alongside the question of whether or not Milton was an allegorist. His *Il Penseroso*, written in the 1630s, evokes melancholy, while it looks back to traditional allegory in Spenserian romance, and thinks of what 'great bards'

> In sage and solemn tunes have sung,
> Of tourneys and of trophies hung;
> Of forests and enchantments drear,
> Where more is meant than meets the ear.

> (lines 116–20, Milton, 1930: 27)

The last line helps to define traditional allegory, and Milton is aware of it. But in relation to *Paradise Lost*, few critics have wished to see Milton continuing Spenserian Renaissance allegory – apart from Kenneth Borris, who reads the epic poem as an allegory illustrating Christianity (Borris, 2000: 253–55, 182–253). He disagrees with Gordon Teskey, who says that heroic allegorism in Tasso, Sidney and Spenser is marked by 'composite characterisation'. Teskey regards the height of allegory, its 'anagogical' state (a term discussed in chapter 1), as 'the image of one body incorporating others'. That is, in the anagogical state, one allegorical figure does not displace others, but stands alongside them, all being representative of a single type: Truth, or Chastity, for example. Teskey argues that the absence of this syncretism in Milton separates him from Renaissance allegory (Borris, 2000: 184).

In *Paradise Lost* the sense of plural and allegorical meanings is displaced by a literality that will not think syncretically of the pagan world existing alongside the Hebrew and/or Christian. An example is the following account of the fall from Heaven of the devil Mulciber. The quotation alludes to the classical myths of Mulciber and then refuses them:

> Nor was his name unheard or unadorned
> In ancient Greece; and in Ausonian land
> Men called him Mulciber; and how he fell
> From Heav'n, they fabled, thrown by angry Jove
> Sheer o'er the crystal battlements: from morn
> To noon he fell, from noon to dewy eve,
> A summer's day: and with the setting sun
> Dropped from the zenith like a falling star,
> On Lemnos th' Aegean isle: thus they relate,
> Erring. ...   (1.738–47, Milton, 1930: 199)

The Greek legend of Hephaestus (Latin: Vulcan), who was thrown out of Heaven, and the Roman legend of Mulciber (a surname of Vulcan, appearing in Ovid, who wrote in 'Ausonian land', i.e. in Italy) is quoted and lingered over. It is then abruptly dismissed, declared to be a lie. The text does not work with the procedures of Renaissance epic or romance, whereby the classical pagan prefigures the Christian. Milton refuses the consolations of symbolism, or rather mortifies them. While that does not make him an allegorist as Benjamin understands the word, it separates him from the idealizing tendency of the syncretizing tradition within Renaissance writing.

But, to follow Benjamin, we will be less interested in the formal aspects of allegory, especially if these are held to support the idea that there is a certain truth outside the work to which the work points, rather than in the idea that allegorical writing is anti-metaphysical, i.e. non-idealizing. Rapaport sees such anti-idealism in Milton, even in his theology. He discusses the episode of Satan meeting Sin, who tells him a story which does not really fit the narrative of the poem and which Satan seems not to know. It is the narrative of Satan's rape of his daughter, Sin, the birth of Death from that union and then Death's rape of Sin, which engenders monsters, and so produces a series of repetitions which can hardly claim any original happening (*Paradise Lost* 2.727–814).

Rapaport connects this progeny to allegory, because each figure stands in a substitutional or supplementary relationship to Satan. One name – Satan, Sin, Death – displaces another. The absence of a single original figure is significant, for it implies that allegory can neither begin from a fixed position nor end with one. Rapaport thinks of Satan in Freudian terms, as narcissistic, which he says is equivalent in this text to being in the state of sin, but above all as a melancholic, since melancholia, in Freud, is narcissistic (Freud, 1977: 259). Satan's loss of Heaven is also the loss of a transcendent position (Rapaport, 1983: 23–56, 37).

Similarly, Milton's rejection of the legends of Mulciber implies melancholia in the poet: Milton turns away from the plurality of thinking that had been possible in Renaissance allegory, towards a single meaning. Something in Satan's mourning and melancholia repeats something in Milton. By the end of *Paradise Lost* Adam and Eve have also had to face this loss of transcendence, and the power of death. At both ends of the epic there is a loss which must be worked through. It recalls a statement of Benjamin's, that mourning is both the mother of allegories and their content (Benjamin, 1977: 230). In Milton's context, that implies that mourning produces further repetitions, each incomplete, each fragmented. Loss of transcendence means the loss of allegory as a form of idealization. Whatever may be Milton's intention, whether he believes he is writing allegory or not, his text is allegorical in that it writes that loss, in the sense that it mourns the absence of completeness and commits itself to fragments with no sense that they can complete themselves. The implications of this will be considered in chapter 7.

6

ALLEGORY, IRONY, DECONSTRUCTION

FROM BENJAMIN TO PAUL DE MAN

In chapter 3 we drew a distinction between allegory and the symbol, noting that the Romantics invested most in the powers of symbolism, while in chapter 5 we saw Benjamin's opposition to this view. As part of a critique of eighteenth-century empirical philosophy, which Coleridge, amongst others, found mechanical and dead, Romanticism emphasized the value of human presence and of transcendental values, downgrading allegory for its mechanical qualities. Romanticism in its turn has been the subject of the critique of deconstruction, which argues that the stress on 'presence' serves another ideology: that of humanism, and the belief in certain central, and, incidentally, Eurocentric, 'human' values. A key move in deconstructive criticism has been to show that the text, whatever it may seem to assert, is premised on absence, on a lack within the speaking subject, who therefore cannot claim to have the 'presence' that much Romantic poetry asserts, as when, for instance, Wordsworth calls poetry 'the spontaneous overflow of powerful feelings'.

What this critique implies for allegory is explored in the work of Paul de Man (1919–83). He argues that allegory recognizes the impossibility, in all writing and speaking, of saying what is intended, and of having a single intention, as well as the impossibility of reading what has been written. He argues that 'the difficulty of allegory is ... that [its] emphatic clarity of representation does not stand in the service of something that can be represented' (de Man, 1996: 51). To explore further the claim that allegory has no referent is the task of this chapter.

The formative work on deconstruction in France is associated with Jacques Derrida (1930–2004). However, deconstruction in America between the 1960s and 1980s was shaped by controversies around de Man, who was influenced by Benjamin's work as it was mediated through the writings of Peter Szondi (1929–71), one of Benjamin's early commentators. It included a response to Benjamin's essay 'The Task of the Translator', with de Man viewing translation as a form of allegory. In the 1960s, de Man became one of the first literary theorists in the Anglo-American world to refer to the *Trauerspiel* study, arguing that Benjamin defines allegory as a void 'that signifies precisely the non-being of what it represents' (de Man, 1983: 35). The relevant passage in Benjamin is as follows: 'this is the essence of melancholy immersion: that its ultimate objects ... turn into allegories, and that these allegories fill out and deny the void in which they are represented' (Benjamin, 1977: 232–33). De Man quotes this from Benjamin during a discussion in which he cites the very stanza from Baudelaire's 'The Swan' discussed above (p. 106). That stanza allows him to claim that allegory starts from 'the loss of reality that marks the beginning of poetic states of mind'. Allegory, then, comes out of absence, but it also turns the objects that it represents into 'non-being'. And of course, allegorical representations themselves lack reality, because they exist only at the level of the signifier.

For de Man, allegory not only lacks a referent, but is generated out of a sense of the loss of a referent. The gulf that now opens up between word and object, language and the world, produces a split between statement and meaning; they do not refer to each other, even if it seems that they do. This is the theme of de Man's influential essay 'The Rhetoric of Temporality' (1969), which we will now explore, before turning to the book *Allegories of Reading*. Later in the chapter I will consider what de Man says on prosopopoeia, or personification, in relation to his essay 'Autobiography as Defacement' from the posthumously published *The Rhetoric of Romanticism*. The last section of this chapter will turn to a consideration of apostrophe, a literary trope which is germane to the process of personification.

'THE RHETORIC OF TEMPORALITY'

'The Rhetoric of Temporality' begins with the Romantic distinction between symbol and allegory, which, like Benjamin, de Man criticizes. But there is a difference: Benjamin's critique of the Romantic symbol came before the outbreak of the Second World War, whereas the young de Man, living in Belgium during the Second World War, collaborated in wartime journalism, whether willingly or unwillingly, with the Nazi occupying forces (McQuillan, 2001: 97–111). Though this has fuelled controversy about deconstruction's real or apparent lack of politics, it is worth speculating that de Man's collaboration must have provided occasions to reflect on the rhetoric of 'organic unity' that feeds fascism, as in nationalist talk of the 'natural unity' that exists between 'man', or the nation, and 'the earth'. The language of organicism, which licenses talk of organic unity within the nation, and which dwells on natural relationships, permits the exclusion of whatever cannot be assimilated into such unity. Foregrounding allegory in opposition to symbolism means rejecting this aesthetic ideology of the organic unity of the work of art, thus aligning de Man with an even more intense version of Benjamin's 'anti-aesthetic' (see Foster, 1983, and see below, p. 161). 'The Rhetoric of Temporality' rejects the idea that the symbol enables the reader to see whole meanings instantaneously, that it illuminates both the comparison and the thing compared. De Man differentiates between symbol and allegory by looking at how these figures relate to *time*. It is the passing of time that makes symbolism impossible because, in de Man's terms, a distinction must be made between 'experience' and 'the representation of this experience' (de Man, 1983: 188).

In this argument, the symbol, 'an expression of unity between the representative and the semantic function of language' (de Man, 1983: 189), assumes a simultaneous, synchronic relationship between the image and the reality, and so implies a 'totality' of meaning (de Man, 1983: 189). In an allegory, which takes the form of a narrative, this cannot be so.

> The meaning constituted by the allegorical sign can ... consist only in the *repetition* ... of a previous sign with which it can never coincide, since it is of the essence of this previous sign to be pure anteriority ... whereas the symbol postulates the possibility of an identity or identification, allegory designates primarily a distance in relation to its own origin, and, renouncing the nostalgia and the desire to coincide, it establishes its language in the void of this temporal difference.
>
> (de Man, 1983: 207)

This extract, which includes a description of what the symbol does, sees allegory as dependent on a series of 'signs' that can only repeat each other. If a narrative sequence, or 'argument', is carried by a series of tropes, no argument can be followed: for tropes, as separate figures, do not relate to each other, being non-coincident with each other, though they appear to follow continuously. They repeat each other, they do not refer back to an origin, which would give identity and meaning. While the word 'void', quoted before in relation to de Man and Benjamin, is noticeable in this quotation, the clue word is 'identity', for this, which the symbol seems to establish through the instantaneous comparison of things through metaphor, cannot be when there is a constant fading of one 'sign' after another, as each succeeds the former in a sequence which cannot, however, be established as such. Where no connection can be made between successive tropes, there can be no thought of identity.

De Man then turns to irony, associating this as a form of discourse with the novel – and so with narrative – though he says that the greatest ironists in the nineteenth century wrote aphorisms, not novels (de Man, 1983: 210). One ironist is Baudelaire, who according to de Man shows that:

> ironic language splits the subject into an empirical self that exists in a
> state of inauthenticity and a self that exists only in the form of language
> that asserts the knowledge of this inauthenticity.
>
> (de Man, 1983: 214)

To unpack this: when a splitting happens, in 'ordinary' or literary
language, between what is said and what is meant, or between
the tropes of language and what the speaker thinks they add up
to, it produces irony. This (as discussed in chapter 3) is a form of
allegory, since it is the classic mode of stating one thing while
meaning another. Irony is usually thought of as being in the
speaker's control in that he or she means both what is said and
what is intended. But for de Man an ironic utterance exceeds, or
differs from, the speaker's intention, and the self that speaks
cannot be in charge of the irony which masters him, and so makes
his speech 'inauthentic'. Trying to reach a full awareness of irony
is impossible, for 'absolute irony is a consciousness of madness'
which can only happen because of the 'double structure of ironic
language: the ironist invents a form of himself that is "mad" but
that does not know its own madness' (de Man, 1983: 216). To try
to stand outside my own utterance would be a form of madness; I
will always be caught out, interrupted, by an irony in my speech
of which I am unaware. Hence de Man quotes Friedrich Schlegel,
referred to in chapter 4, on irony as 'a permanent parabasis' (de
Man, 1983: 218). Here, 'permanent' implies something repeated
again and again, while 'parabasis' means 'interruption'. Kathleen
Wheeler illuminates Schlegel's definition by saying that within a
text irony works as 'a continual self-consciousness of the work
itself' (Wheeler, 1984: 20). Irony, surfacing as parabasis repeat-
edly within a text means that the text's discontinuity with itself
is constantly being advertised, so that the text is, actually, 'mad',
disconnected, and ecstatic in the literal sense in that each part of
it stands outside those parts surrounding and succeeding it.

De Man illustrates the 'temporal structure of allegory and irony'
with an analysis of one of Wordsworth's 'Lucy' poems (1799):

> A slumber did my spirit seal;
> I had no human fears:

She seemed a thing that could not feel
The touch of earthly years.

No motion has she now, no force;
She neither hears nor sees;
Rolled round in earth's diurnal course,
With rocks, and stones, and trees.

(Wordworth, 1936: 149)

In this lyric, two stages are posited. There is, first, a gap in time, for in the first stanza, where the verbs are all in the past, the 'I' said that he thought of the woman ('she') as a thing, and 'now' she is a thing. But it should be noted how the second stanza, which records the point that the woman is dead, and therefore a 'thing', makes the word 'thing' in the first verse ironic. Yet de Man insists that thinking 'then' of the woman as a thing was not ironic and his reading shields the 'I' from an accusation of blindness: 'the text is clearly not ironic' (de Man, 1983: 223). Also, as speaking 'now' from the standpoint of the second stanza, the 'I' is not wrong either, for he sees things as they are. But that poise of the subject, which gives him his identity, and ability to see things as they are, depends on the break between the verses, which passes over the death of the woman. The gap constitutes the space of death and points to a separation taking place in and because of time passing, which, however, the poem is reluctant to admit; so it will be noted how lightly the passing of time is implied in line 4.

De Man locates the practice of allegory in his emphasis on 'duration as the illusion of a continuity that it knows to be illusionary' (de Man, 1983: 226). The death within the 'gap' of the woman, the poem's 'she', is homologous to the gap that takes place between each sign or trope in utterance, which severs them from each other. Because the poem says nothing in and about the gap, it seems to repress its allegorical structure, allegory being the mode of utterance that knows nothing else than that a temporal difference marks each of its stages. This allegoric structure, once recognized, brings out an irony otherwise concealed: that the subject's serene poise and identity – which makes the poem 'Romantic' – is preserved only by a trick, the effacement of the details of the gap, which is the effacement of allegory. Undoing identity in that way undercuts the most fundamental premise of the Romantics: belief in the 'I' marked by a creative imagination. It replaces presence with absence. De Man's definitions of allegory and irony have in common the sense that all tropes undo identity. The assertion of the 'I' as an identity must bypass allegory, whose 'rhetoric of temporality' does not allow the subject to think of itself in a full, self-consistent mode.

De Man's essay 'The Concept of Irony' (1977), posthumously published, returns to Schlegel on irony as 'permanent parabasis'. It completes the definition, saying that the narrative which is undone by irony is that 'resulting from the tropological system' so that 'irony is the permanent parabasis of the allegory of tropes'. A footnote by the editor, Andrzej Warminski, which originates from an oral comment made by de Man, glosses this: 'irony is (permanent) parabasis of allegory – intelligibility of (representational) narrative disrupted at all times' (de Man, 1996: 179). What is the allegory of tropes? The 'of' must be read in two ways, as a *double genitive*: it means both allegory as a narrative which is composed of figures of speech, which is, roughly, the way in which allegory is usually understood, and it means what de Man has said above: that tropes which are always different from each other, form, in the way they are laid alongside each other, an allegory, in the sense that they each say something 'other' from each other; which is, again, a definition of allegory. On that basis, all writing, for de Man, is allegorical. And what of the reference to irony? Irony disrupts, undoes, this 'allegory of tropes' by breaking up the apparent coherence and systemacity within a narrative that is composed of tropes; at each stage irony shows that there can be no *essential* connection of one trope to another. The gap in the middle of the 'Lucy' poem, which a 'traditional' reading would see as an example of Wordsworth's power of understatement, is ironic, because it separates both the speaker's utterance and identity from stanza to stanza. There cannot be a narrative which so unites the speaker's experiences from the first to the second stanza.

So, any 'theory of irony is the undoing of any theory of narrative' (de Man, 1983: 179). Allegory, we have said, is connected with narrative, since the latter depends on a relationship between signifiers following each other in a temporal sequence. But an allegory *of tropes* breaks up the unity of this temporal flow. We think that narrative provides a sequence of similar forms of language which can be put together, and which, taken together, may refer to a reality outside themselves, and fail to read literary language as successive tropes which necessarily deviate from each other. De Man concludes by broadening his discussion from narrative to history, which as a form of discourse, both self-reflexive and following its own logic – what de Man calls its 'dialectic' – is undone by irony as parabasis, because both 'the reflexive and the dialectical are the tropological system' (de Man, 1983: 181). The reflexive is the mode of the lyric poem, the dialectic that of narrative history, but both are constructed by tropes and it is impossible to stand outside them.

ALLEGORIES OF READING

For de Man, all texts are implicitly allegorical – an issue central to *Allegories of Reading* (1979), a study which he says began as historically based, but which ended up as a 'theory of reading'. De Man distinguishes between narrative that thinks it is representation and narrative that shows itself to be 'temporality', and so he breaks with the naivety of thinking that the text can represent, or narrate. Such allegorical discourse, as a series of tropes where 'the trope is not a derived, marginal, or aberrant form of language but the linguistic paradigm par excellence' (de Man, 1979: 105) emphasizes that narrative is 'rhetoric'. In chapter 2, we saw that classical rhetoric names the system of tropes and figures and the techniques that writers devised which enabled them to use oratorical eloquence and persuasion.

> Considered as persuasion, rhetoric is performative, but when considered as a series of tropes, it deconstructs its own performance. Rhetoric is a *text* in that it allows for two incompatible, mutually self-destructive points of view, and therefore puts an insurmountable obstacle [what deconstruction elsewhere calls an 'aporia'] in the way of any reading or understanding.
>
> (de Man, 1979: 131).

This passage is not difficult once it is understood that 'performative' language (a term deriving from the philosopher J. L. Austin) brings about a state of affairs, and thereby creates a new situation. Rhetoric is performative in this sense, but because it comprises discontinuous tropes it undoes its own performativity and illustrates the point that its language is only persuasion, not 'truth'. One way, rhetoric aims to create a new situation; in another way, it undoes it, producing an 'undecidability' which affects the reading of any text. Reading cannot stop with this 'simple antithetical relationship between referent [what the text is saying] and figure [i.e. trope]' (de Man, 1979: 200) because it must go on to recognize that the referential sense is also a figure, a trope. We always have one more trope than we want, and the text becomes 'the allegorical narrative of its own deconstruction' (de Man, 1979: 72), which means that whatever the text narrates, it also narrates that it cannot say what it narrates.

Discussing passages in Proust where the narrator is engaged in reading, where the meaning which he 'reads' is not necessarily the meaning which is stated, and focussing specifically on the passage where the narrator 'reads' pictures of Giotto's frescoes of virtues and vices (see above, chapter 3), de Man speaks of 'the possibility of including the contradictions of reading in a narrative that would be able to contain them. Such a narrative would have the universal significance of an allegory of reading' (de Man, 1979: 72). Proust's text demonstrates this, and we must think of an 'allegory of reading' in terms of the following three axioms:

1. A text shows the impossibility of reading it for its referential value, for its ability to represent literal events. On that basis, and following the 'double genitive', an 'allegory of reading' is also a reading of allegory, deciding that the text *is* an allegory.
2. A text shows that when we read, we do not read the text but our version of it. De Man points out that the interpretation that Giotto's figure of Charity means Charity is, because of contradictory signs in the portrait itself, only secured, ultimately by Giotto writing KARITAS above the pictured personification. Nothing in the actual portrait can stabilize meaning: 'the allegory of reading narrates the impossibility of

reading' and in the plurality of signs, the word 'reading' is 'deprived of any referential meaning whatsoever' (de Man, 1979: 77). What does 'reading' mean? We can only read tropes, figures.

3. The reading is not just an allegory of the text, but an allegory of the referential meaning. The text will always record a split between reading and understanding. Reading means reading an allegory of the text. Understanding can only be of another allegorization of the text. Reading and understanding will never coincide: 'Proust is the one who knows that the hour of truth, like the hour of death, never arrives on time, since what we call time is precisely truth's inability to coincide with itself' (de Man, 1979: 78). (If I explain something to you, and you then say 'I see', the time gap between these two means that we are not coinciding, not talking about the 'same' truth; one truth becomes an allegory of the other.)

Metaphor, which de Man aligns with the symbol, substitutes one meaning for another, and the union of the two terms produces a 'totality' that in chapter 6 we associated with the symbol. Allegory, however, does not allow such substitutions. Every comparison is a catachresis: it gives

> a proper meaning ... by using a literal sign which bears no resemblance to that meaning and which conveys in its turn, a meaning that is proper to it but does not coincide with the proper meaning of the allegory.
>
> (de Man, 1979: 74)

The proper meaning is deviated from by a traditional and figurative use of language, as inevitably happens when a statement is transposed into, and framed within, the terms of a particular literary genre. The troping form of language that is then employed, which belongs to the particular 'lexicological and grammatical code' of the text (de Man, 1979: 201), supplies a further set of catachreses, in addition to the tropes seen already to be inherent in all narrative utterance, and which constitute the 'allegory of tropes'.

Obviously, no totality can be reached this way. The text has become an allegory of the 'impossibility of reading'. The following passage, on Rousseau's *Julie* (and which contains the last quoted phrase), speaks of a 'final reading' which would allow for the emergence of a single meaning, except for something that we have already discussed: the presence of an ironic excess within the text. This announces the impossibility of totality, for if that excess could be accounted for, the supplementary material which did so would itself be a text full of the rhetorical devices of narrative. And that would have to be accounted for, in its turn.

> The paradigm for all texts consists of a figure (or a system of figures) and its deconstruction. But since this model cannot be closed off by a final reading, it engenders in its turn, a supplementary figural super-position which narrates the unreadability of its prior narration. As distinguished from primarily deconstructive narratives centred on fig-ures and ultimately always on metaphor, we can call such narratives to the second (or third) degree allegories. Allegorical narratives tell the story of the failure to read whereas tropological narratives ... tell the story of the failure to denominate. The difference is only a difference of degree and the allegory does not erase the figure. Allegories are always allegories of metaphor, and, as such, they are always allegories of the impossibility of reading.
>
> (de Man, 1979: 205)

This statement differentiates between allegorical narratives – whose structure has been discussed – and tropological narratives, which consciously rely on metaphor, and which attempt to think synchronically (as with the use of symbolism). But no metaphor can nominate, or dominate (the pun in de Man's 'denominate'), nor can it secure a totality of meaning. Allegories show that the metaphor which is intended to clinch a meaning only generates another, other, sense, and so yields the impossibility of reading. That impossibility, then, may be defined and summarized in this way, and it is the point behind all de Man's terminology: *as the impossibility of knowing, or of naming, something or someone, or of being able to control the otherness of an other*. To continue with reading or rereading shows the impossibility of reading the same text over and over again, as the text, already discontinuous, is put into one allegorical framework after another in the process of finding a metalanguage for it, i.e. a language to explain it (Miller, 1989: 155–70). De Man's sense of allegory is that it is, indeed, deconstruction, for 'allegory' names that which makes the text other than what it seems to be.

De Man's argument asserts the impossibility of reading a text for a univocal meaning. It differs from Derrida, whose work shows a commitment to an active process of deconstruction, which will expose the metaphysical/ideological underpinning of the text, whereas for de Man the literary text already disallows the possibility of such ideology taking hold. Critics of de Man's politics often point out that the theory cannot account for the point that ideology still *does* take hold, despite the tendency of language to deconstruct the propositions contained within it; de Man's criticism takes place in a social void – of all critical theorists, he is least concerned with anything approaching 'cultural studies'. But there is something more intense in de Man's approach to allegory, which will be examined in the following section.

PROSOPOPOEIA

As a prelude to thinking again about de Man, we may recall our discussion of personification in chapter 3, and the definition of a person as given by Thomas Hobbes in *Leviathan* (1651) will remind us of 'persona' (Latin: 'mask') and so of personification:

> A person is he whose words or actions are considered, either as his own, or as representing the words or actions of another man, or of any thing to whom they are attributed, whether Truly, or by Fiction. ...
>
> The word Person is latine: instead whereof the Greeks have prosopon, which signifies the *Face*, as *Persona* in latine signifies the *disguise*, or *outward appearance* of a man, counterfeited on the Stage; and sometimes more particularly that part of it, which disguiseth the face, as a Mask or Vizard: And from the Stage, hath been translated to any Representer of speech and action, as well as in Tribunalls, as Theatres. So that a *Person*, is the same as an *Actor* is, both on the Stage and in common conversation, and to *Personate*, is to *Act*, or *Represent* himself, or an other ...
>
> (Hobbes, 1968: 217)

In Hobbes' chapter, called 'Of PERSONS, AUTHORS, and Things Personated', a 'person' is someone who personates himself or somebody else, or who stands in for some institution (such as the university, or the law, or the government). Hobbes gives a definition of the word 'prosopopoeia' as the mask, or disguise, which the actor puts on. To act is allegorical: it is speaking the words of another, perhaps on stage, or whenever we have to speak in a way which represents ourself or another person. Anyone who feels that their social interactions necessarily involve different forms of falsity will appreciate that for Hobbes being a person is the same as being a hypocrite, for the Greek 'hypocrite' means an actor.

Hobbes does not believe in the human subject who precedes such interactions; nor, it seems, does de Man, nor Nietzsche, who will be quoted later in this chapter. For each, a 'person' is a fiction (what Hobbes calls an 'artificial man') and the concept of the individual subject or person is created through the power of language which creates the subject. In the essay 'Hypogram and Inscription' (1981), de Man discusses personification through discussion of prosopopoeia, which he calls 'the trope of apostrophe' (de Man, 1986: 44). Prosopopoeia he calls 'the master trope of poetic discourse' (de Man, 1986: 48). An apostrophe is an address to what is faceless and formless. It uses the vocative mode, frequent in the classical ode and surviving in poems such as Ben Jonson's 'To Penshurst', just as in Romanticism Blake addresses the 'Tyger', or writes 'O Rose thou art sick!', Shelley addresses the West Wind, or the skylark, and Keats addresses the Grecian Urn: 'thou still unravished bride of quietness'. An outstanding example of apostrophe is 'Andromâque, je pense a vous' – 'Andromache, I think of you' – the opening line of Baudelaire's 'The Swan'. Apostrophe would have no validity were it not for the opposite possibility, that of producing, in contrast, the idea of the absent, or dead, or silent entity, speaking of itself as though it was a human figure, through prosopopoeia, or personification, through a mask which it has been given. This supreme form of allegory de Man sees operating through a genre such as autobiography, in which an author speaks as though his life was completed, as though he was already dead.

In the essay 'Shelley Disfigured', de Man discusses the narrative poem *The Triumph of Life*, which Shelley (1792–1822) left as a fragment at his death. In this poem, the 'I' hears about the lives and deaths of people, deriving its inspiration from Dante, hearing about the deaths of those who, in *Inferno*, speak from beyond the grave. De Man refers to

> the endless prosopopoeia by which the dead are made to have a face and a voice which tells the allegory of their demise and allows us to apostrophize them in our turn.
>
> (de Man, 1984: 122; Shelley, 2002)

De Man implies that to write is to create a mask for whatever it is that speaks in the text, transforming the speaker into a person. In Dante, or in Shelley, or in autobiography generally, the dead are made to speak. With autobiography, writing creates a textual face for the subject to speak of his/her life, so that the face de-faces, or disfigures, the life that emerges; the concept of the 'person' created does an injustice to the subject spoken of. The narrative emerging from each mask in *The Triumph of Life* de Man calls 'the allegory of their demise', which phrase means the story of how they died. Here 'allegory' may be taken to mean 'narrative' as a series of substitutive figures, or the narrative of their death rendered fictively, for no-one can speak in the present of how they died, unless their 'death' is allegorical not literal. However the phrase is understood, whoever speaks of his or her death does so from the other side of a central gap, like that between the stanzas of 'A slumber did my spirit seal'. The gap, which means that there is no direct, immediate speech, makes all speech 'other' than what it purports to be, thereby challenging the claim to fixed or unitary meaning: if the person speaks, that does not make them a single subject; but rather, a divided one.

Apostrophe addresses the entity which is to be given a mask, thus indicating that apostrophe and prosopopoeia circulate in relation to each other. In a fascinating essay, 'Autobiography as Defacement', de Man quotes from the first of Wordsworth's prose pieces called 'Essay on Epitaphs', published in 1810. It is an example of de Man locating a moment in a Romantic text that works against the customary affirmation of presence and life. De Man writes:

... the epitaph, says Wordsworth, 'is open to the day; the sun looks down upon the stone, and the rains of heaven beat against it'. [Wordsworth, 1974: 59.] The sun becomes the eye that reads the text of the epitaph. And the essay tells us what this text consists of, by way of a quotation from Milton that deals with Shakespeare: 'What need'st thou such weak witness of thy name?' [Wordsworth, 1974: 61.] In the case of poets such as Shakespeare, Milton or Wordsworth himself, the epitaph can consist only of what he calls 'the naked name' [Wordsworth, 1974: 61], as it is read by the sun. At this point, it can be said of 'the language of the senseless stone' that it acquires 'a voice', the *speaking* stone counterbalancing the *seeing* sun. The system passes from sun to eye to language as name and as voice. We can identify the figure that completes the central metaphor of the sun and thus completes the tropological spectrum that the sun engenders: it is the figure of prosopopoeia, the fiction of an apostrophe to an absent, deceased or voiceless entity, which posits the possibility of the latter's reply, and confers upon it the power of speech. Voice assumes mouth, eye, and finally face, a chain that is manifest in the etymology of the trope's name, *prosopon poein*, to confer a mask or a face (*prosopon*). Prosopopoeia is the trope of autobiography, by which one's name, as in Milton's poem, is made as intelligible and memorable as a face. Our topic deals with the giving and taking away of faces, with face and deface, *figure*, figuration and disfiguration.

(de Man, 1984: 75–76)

Wordsworth's meditation on tombstones and their poetic inscriptions alludes to the sun beating down on the tombstone and the rain weathering it. De Man calls the sun an 'eye', so intensifying the personification, and moving, in a metonymic 'chain', towards giving the sun a face. At the same time, the tombstone, with its epitaph, which as part of a monument relates to the emblem tradition, is allegorical both because of that and because it speaks, in prosopopoeia, in an apostrophe, to the passer-by. It solicits attention by the words on the epitaph: 'Pause, courteous stranger' [Wordsworth, 1974: 54]. The passer-by who reads the stone for the name, which Wordsworth says may be the stone's sole inscription, then 'sees' a face that speaks but which is simultaneously under erasure, being defaced, defigured, because Time, a personification here, will eventually make the epitaph/name unreadable.

The inscription on the tombstone gives the deceased's auto-biography; the name itself may constitute an autobiography. As the inscription speaks in an act of prosopopoeia, it can be said that this, and every other form of autobiography, gives a 'face', while the face, the writing on the tombstone, is de-faced. De Man interprets this to mean that autobiography can never be full; it takes away knowledge of the subject while giving it. Auto-biography, a concept historically associated with Romanticism, and the ability to speak of the self as marked by a self-identity, extending through time, delivers an account of the self as dead, like the writing on a tombstone. This associates it with allegory, which, as a figure giving a face, defaces, or disfigures what it describes.

De Man's word 'figure' should recall, for contrast, Auerbach on *figura*, discussed in chapter 2. For him, 'figura' refers to the idea that one event or person prefigures another, so that any event may be used to speak of another. The word 'figura' connects to a word which means a face (*OED*), and with this word we return to Hobbes, who sees a face as a 'disguise' and people as mere person-ifications. The philosophers Gilles Deleuze and Felix Guattari argue that the idea of the face has been encoded into all ways of seeing landscapes and forms of reality, so that everything appears as though facialized: the face is a controlling figure (Deleuze and Guattari, 1988: 167–91). The idea of the face is all-pervasive, then, and its use in allegory is one instance of it. It has appeared constantly in this book. It emerged as an image with *The Nether World*. There were the masks in Bronzino's painting; there is the skull for Benjamin. Painters, and, in the nineteenth century, Dickens, were interested in physiognomy, which itself develops from an idea that emotions may be written on the face, in which case it is a question of interpreting, reading, the face. The absence of face in the white whale, Moby Dick, makes him an especially teasing figure of allegory and a complex mask. Because the mask covers the face, allegory is inseparable from questions of disguise, false seeming and hypocrisy. The argument of the medievalist Daniel Poirion (Poirion, 1999: 13–32) is that allegory gives no sense of the other, because the face it turns towards the narcissistic self is always illusionistic. With de Man, the word 'figure' implies that tropes in language give a face to that which has no single face, and there is no other way of bringing out, or bringing back, an event or person than through rhetorical figures. In 'Shelley Disfigured', 'figuration is the element in language that allows for the reiteration of meaning by substitution' (de Man, 1984: 114–15). The substitutive nature of language again recalls a potential within allegory: saying one thing actually says another. For de Man, there are only substitutive moves in language, which figure and disfigure at once. Benjamin, it will be recalled, had said that mourning revives the dead world in the form of a mask, one which, as Ahab thinks in *Moby-Dick* (see above, p. 90), may be all there is in the world, lacking a face behind it. This suggests that prosopopoeia comes out of mourning, a state which for Benjamin is akin to melancholy, as mourning must obviously include melancholy. Prosopopoeia, as a dominant trope in language, creates something which is manifestly only a mask; a state of loss, of mourning, creates the illusion of the separate, real other 'person', through the power of allegory.

APOSTROPHE

In this final section, we will consider the 'apostrophe', as a rhetorical trope inseparable from personification. But first, it will be worth quoting Nietzsche, from an early essay, *On Truths and Lies in the Extra-Moral Sense* (1874), where he poses and answers the rhetorical question:

> What, then, is truth? A mobile army of metaphors, metonyms, and anthropomorphisms – in short, a sum of human relations, which have been enhanced, transposed, and embellished poetically and rhetorically, and which after long use seem firm, canonical, and obligatory to a people ...

> (Allison, 1983: 167)

The quotation supports de Man's point that all language tends towards allegory, or, as de Man puts it, discussing Nietzsche and lyric poetry, 'turns trope into anthropomorphism' (de Man, 1984:

261). For Nietzsche, the point is that language anthropomorphizes reality: gives to all of it a human aspect, personates it, as Hobbes would say. Chapter 3 discussed Blake on animism, which made it a mark of poetic genius to find all objects to be characterized by the divine; there, we also looked at Freud on anthropomorphism. In the alienated atmosphere of capitalism, it is the commodity which is invested with divine attributes. In the quotation from Nietzsche, something different from Blake is described, in suggesting that language creates allegories because of its tendency to interpret reality, to make comparisons, and to create in each sentence an agent, or Hobbesian actor, who does something. For that reason, personification and prosopopoeia become inevitable tropes within language. If personification is called by Hillis Miller 'the fundamental trope of narrative' or integral to western poetry (Miller, 1990: 79; Culler, 1981), that implies that the tropes within language generate narrative possibilities.

On that basis, the lyric poem, which uses apostrophe so much, and anthropomorphizes what has no substance, in that it ascribes hands, feet, eyes, and faces to formless entities, develops the tropes which construct it initially. But de Man's version of deconstruction insists that the fiction inherent in apostrophe is that the text is *not* allegorical in its assumed anthropomorphism. We should develop this point here. For Jonathan Culler, apostrophe has several functions:

1. It assumes a relation between two subjects (not subject and object), so that the subject speaking gains a presence by being enabled to speak to an 'other', even though the other has no actual literal being.
2. Also, since it is such a standard trope, it may be 'the pure embodiment of poetic pretension: of the subject's claim that in his verse he is not merely an empirical poet, a writer of verse, but the embodiment of poetic tradition and of the spirit of poesy' (Culler, 1981: 158). And so it can also be a palpable fiction which announces its fictionality.
3. Third, addressing the other can, in addition, mean speaking to an aspect of the self, making the apostrophe an act of interiorization and solipsism. It increases the subject's sense of self,

consolidating its belief in its identity. (There is no 'other' that the speaking 'I' is addressing.)

4. The address creates a time of the apostrophe: it seems to take place in a moment, with the kind of simultaneity and immediacy that is associated with the immediacy of the symbol. Apostrophe seems, therefore, anti-allegorical. This immediacy is in spite of the point that it seems to put everything into a synecdochal relationship, where things are described primarily in terms of their parts. Actually, the synecdoche seems to suggest the complete presence of what is addressed. When Wordsworth apostrophizes, in the last verse of the 'Ode: Intimations of Immortality', 'And O ye Fountains, Meadows, Hills, and Groves', he links these various parts of nature into a synecdochal relationship with each other as if the parts added up to a whole, to a totality, which exists in the poet's mind (Culler, 1981: 164).

Culler therefore contrasts lyric poetry, which uses apostrophe, and narrative poetry, which, following de Man, has the allegorical structure defined earlier in discussing 'The Rhetoric of Temporality'. One example of the special time frame set up in the lyric is the elegy, of which Milton's 'Lycidas' (1638) is a good example. This was written in commemoration of the death by drowning of a minor poet, Edward King, and it is full of apostrophes, four obvious examples of which follow:

> Yet once more, O ye Laurels, and once more
> Ye Myrtles brown, with Ivy never-sear
> I come to pick your Berries ...   (1–3)
>
> But O the heavy change now thou [i.e. King] art gon,
> Now thou art gon and never must return!   (38–39)
>
> Where were ye Nymphs when the remorseless deep
> Clos'd o're the head of your lov'd Lycidas?   (50–51)
>
> O Fountain Arethuse, and thou honour'd floud,
> Smooth-sliding Mincius. ...   (86–87)
>
> (Milton, 1930: 38–40)

The first of these addresses is to the trees, which symbolize poetic achievement in that the poet is garlanded by wreaths from laurel trees. The fruit of these trees is not ripe and the poet claims that he is not mature enough to write. In the second address, the dead poet is addressed under the fictional name of Lycidas, and his death is negated by the apostrophe. In the third, entirely mythical sea-nymphs are apostrophized, though they were unable to stop Lycidas from being drowned at sea. In the fourth, the spirits of rivers are addressed, as the symbols of the inspiration of pastoral poetry, and we may recall that the Greek 'pastor' means 'shepherd'.

The apostrophe animates, and anthropomorphizes, everything: the poem speaks about, and to, a dead person, and moves backwards and forwards between mourning and consolation, so that Lycidas, though dead, is also presented as alive. A last example from the poem brings out the fictive nature of everything:

> Weep no more, woful Shepherds, weep no more,
> For Lycidas, your sorrow, is not dead ...
>
> (165–66)

But there are no 'shepherds' since they are fictional creations necessary for a pastoral poem. Not only is Lycidas not alive, those who are said to mourn for him have no existence either. But the elegy, in using apostrophe, seems, in this way, to be the exact opposite of the *Trauerspiel*, with its emphasis on death, even though, like it, *Lycidas* begins in mourning. The difference is that *Lycidas* ends denying death. The apostrophe, apparently claiming totality, through its inclusive references to nature, refuses the irreversibility of loss. Though as a form it may be linked with personification allegory, which it calls into being through its address, apostrophe attempts to be anti-allegorical in denying death, in conjuring up a presence out of absence. It could be said that the poem approaches the condition that Romantic symbolism aspires to.

Yet, despite this, apostrophe and prosopopoeia may both be allegorical in the sense which Benjamin suggested, and which de Man follows: that they associate with death, and with writing as disfiguring, defacing. An example may be given from Keats's

'Ode on a Grecian Urn' (1819), a Romantic text whose structure obviously depends on both apostrophe and prosopopoeia, and in which the urn is normally classed as a symbol. I quote the first and the last two stanzas:

> Thou still unravish'd bride of quietness,
> Thou foster-child of silence and slow time,
> Sylvan historian, who canst thus express
> A flowery tale more sweetly than our rhyme:
> What leaf-fring'd legend haunts about thy shape
> Of deities or mortals, or of both,
> In Tempe or the dales of Arcady?
> What men or gods are these? What maidens loth?
> What mad pursuit? What struggle to escape?
> What pipes and timbrels? What wild ecstasy?
> [...]
> Who are these coming to the sacrifice?
> To what green altar, O mysterious priest,
> Lead'st thou that heifer, lowing at the skies,
> And all her silken flanks with garlands drest?
> What little town, by river or sea shore,
> Or mountain-built with peaceful citadel,
> Is emptied of this folk, this pious morn?
> And little town, thy streets for evermore
> Will silent be, and not a soul to tell
> Why thou art desolate, can e'er return.
>
> O Attic shape! Fair attitude! With brede
> Of marble men and maidens overwrought,
> With forest branches and the trodden weed;
> Thou, silent form, dost tease us out of thought
> As doth eternity: Cold Pastoral!
> When old age shall this generation waste,
> Thou shalt remain, in midst of other woe
> Than ours, a friend to man, to whom thou say'st,
> 'Beauty is truth, truth beauty,' – that is all
> Ye know on earth, and all ye need to know.

(Keats, 1970: 532–38)

The poem's first three lines apostrophize the urn – which speaks of death because its use was, typically, to contain ashes – in three different ways, and they question it. Yet there is an equal insistence in the first two lines that the urn is silent, despite the word 'express' which implies communication. Silence, referred to in the second line, and not broken despite the evocation of sound in the last line, is emphasized again in the second stanza, through the 'soft pipes', which are apostrophized, as though they were playing themselves. In the third stanza the melodist is 'for ever piping songs for ever new'. The fourth stanza uses the word 'silent' again, and again asks questions. To the six questions of the first stanza are added a further three. And they include a further apostrophe within the overall apostrophe to the urn. Now not just the urn but the figures within it are addressed: the priest, and the town where the people have come from. And that is not even visible on the urn, only imagined. The town has, or had, only a temporal existence; the urn a timeless one, hence its value as a symbol.

In asking questions, Keats seems to follow a practice usual in apostrophe, but it is unusual that the poem insists that no answer can come from the silence: it is as though the poem incorporates death into the apostrophe. Acceptance of death, indeed, occurs throughout the second, third and fourth stanzas, culminating in speech to both what is dead, i.e. all the inhabitants of the town, and to what is absent, i.e. the town itself. It seems to identify itself with death, moving into death itself, as that from which it cannot 'return'. The word 'turn', it should be noted, is exactly the same as 'trope'; and recalling de Man it may be said that the death which the urn records allows for no further 'troping', no more substitute figures of speech, no more allegory.

However, in the last stanza the urn, which is still apostrophized in four different ways, and identified with death through the words 'marble' and 'cold', speaks in a prosopopoeia which breaks with the apostrophe, which, as we have seen, presupposes the animated quality of what is addressed. And that confirms the difference between apostrophe and prosopopoeia: the first denies death, the second affirms it (Riffaterre, 1985: 108). The urn's rhetorical, prosopopoeic statement: 'Beauty is truth, truth beauty' turns or reverses the two substantives, beauty and truth, in a chiasmus which de Man would call a tropological substitution, because each term substitutes for the other, neither completing the other. If beauty 'is' truth, neither term can be said to be substantial, real; both are tropes, figures of speech. The persuasion within the statement comes from nothing but the chiasmus, which occurs not only with the words 'beauty'/'truth', but in the 'turn' of the line which yields the repetition 'that is all / Ye know on earth, and all ye need to know'. This rhetoric is the voice of death in coming from the urn in a prosopopoeia; implying the impossibility of going further than substitutive reversals. Reading offers nothing but such reversals, and their effect is the death of the reader.

'Ode on a Grecian Urn' could be claimed to be an allegory on the strength of its insistent personifications: for example, the pipes, the youth who is the absolute personification of the 'Lover', and the urn itself, are all fashioned into the type of 'pastoral'. But in this chapter's terms, it is an allegory in showing that apostrophe does not produce the poetic self who writes as authoritative and commanding; the final prosopopoeia is unable to deliver any message of life. The Grecian Urn may be thought to be a symbol, since it produces such relentless questioning of its essence, and since its being cannot be explained, but because its being is inseparable from death it is thereby removed from the essence of symbolism. Because the urn has writing on it, suggested in the word 'legend', it may also come close to allegory in Benjamin's sense, in that it cannot quite be read. Because the poem implies that there can be no more than a relentless questioning of language, where one figure observed on the urn substitutes for another, it seems that it becomes allegory in de Man's sense, in that one trope after another suggests an absence. And that absence, which generated the need to write the poem in the first place, is also that to which the poem leads.

The title 'Ode on a Grecian Urn' contradicts the first line of the poem, since it says it is not an apostrophe (it is not 'Ode to a Grecian Urn'). Its ambiguity about whether the urn figures life (apostrophe) or death (prosopopoeia) should be compared with the Wordsworth poem discussed above, 'A slumber did my spirit seal', which may emphasize death even within the word 'diurnal'. The comparison brings out an ambiguity which makes the Romantic backing of the symbol so poignant. Romantic language now seems based on knowledge of death and absence, not life and presence, and becomes associated with melancholy and mourning, like 'The Ancient Mariner' (chapter 4). De Man's reading of allegory recalls this point. It means that the Romantic lyric must be seen not as affirming the power of the natural world, but as denying the possibility of any external reference at all. Discovery of this produces no complacency since de Man sees the Romantics as haunted by that sense of loss, or death, the message 'expressed' from the allegorical urn.

7

MODERN ALLEGORY

This last chapter looks at allegory in some twentieth-century versions, and follows on from insights discussed in chapters 5 and 6. It concludes with discussion of the idea of allegory, but we cannot hope to arrive at any finality here; we can only think of further questions which need consideration.

Modern criticism and practice has extended the arguments of Walter Benjamin and Paul de Man, developing the concept of allegory as part of a critical vocabulary throughout literary and cultural studies. Some critics, such as James Paxson, have used de Man to reread texts of traditional allegory to show how these new insights have the potential to disturb earlier ways of reading them (Paxson, 1994). While some approaches have concentrated on allegory as an element in the content of fiction, others have argued that all writing is allegorical, or that no text is free of it (Fletcher, 1964: 8). This has been a division which this study has tried to bring out.

In his book *Metahistory* (1973), the historian Hayden White argues that the consciousness of nineteenth-century historians was informed by four strategies, of thinking through the four tropes: metaphor, synecdoche, metonymy and irony. No narrative of history could be empirical, or non-figurative; to write history in narrative form entails working with one of these modes, which in turn structures both thought and narrative. These four terms imply allegory since each literary mode implies others; the narrative means what it says *and* is overcoded with another narrative that is dependent upon the choice of trope. White would not, of course, go so far as de Man in the claim that tropes undo narrative. In later writings, White returns to the theme, quoting the philosopher Louis Mink that 'narratives contain indefinitely many ordering relations, and indefinitely many ways of *combining* those relations. ... a historical narrative claims truth not merely for each of its individual statements taken distributively, but for the complex form of the narrative itself'. White adds that to put those individual statements together is allegoresis: allegorical interpretation. 'What else' he asks, quoting Marx's opening of *The Eighteenth Brumaire of Louis Bonaparte* (1852), 'could be involved in the representation of a set of real events as, for example, a tragedy ... or farce?' (White, 1987: 45–46). Perceiving the events of 1848–51 in France to be a farce, in contrast to the tragedy of the earlier French Revolution (1789), Marx deliberately articulates them in farcical, excessive language: the work is an allegory of what it describes and what it has allegorized. White's argument implies that to go from listing historical events to seeing them as having generically specific forms – first as tragedy, then as farce, as Marx says – is a move from literality to 'a figural account, an allegory'.

White's thinking silently alludes to Auerbach, but engages in dialogue with Paul Ricoeur, who believes that it is temporality which enables 'narrativity'; while narrativity is 'the language structure that has temporality as its ultimate referent' (Ricoeur, quoted in White, 1987: 52). The knowledge and experience of time constrains narrative, which is therefore a figure, an allegory, expressing a relationship towards temporality. It emphasizes that the narrative exists in time. If it did not, then there could be a complete plot, but because a narrative refers back, ultimately, to time as the referent, and is structured by that time, which, of course, has not finished, then it contains within it the allegory of its own incompleteness. A narrative is an allegorization of being within time.

White says that the necessity to think forwards, as Marxism requires, involves an ability in the present to reconfigure the past, to 'emplot' it differently. He uses Auerbach's account of Dante to illustrate what it might mean to 'emplot' the past differently. 'Just as for Dante the afterlife was a fulfilment of a figure of a given worldly existence, in history, every age or epoch was regarded as a fulfilment of a figure of some earlier age or epoch. The meaning of its present was its completion of what had been prefigured in the past' (White, 1987: 151; see also White, 1999: 87–100). The past becomes an allegory of the present when seen as prefiguring it, and the present also becomes allegorical, because though past events are fixed, their meaning is not; Dante's encounters with dead souls in the present reopen and reread the past, which means that the present (as the result of the past) becomes prefigured differently.

ALLEGORY IN POSTCOLONIALISM

The American Marxist critic Fredric Jameson has been deeply influenced by the idea of 'allegorical interpretation', which, he says, in the conditions of postmodernism requires 'a kind of scanning that, moving backwards and forth across the text, readjusts its terms in constant modification[,] of a type quite different from our stereotypes of some static medieval or biblical decoding' (Jameson, 1986: 161). Phenomena within postmodern reality cannot be interpreted statically; they require a thinking which is relational, and which rereads one text, or one feature of a text, in the light of another, shifting the interpretive value to be given to each part accordingly. Similarly, White, and Auerbach before him, had thought of being able to ascribe a different value to a past even in relation to the present. But what stands out in Jameson is the conviction that present texts can be interpreted, that the term 'allegory' remains relevant. For example, he sees texts which are not in formalist terms allegories as nonetheless allegorical in contending that 'All third-world texts are necessarily, I want to argue, allegorical, and in a very specific way: they are to be read as what I will call *national allegories*' (Jameson, 1986: 67). This rejects Paul de Man's sense that allegorical modes illustrate a resistance to communication and meaning. Calling postcolonial texts 'allegories' shows Jameson attempting to validate literature which he calls, in comparison to first-world texts, 'under-developed' (Jameson, 1986: 65). For Jameson, 'the story of the private individual destiny is always an allegory of the embattled situation of the public Third-World culture and society' (Jameson, 1986: 67). The 'third world' is defined by its 'experience of colonialism and imperialism'; its present choices are always deeply compromised, and the evidence of that is found as the referent of the national allegories that postcolonialism produces.

This reading gives a determinate meaning to allegory, and a prescriptive view of what writers should treat. As a view it was criticized, for instance by Aijaz Ahmad, first for Jameson's binary opposition between 'first' and 'third-world' literature, and second for the essay's slighting of the different ways in which countries have been brought into global capitalism (Ahmad, 1992: 95–122). Ahmad points out that the bifurcation between private and public worlds which marks the 'first world' also has affected 'third world' countries, so that a 'Third World' text cannot be assumed to generate stories relative to the private sphere which can then be allegorized by relating them back to the public or national sphere. Ahmad replaces the idea of the nation with that of the 'collectivity' and finds no less allegorization in relation to culture in the United States in the texts of, for instance, Thomas Pynchon, Ralph Ellison and Adrienne Rich (for Pynchon and allegory see Quilligan, 1979: 42–46). He says that neither a US woman nor a US black writer could speak so generally about the nation; they lack the access to it that is found in Jameson's more metropolitan-based theory. This, for Ahmad, suggests something about the presence of pockets of third-worldism within the USA. Ahmad's point could be extended to say that the view that texts are allegories necessarily idealizes, in subordinating gender and race differences.

Jameson contends that writing always bears the marks of politics, consciously or not. In *The Political Unconscious: Narrative as a Socially Symbolic Act* (1981), he argued that there was a politics buried under the surface of texts, which, appearing within the text as a symptom, points to what operates below its surface. Novels bear unconscious witness to a political crisis which cannot be stated openly because the writers of those texts are not fully aware of what structures them. If we read the text for symptoms of that crisis, remembering that symptoms are, in a medical sense, both real and symbolic of something else which is hidden, then this approach, taking narratives not for what they say, but for what they cannot say, looking at the gaps within them, will give us another sense of how texts say one thing while saying another. Yet here the criticism of Jameson by Gayatri Spivak is relevant. She argues that Jameson opts for a single buried unconscious narrative which is the referent of the text. Jameson's desire to allegorize produces allegory's most dangerous tendency: moving towards a single, overarching, even totalizing meaning. For Spivak, Jameson assumes he knows what the allegorical referent of the text is before reading, and consequently this determinate account erases those who are not subjects of the history that Jameson narrativizes: such as women, gays or lesbians, and other racial groups. To the single allegorized political unconscious that she sees Jameson speaking for – whether in European fiction or in third-world texts – Spivak says that 'the only figure of the unconscious is that of a radical series of discontinuous interruptions'. She finds in postcolonial writings 'the story of interruptions, a repeated tearing of time that cannot be sutured' (Spivak, 1999: 208), adopting Paul de Man's terms about 'permanent parabasis' (see above, p. 134). These other figures, who will never find a place inside the 'national allegory', enter the text and upset or uproot it: Spivak agrees with Paul de Man in defining the unconscious in terms of parabasis, and she moves from irony to allegory as parabasis (Spivak, 1999: 156, 337, 430). For her, the repressed unconscious appears in allegorical forms, forms of 'other' speaking which cannot be pre-known and therefore interpreted. These other voices have been silenced; what they would say cannot be known. Jameson's political unconscious, because it has a determinate referent, pre-known and appearing allegorically, she sees as a nostalgia for a 'totality'. The use of 'nostalgia' recalls Paul de Man's critical use of it (see above, p. 131); it suggests the desire to have started from a pure, single 'origin' which would enable a unified, total way of seeing reality, not one marked by recognition of irreducible differences.

Claiming to be writing allegory now, and thinking what allegorical interpretation means now, depends on defining a particular theoretical approach. Several critics resist the idea of allegory, much on the lines discussed at the beginning of the Introduction. Derek Attridge sees its dangers when he discusses *Waiting for the Barbarians* (1980) by the South African novelist J. M. Coetzee (b.1940) in a chapter called, provocatively, 'Against Allegory'. He responds to a dialogue in the novel where the 'I' of the text, a local magistrate in an unspecified country, speaks to the quasi-fascist Colonel (one of the 'barbarians') about his interest in old, aboriginal, slips of wood containing an unfamiliar script which the magistrate has been deciphering. The magistrate says that the slips

> form an allegory. They can be read in many ways. Together they can be read as a domestic journal, or they can be read as a plan of war, or they can be turned on their sides and read as a history of the last years of the Empire – the old Empire, I mean. There is no agreement among scholars about how to interpret these relics of the ancient barbarians. ... I found [this set of slips of wood] not three miles from here in the ruins of a public building. Graveyards are another good place to look in, though it is not always easy to tell where barbarian burial sites lie. It is recommended that you simply dig at random: perhaps at the very spot where you stand you will come upon scraps, shards, reminders of the dead ...
>
> (Coetzee, 1980: 112)

This passage has often been taken as metalinguistic, indicating to the reader how they should read: by taking the novel as allegory. While Attridge accepts that this may be necessary, insisting that he is not opposed to allegorical reading (Attridge, 2004: 63), he criticizes readings which accept allegory in Coetzee. He argues that they universalize the text and diminish its immediate political context by making the narrative describe a universal human condition. He says that reading allegorically diminishes the 'event' of reading the text; the point that the text means and communicates in an immediate way which the reader responds to, and responds to differently each time the text is read, because each time a text is read the reader is doing something different, each (re)reading being a singular event. If the meaning is underpinned by allegory, he argues that that 'event' is diminished. Last, Attridge argues that allegory 'deals with the *already known*, whereas literature opens a space for the other. Allegory announces a moral code, literature invites an ethical response' (Attridge, 2004: 64). It is not difficult to see a similarity here with arguments raised against Jameson: that his version of allegory also deals with 'the already known'.

Some of Attridge's charges against allegorical readings repeat strains in Romantic criticism. They rest on a sense of allegory ignorant of either Benjamin or de Man, neither of whom would say that allegory deals with that which is already known. Coetzee's passage, however, is conscious of Benjamin in three ways; first in its sense that the writings of the 'barbarians' do not have a single determinate meaning, that they are, instead, infinitely suggestive; second, that the writings are fragments, and derived from death. They speak of what has been cut off; they associate with the point that 'the air is full of sounds and cries' (Coetzee, 1980: 112) and that these 'cries of the dead ... like their writings, are open to many interpretations' (Coetzee, 1980: 112), not to one single buried narrative. Third, they associate with the *Trauerspiel* in that the 'allegorical sets' are associated with the ruins of public buildings – those used to maintain a previous empire – and burial sites. Allegory is, as for Benjamin, the record of what is 'untimely, sorrowful, unsuccessful', and to revive the dead world in these slips of wood is one form of a mask by which the dead speak to allegory's 'confused investigator'.

Benjamin's insights, pairing allegory with melancholia and failure, not with achievement, become richer when politically inflected by the experiences of the oppressed and beaten in South Africa; as Spivak knows, allegory as parabasis is associated with what is radically excluded, i.e. with that which will never appear positively in postcolonial narratives, with their attempts at formulating a single inclusive narrative to counter colonial narratives. Attridge's method of reading literature as a 'singular event' is important, in its resistance to allegorical interpretations of Coetzee which are little more than standard hand-me-down postcolonial exegeses of the text; similarly, his insistence on literality contests a tendency in allegoresis to deny the literality of the text and hence its singularity. But allegory, because it does yield the sense of the text as 'other', is exactly what allows for the emergence of singularity. If we take a text Attridge mentions, Thomas Mann's *Doctor Faustus* (1947), and read it as an allegory of events in twentieth-century Germany, it is true that there are certain elements in it which read like a *roman à clef*, and which therefore suggest a determinate meaning, but the text cannot be reduced to that. Successive readings confirm that we cannot read it in one, but in plural ways, and that is also part of the singularity – the event – of reading.

The introduction suggested that reading involves choices. Allegorical reading can constrain choices of how to read, as it does in Attridge's sense of allegory, perhaps by omitting the literal sense of the text. But reading for allegory can also suggest new strategies of reading that present new possibilities for interpretation. The scene in Coetzee's novel in which the magistrate is called upon to interpret the cache of wooden slips is significant: his interrogators, the barbarians, are ready to transcribe his expected 'confession': that the slips are coded messages which have been sent to him by 'barbarian' conspirators. Yet the magistrate, though he is unable to divine any original or intended 'meaning' from the slips, is nonetheless able, precisely because he recognizes their susceptibility to numerous interpretations, and the point that it may no longer be possible to interpret them, to see them in a way which gives insight into the transience of the current empire and its attempt at monologic control. It (as a collectivity of barbarians) will disappear, and so will the body of meanings associated with it. Throughout, the magistrate reads and interprets; the quest to read the unreadable slips leads to insights about the nature of power, that it is to be seen as already ruined; this access to insight is not necessarily related to the actual meanings on the slips of wood, whose message is allegorical, being real but other than what might have been originally intended. Where fragments suggest the impossibility of reading a text for a single isolatable truth, we may call this allegory, for want of a better word, 'postmodern'.

POSTMODERN ALLEGORIES

The main difference between traditional allegory and 'postmodern' allegory is that whereas the first assumes a system of thought which may be extracted from the allegorical level of the work, the latter does not; there may be scraps of meaning, but no assumption can be made of an underlying coherent meaning. From this standpoint, current discussions of allegory relate closely to contemporary deconstruction and the work of Paul de Man. In an essay, 'The Allegorical Impulse: Toward a Theory of Postmodernism', the art critic Craig Owens, as if remembering sixteenth-century emblems, calls the image a rebus. This is exactly how Freud had described a dream: 'a picture-puzzle, a rebus' (Freud, 1976: 382), a pictorial image which when explained turns out to be a word. The rebus is, then, a form of writing, as is a dream, which is a form of allegory (White, 1999: 101–25). For Owens, 'allegory occurs whenever one text is doubled by another' (Owens, 1992: 53). In this argument, allegory's imagery – as in a dream – has been appropriated, taken out of its functional context where it had meaning, and to which another meaning is now attributed. The earlier image works as a palimpsest, which is supplemented by something else. Owens' idea that 'in allegory, the image is a hieroglyph; an allegory is a rebus – writing composed of concrete images' (Owens, 1992: 57), derives consciously from Walter Bejamin, and also perhaps from the sense that the hieroglyph gained in expressionism, as in the paintings of Ernst Ludwig Kirchner (1880–1938), one of the original members of the Berlin Brücke group (1906–13). In 1920, Kirchner called his calligraphy 'hieroglyphs', meaning that 'in the sense that they represent natural forms in simplified, two-dimensional forms and suggest their meaning to the onlooker. Feeling constantly forms new hieroglyphs, which emerge from what is at first sight a confused mass of lines, and become almost geometrical symbols' (Dube, 1972: 40). This is an art of omission and simplification and suggestion which may be compared with the 'hieroglyph' as this is used in discussions of film, where it may be defined as the appearance in the visual field of a cipher of unstable meaning, representing something unknown, a shape constantly re-articulating itself, and, puzzling like a rebus, complicating the sense that everything can be known within the film narrative (Conley, 1992).

Owen's argument virtually aligns allegory with postmodernism, in its interest in parody or pastiche, montage and collage. Another example is the 'double-coding' that Charles Jencks sees at work in postmodern architecture, where local and more non-local 'contemporary' references appear side by side, or where the architect's own tastes and professional skills are articulated with the tastes of their clients (Jencks, 1991: 12). Postmodernism in this account belongs to what Hal Foster called the 'anti-aesthetic'. The term refers to the critique of form and beauty as these are traditionally presented when it is argued that works of art have an organic, symbolic relationship with what they describe and embody. If art is now 'anti-aesthetic', it cannot think symbolically, or say that a concept can be expressed through a symbolic object. This makes postmodern art allegorical; the image is no longer thought of as describing, or representing, a pre-existent world. The fragment stands for anything, nor is there anything but fragments, whose being declares the absence in them of inherent meaning, since 'any person, any object, any relationship, can mean absolutely anything else' (Benjamin, 1977: 175).

Adorno has applied this concept to Mahler's modernist music. Music may be seen as writing which is allegoric in structure, partly because music cannot be seen as metaphor, but only metonymically, that is, as it exists in time. Yet it is impossible to grasp entirely a movement of a Mahler symphony, for instance, in the time it takes to play it. Adorno's study of Mahler (1860–1911) is heavily influenced by Benjamin; it sees Mahler as disintegrating forms into fragments. Listening to his symphonies means being jolted from lyrical art-music to brash march tunes, to the Austrian *Ländler*, to fairground music, to vocal music of extraordinary innocence; to hear both cowbells and a sledgehammer in Symphony no. 6 (1906), for instance. In this sense of music where there is no inherent fitness, the word 'catachresis' applies: Mahler's ironic mode shows that there is no inherent fit to music, no appropriate structure to which it must belong. Raymond Monelle, using a distinction from Umberto Eco between the open work and the closed work, finds a definition of the first to be that it presents a discourse on other works. 'This inclusiveness of the open work is a certain mark of its potency. Mahler's symphonies may form a discourse on the waltzes of Lanner [The Viennese Joseph Lanner (1801–1843) generated the waltz fever of the nineteenth century: the *Ländler* preceded the waltz] but it is hard to imagine the reverse' (Monelle, 2000: 207). Mahler seems to include in his music that which is not music: Adorno refers to the 'threatening, asphyxiating effect' produced by the scherzo, the second movement of Symphony no. 6, which moves from a *Ländler* to a deliberately 'old fashioned' (*alterväterlich* – so specified in the score) – minuet (an eighteenth-century form), heard in the trio section (Adorno, 1992: 103). Mahler moves from a more modern style, but one which is associated with the country, to an older one which is, however, associated with the urban mode. The music of the *Ländler* associates with the symphony's first movement, commenting on it: music becomes quotation, parody and catachresis. Monelle finds the dance code to be mixed from the start of the music with a march code; the result is that while the dance moves, the march seems static (Monelle, 1992: 318). For Adorno, the conjunction is like a nightmare, while the fragmentation is one way in which the piece seems allegorical.

Deconstructive architecture, playing on motifs of fragmentation, as with Frank Gehry's Guggenheim museum in Bilbao (1997), or Daniel Libeskind's Jewish museum in Berlin (2002), questions in its form the concept of the complete building which stands to hold, and to represent as a museum, a single idea with institutional status. The postmodern museum building rather implies that the museum can only ever be what Coetzee calls 'the ruins of a public building', its nationalistic, or conceptual, or symbolic value ruined inside a labyrinthine space which confuses any single identity. The museum as ruin is capped by the building's architecture, whose design affirms the 'anti-aesthetic', questioning the idea that a single museum can house a single, ordered, idea. Libeskind's design for the Jewish Museum is an image of what it contains (the ruins of a people who suffered genocide). Considered as allegorical, it points to something which is 'other' to the discourse within the city where it exists.

The difference of allegory from symbolism is based on the deconstructive sense that metaphor, constructed out of the ideological assumption that one thing can be compared to another, and out of the belief that there can be 'natural' resemblances, is always catachresis. Nietzsche's 'autobiography', *Ecce Homo*, describes the inspiration that stimulated his writing of *Thus Spake Zarathustra*:

a gale of a feeling of freedom, or absoluteness, of power, of divinity. – The involuntariness of image and metaphor is strangest of all; one no longer has any notion of what is an image or a metaphor: everything offers itself as the nearest, most obvious, simplest expression. It actually seems, to allude to something Zarathustra says, as if the things themselves approached and offered themselves as metaphors ('Here all things come caressingly to your discourse and flatter you; for they want to ride on your back. On every metaphor you ride to every truth ... Here the words and wordshrines of all being open up before you; here all being wishes to become word, all becoming wishes to learn from you how to speak').

(Nietzsche, 1967: 300–301)

Nietzsche quotes from his own *Thus Spake Zarathustra* Part III, 'The Return Home' (Nietzsche, 1976: 295), as though it was Zarathustra who was speaking. Zarathustra describes the loss of distinction that takes over in writing, which means that there is no point in reaching for figurative language to get inspiration, because all language is figurative. In one image things want to ride on Zarathustra's back (as if he were a horse), but in the next moment he is borne on the back of every metaphor, as if it was not clear which was Zarathustra and which was metaphor. And 'all things' are, in any case, language, because Zarathustra is himself a figure, a creation of language; Nietzsche is simply describing the loss of all ability to say exactly what is going on in language. This abolishes the idea of preset comparisons, and traditional metaphor and allegory together, alongside the Platonic account that 'ideas' precede 'language'. Similarly, Deleuze and Guattari draw attention to the refusal of metaphor in Kafka. They quote a diary entry of 1921: 'Metaphors are one of the things that makes me despair of literature' (Deleuze and Guattari, 1986: 22). Metaphor homogenizes, brings things back to a familiar ideological perspective, to what is already known, in contrast to 'metamorphosis', which changes everything. And so in Kafka's *Metamorphosis*, when Gregor Samsa wakes from unsettling dreams to find that he has been turned into a monstrous vermin, he has changed into a thing that can never be re-assimilated, made familiar (Kafka, 1996: 3).

Does Kafka write allegories in *Metamorphosis* or *The Trial*? It is not possible to decide this conclusively, but here are some possible answers:

1. Yes, if we think of writing as other-speaking, in a way which may defer the direct statement of meaning, in which case all writing is allegorical.
2. Yes if that recognizes that the text cannot amount to more than a fragment.
3. Yes, if it means that the writing is opposed to realism, where we know what the bounds of probability are.
4. Yes, if we mean that the text is suspicious of metaphor. Though some critics have wished to say so, becoming a monstrous vermin is not a metaphor for Gregor Samsa's dull life at the office, or the state of being Jewish in anti-Semitic Prague. If metaphor creates *resemblances*, this, if it is allegory, creates *difference* and something new, because instead of asserting similarity there is a taking away of meaning, which may be at the heart of what allegory is: a way of concealing meaning, removing familiar meanings. The old and familiar associations of what vermin are and what comparisons are fit for them disappear. In this respect there may be a difference between allegory and personification; allegory tends to make meaning disappear behind a veil, whereas personification brings meaning forward in a recognizable form.
5. No, if we think of traditional allegory, because that would mean that Kafka was writing a text that could or should be interpreted otherwise than as written. 'Monstrous vermin' does not allegorize anything. This statement is only to be interpreted literally. Benjamin discusses Kafka in relation to the 'Halakah' – the Law – and the 'Haggadah' – the mystical-poetic tropings and free elaboration that appears in writing in relation to the Jewish Law, the Torah. For Benjamin, Kakfa 'sacrificed truth for the sake of clinging to its transmissibility, its haggadic element' (Benjamin, 1970: 147). Joseph K in *The Trial* is told by the priest that he doesn't have to consider everything true, he just has to consider it necessary, to which Joseph K replies that this means that 'lies are made into a

universal system' (Kafka, 1998: 223). The priest does not quite accept this; he says that it is not a question of truth or falsity; language does not refer to a system either true or false. Kafka risks everything in his writings so that there may be the transmission of something that does not depend on something prior to it. *Metamorphosis* is a troping that does not rest on a prior text. In that sense, Kafka is in no sense a traditional allegorist.

Nietzsche and Kafka, Benjamin and de Man work with language and thinking as non-representational, not 'about' the real world which can be described through a language and which can be decoded through a metalanguage. Simile and metaphor both assume that literature is a form of representation, or mimesis; they imply that the literary text imitates life. We can summarize by saying that allegory is not a 'speaking other' which differs from some anterior given statement. Images become allegorical in this context by being always 'other', not underpinned by some reality with which we are familiar.

FOR AND AGAINST ALLEGORY

Earlier sections in this chapter have considered modern allegory, completing the historical survey which ended in chapter 4, but I conclude with thinking of allegory in more formal terms. What are the justifications for allegory; what problems does it address, or leave the reader with?

Saussure and Roman Jakobson view language as working in two ways: one on a horizontal axis, in a metonymic chain, associating letter with letter and word with word in an onward pattern of substitutions, while the other, vertical axis is that of metaphor, which combines and condenses terms which are alike (see glossary). Metaphor puts together words with similar meanings, while metonymy associates term with term in a sequential pattern, one term succeeding or substituting for another. For Jakobson, 'the poetic function projects the principle of equivalence from the axis of selection into the axis of combination', which means that in literary language the metaphoric use of language is inserted into the metonymic sequence, the axis of combination, and so interrupts it and changes it (Jakobson, 1960: 358). Joel Fineman's essay 'The Structure of Allegorical Desire', obviously indebted to de Man, uses Jakobson to argue that 'it is always the structure of metaphor that is projected onto the sequence of metonymy, not the other way round, which is why allegory is always a hier-archizing mode, indicative of timeless order, however subversively intended its content might be … in deferring to structure it insinuates the power of structure' (Fineman, 1981: 32–33). Alle-gorical personifications, condensing several features into one image, are sufficiently like the structure of metaphor to make it possible to create hierarchies, timeless personified entities which move within a narrative sequence, presenting abstractions in a way which gives them a sole, unquestioned dignity. Viewed from this perspective, allegory may be considered as inherently conservative (Greenfield, 1998: 18).

However, against this, allegory is also open-ended. The metonymic axis of language shows one term displacing another term and so on in an endless sequence. Fineman, quoting Fletcher, connects this with the assertion that allegory need never end (Fineman, 1998: 40; Fletcher, 1964: 174–80). Langland and Spenser, despite their historical grounding, exemplify allegorists who cannot come to a close. Fineman discusses a line from Chaucer's 'General Prologue' to *The Canterbury Tales*, which states that with the coming of April and its quickening effects, 'thanne longen folk to goon on pilgrimages' (line 12, Chaucer, 1990: 23). Fineman discusses this line as showing a desire for origins, as if the 'folk' who travel wish to discover an origin for their existence in the shrine of St Thomas at Canterbury, because the relics of St Thomas have helped them 'whan that they were sick' (line 17). But since the pilgrimage to Canterbury is a journey towards what has yet to be experienced, as well as a narrative device to enable stories to be told, the journey is also a desire to know, which finds its equivalence in allegory and in allegorical interpretation.

Longing for knowledge begins, for Fineman, with taking allegory as 'continued metaphor', a definition with which this book started. But placing the emphasis on allegory as, essentially, metaphor, Fineman argues that the allegorical desire begins not from a firm point of origin, but rather from a gap, an emptiness which is signalled by the point that we must start, not from the thing itself, but from metaphor. Desire, then, is motivated by absence, or lack, what Fineman calls 'a fracture at the source':

> Distanced at the beginning from its source, allegory will set out on an increasingly futile search for a signifier with which to recuperate the fracture of and at its source, and with each successive signifier the fracture and the search begins again: a structure of continual yearning, the insatiable desire of allegory.
>
> (Fineman, 1981: 45)

The desire to know, which produces allegory, also engenders allegorical interpretation (allegoresis). Fineman includes psychoanalysis under the heading of allegoresis, interpreting behaviour and the patient's language which it regards as allegory; psychoanalysis, like allegoresis and allegory, is fascinated by new knowledge, rather than simply explaining older knowledge in a new form. In chapter 1, allegoresis was seen to predate writing actual allegory: allegorical *writing* is prompted by the ability to perform or undertake allegorical *interpretation*. It is as though writing allegory embodies an urgent desire further to explore the origin, to uncover what psychoanalysis calls 'the primal scene'. But if allegorical writing and allegorical interpretation are part of the same process, the desire to know cannot be reduced to just one process, for it also includes the desire to conceal. Allegory, saying one thing while saying another, hides as much as it shows. Allegorical interpretation, while perhaps revealing a truth that allegory seems to seek, can never reach it; it can only generate further allegorical writing.

The metonymic axis of language engenders the repetition of things, as one signifier displaces and substitutes for another, while seeming similar to it. This makes repetition a feature of allegorical narratives. Freud's *Beyond the Pleasure Principle* (1920) associates repetition with the 'death drive', which is the impulse within the organism to move in a deliberate but unconscious manner, following 'its own path to death' (Freud, 1977: 311). He presents the paradigmatic form of this repetition in the boy throwing away and retrieving an object (the cotton reel) with the words *Fort*! and *Da*!

('gone' and 'here'), in a pattern of withdrawal and reappearance, deferral and return, hiding and revealing. This repeated motion, of delay and advance, has been compared to narrative progression (Freud, 1977: 283–86; Brooks, 1984: 90–112). If a pattern of repetition structures narrative movement, this relates to something familiar in allegorical narratives, their ability, as with Spenser, to repeat, from canto to canto, personifications who are only minutely different from each other. But this repetition has the quality of supplementing something that cannot stand alone with its own independent authority. In Herman Rapaport's reading of Satan, Sin and Death in *Paradise Lost* we observed a set of abstract allegorical personifications who exist in a pattern of repetition which they do not seem to fill out, to make complete. Allegory shows itself as comprising fragments, insufficient to reach the fullness of the symbol, or to state a single, originating proposition convincingly. Allegory demonstrates its substitutive nature, its inability to complete, but it also questions the adequacy of those forms of writing that it is imagined can achieve 'totality'. Allegory can never reach the 'totality' proposed in the symbol, and this is why Benjamin compares the allegorist with the collector, who must go on adding and adding without ever coming to completeness, like Coetzee's magistrate, who collects the slips, fragments of a bygone culture, in a spirit opposite to that of the historian collecting data. The collector 'takes up the struggle against dispersion':

> The allegorist is, as it were, the polar opposite of the collector. He has given up the attempt to elucidate things through research into their properties and relations. He dislodges things from their context and from the outset, relies on his profundity to illuminate their meaning. Nevertheless ... in every collector hides an allegorist, and in every allegorist a collector. As far as the collector is concerned, his collection is never complete; for let him discover just a single piece missing, and everything he's collected remains a patchwork, which is what things are for allegory from the beginning. On the other hand, the allegorist – for whom objects represent only keywords in a secret dictionary, which will make known their meanings to the initiated – precisely the allegorist can never have enough of things.
>
> (Benjamin, 1999: 211)

If the tropes of allegory cannot 'add up', then that is a source of the melancholia associated with the form, and it prompts study of the psychology of those who think allegorically. Perhaps, following Angus Fletcher, the psychological character is compulsive, because he suggests that the typical agent in an allegorical fiction is daemonic, like Ahab in *Moby-Dick*, working obsessively, dominated by anxiety or by paranoia (Fletcher, 1964: 279–303). Freud would agree: paranoia produces projection, one of the basic promptings towards personification. Hence, for Fletcher, the consideration of such obsessional behaviour involves proposing a link between allegories and journeying, or pilgrimage, or questing, as in Spenser. The obsessional damned souls of Dante's *Inferno* – for example Farinata (see chapter 1) – provide further examples. There is a sense of psychic possession at work in the writing of allegory, which prevents the obsessive who is the subject of the allegory, like a pilgrim, or Ahab on his voyage – not coincidentally, allegory often has hard journeys as its subject matter – from taking a short cut or avoiding difficulties. Allegory accepts and depicts irresistible drives: we can think of how these appear in Bronzino's *Allegory*, or in the confession made in 'A Poison Tree', and we can recall Chaucer's Pardoner, driven tragically in every respect, both in ways he knows and in ways he does not.

As a corollary to allegory as obsessional, Fletcher also refers to the *idée fixe* as a characteristic of allegory, and to compulsive behaviour and rituals which are typical in allegory. He says that allegory characteristically draws on magic names, or magical practices and that it is fascinated by system building, creating dream mythologies. Here, the medieval interest in cataloguing numbers, and explaining the meaning of lists of names or qualities painstakingly gathered, is relevant. Insofar as allegory is on the side of the daemonic, and even the supernatural, it is, for Fletcher, the opposite of a mimetic, Aristotelian art, which deals with empirical reality (Fletcher, 1964: 67).

In Fletcher's taxonomy of characteristics displayed by allegory, the last is 'ambivalence', a quality which fascinated Freud, prompting him to discover, for instance, 'the antithetical meaning of primal words' (Freud, 1957: 155–61). The important words mean what they say and the opposite. Ambivalence, loving and hating at the same time, is familiar in psychoanalysis, beginning from Freud's essay 'Instincts and their Vicissitudes' (1915). That allegory is a mode that displays ambivalence is apparent because the form 'always demonstrates a degree of inner conflict' (Fletcher, 1964: 301). This appears in divided subjects, shown as virtues paired with vices, and with personifications who are always associated with matching, antithetical forms, as in Giotto's figures in the Scrovegni chapel. The obsessional, repetitious and ambivalent behaviour which appears in allegory is matched, in Fletcher's reading, by the impulse which creates or writes the form: an authoritarianism that is compulsive and that is fascinated by structure.

Allegory seems both creative and imprisoning, creative of fixed states which mis-name the subject. If personifications are recognizable and fixed, then that conservatism lies behind Fletcher's concluding remark that 'allegories are the natural mirrors of ideology' (Fletcher, 1964: 368). What does allegory do to identities, including gender identity? Women are often the special subjects of allegory; examples for this which have been glanced at in this book include the Rose in *The Romance of the Rose*, Spenser's Acrasia and women in Courbet's artwork. It has been argued that this idealizing is a way of denying the actual qualities of women, and it invites the question, discussed in part in chapter 4, of whether women have found a role for allegory. Benjamin and de Man have linked allegory with 'anti-aesthetic' arguments, especially in their contrasting it with symbolism, but how does this argument, which also presses towards seeing all writing, including history and autobiography, as allegorical, work in relation to actual, formal allegories? There is a clear problem here. In one reading, allegory is 'speaking other', speaking in a way which fragments comparisons, and does not consolidate them. Here, it is the name of a writing which destabilizes. But it may also reinforce accepted ways of seeing, which is why many readers distrust it.

The 'new historicist' critic, and Freudian, Howard Bloch, reading medieval texts, has discussed the fascination with castration in medieval *fabliaux* (tales which show urban life, as opposed to romance, and which work in non-ideal terms). In the case of Chaucer's Pardoner, there seems to be a relationship between his incessant storytelling, which includes his confession, and the point that he bears with him old relics which he says are genuine bones of saints, but which are obviously fake. The point that he is a eunuch, his body incomplete, gives him, perhaps, the impulse to try all the time to supplement his being with fragments that can never reach a whole, never give him completeness; that may well have to do with the point that he does not belong with the 'heteronormativity' of the other pilgrims. It certainly suggests the fascination of his obsession. The insight may be paired with Fineman on allegorical desire and Fletcher on compulsive behaviour, and suggest further motivations to allegorize, and reasons why readers should respond to its drive.

ALLEGORY VERSUS PERSONIFICATION

A conclusion, however provisional, to a consideration of the value of allegory should also distinguish terms. A history has been traced within this study, of texts being interpreted allegorically, because of a determination to read below the surface of the text, and of allegory being defined as a rhetorical device within language which exploits the gaps between words and meanings. In the twelfth century, writers began crafting allegories, texts with plural meanings. Characteristically, the device deployed was personification, giving life to abstract ideas by endowing them with a mask. Whereas allegoresis draws attention to hidden or abstract meanings, and allegory stresses that the surface meaning is not the ultimate quarry of interpretation, personification emphasizes the face which appears, which is, by definition, the surface meaning. In this way, allegory and personification work, characteristically, in opposite modes.

Personification has been sufficiently important in dictating attitudes to allegory and to ways of reading for it to require another, final comment. Chapter 2 discussed Bronzino's picture, using the interpretations of Erwin Panofsky (1892–1968), the art historian associated with the Warburg Institute when it opened in Hamburg in 1926, founded by Aby Warburg (1866–1929). Panofsky, like Fritz Saxl (1890–1948) and E. H. Gombrich (1909–2001) was associated with studying 'iconology' in Renaissance art. Warburg was fascinated by personification; his writing began with a doctoral study of Botticelli in relation to pagan classical sources. He was interested in images as expressive of an innate human need to objectify that which could not be derived from 'real' life. Images personifying human feelings were not representations of something in the real world, but emerged from a compulsion to objectify and represent feelings as independent beings. As a result, the concept of empathy (*Einfühlung*), 'feeling one's way into something', emerged, as conceptualized in the nineteenth century by Robert Vischer (1847–1933), and as used by the Viennese art critic Aloïs Riegl (1858–1905), a significant influence on Benjamin in his writings on the baroque. Reigl took baroque art to show, like Mannerism, a conflict between subjective feeling and objective form, the former resisting, not being contained by, the latter. The evidence for this was apparent, through empathy, by looking at the sculpture, or architecture, or painting itself.

Empathy implies projecting a corporeal state similar to the viewer's own onto the object to be interpreted in the painting; thus making it reflect states of mind in the viewer. Its danger is that it regards visual images as the expression of how the subject engages with the world. In this it is similar to fetishism, which invests dead objects with imaginary life. Indeed, Gombrich uses the word 'fetishism' when discussing the symbolic image. He says that a motif in a picture by Bosch may *represent* a broken vessel, *symbolize* the sin of gluttony, and at the same time *express* an unconscious sexual fantasy of the artist. Nonetheless, distinctions between representation, symbolisation and expression cannot be upheld. 'We know that in magical practice the image not only represents an enemy but may take his place (the very word "represent" still has that dual meaning). We know that the word "fetish" not only "symbolises" fertility but "has" it' (Gombrich, 1972: 124–25). The object symbolized in the work of art, Gombrich argues, is capable of having an absolute reality as well as being 'only' a sign. But if so, there is also the possibility of 'reading in', constructing the symbol's significance as real. Reading for symbolism, working from empathy, is open to the objection that it does not respect the otherness of the other, but sees the self in the other. To identify an object in a work of art and to say what it expresses becomes a way of personifying a desire *within the viewer, or reader*. This returns us to the obsessional desire discussed by Fletcher.

We must, then, distinguish between allegory as a concept and personification allegory. Allegory comprises a discourse which thinks in terms of the 'other', which, is, of course, part of the etymology of 'allegory'. The 'other', as different from me, is what I cannot claim to be able to control, describe adequately, or know, or 'empathize' with. Personification works by making identifications, and claims implicitly, by its existence, that it can conceptualize, or visualize, or realize, the 'other' in a particular form: as Revenge, or as Sleep. It creates an image, and makes it a fetish, expressing something in the self. This, because it is created by the person who makes the visualization, is not 'other', but a way of rendering 'otherness', or difference, in terms which make it the image of, and expression of, the views of the person who has the power to create it. Hence, recalling the discussion of the New Testament in the Introduction, and St Paul's reading of the Jews in contrast to the Christians, it may be said that this, even if it is not a pure case of personification, is, amongst much else, a way of negating the 'otherness' of those outside Christianity. More, it makes them 'other' in such a way that they seem to be outsiders, beyond consideration. Personification becomes an imposition of the subject onto the other, a way of projecting feelings onto the outside and making them seem to be universal representations of reality.

The mask in its fixity may be like Hobbes' 'person', speaking the words of another, like an actor, or it may be that which withholds itself from declaring the 'truth' behind it. To be held by the power of allegory is to be caught by the question: is the reader, or viewer, captivated and controlled by what is merely a play of masks, or is there is something else, other, speaking differently from the hegemonic text, and if so, how can that can be heard? The mask speaks through prosopopoeia: but is the speech that of the other? Or is it how the mask has been made to speak? In that teasing question lies one of the abiding fascinations of allegory.

Glossary

Allegoresis Commentary, either on a text regarded as an allegory (e.g. Homer's epics), decoding what has been encoded, or drawing out language as inherently allegorical: 'the "other" named by the term *allos* in the word "allegory" is not some other hovering above the words of the text, but the possibility of an other, a polysemy, inherent in the very words on the page' (Quilligan, 1979: 26). Thus 'allegoresis, elder cousin to narrative allegory, begins by saying that texts are, superficially, lies; they must be interpreted, or "allegorised" into telling the truth' (Quilligan, 1979: 46).

Apostrophe Greek: 'a turning away' – in speech, or writing, a sudden breaking off from a previous discourse and addressing some person or thing, absent or present.

Catachresis '[T]he inexact use of a like and kindred word in place of the precise and proper one', occurring when 'words of kindred, but not identical meaning have been transferred on the principle of inexact use' (Cicero, 1954: 342–43).

Conceit A concept, or an image, applied to a figure of speech which finds an unusual parallel between two dissimilar things; an intricate metaphor, or witty (quick-witted) comparison. Sometimes, in Renaissance and seventeenth-century poetry, it is associated with the comparisons that emblem books allowed, as also with the idea in rhetoric of the use of verbal ingenuity in speech.

Deconstruction A name given to the critical practice of Jacques Derrida, and, in America, of Paul de Man, which shows how meanings in texts are produced ideologically and which considers the Western philosophical and literary tradition as that which gives authority to the subject, to 'presence' and to utterance as complete and self-knowing (logocentric). For a summary, see Spivak (1999: 423–31).

Figura ('shape') For Quintilian, a figure (a way of speaking, a trope) is 'a shape of speaking altered by some art' of rhetoric (*arte aliqua nouata forma dicendi* – *Institutio Oratio* IX.1.14). For Paul de Man, 'the figurative structure … characterizes language as such' (de Man, 1979: 105). 'Figura' is used by Erich Auerbach to show how one person or event foreshadows another: figural interpretation differs from allegorical interpretation through the historicity of the *figura* representing something later on – in *figura*, both the sign and what it figures are historical.

Iconography (Greek: 'eikon', 'likeness') Iconography studies the subject matter, not the form, of the work of art, and proceeds particularly by looking at its images, which it identifies, describes and classifies; Erwin Panofsky develops the term as **iconology**, which puts the study of such subject matter into a historical context, and interprets it as symbolic of the age.

Image (Latin: 'imago', 'copy' or 'likeness') Here, a comparison, metaphor or trope. An 'image', which shares a root with the word 'imitate', meant, till the eighteenth century, 'artificial image or representation' and 'imagine' and 'imagination' were derived from it. The Greek 'phantasia' – a making visible – produced the English 'fantasy', 'fancy', 'fantastic'. The faculty of making mental pictures was assigned in Aristotle's thought to the sensitive, not the rational, soul, so it was seen as a comparatively lowly ability. (The Latin 'phantasia' meant 'vision'.) Phantasy was identified with imagination; the shorter form, 'fancy', appeared in the fifteenth century. Coleridge distinguishes fancy and imagination in *Biographia Literaria* chapter 13 and Furbank (1970: 30) argues that with Coleridge 'image' came to mean 'metaphor' or 'simile'.

Irony (Greek: 'dissimulation') An ironist says less than he thinks or means (in a spirit of modesty, Aristotle thought). If allegory says one thing and means another, it is a form of irony. In Roman writers and later, it became part of rhetoric: descriptive of a way of speaking. Renaissance theorists distinguished irony and allegory on the basis that irony, unlike allegory, does not depend on metaphor, and there is another difference: that to miss irony implies a serious misunderstanding, but it is never regarded as essential to see allegory in a piece of literature (indeed, it is often argued that a work fails if it can only be seen, or has to be seen, allegorically). An allegory/irony distinction does not hold with Paul de Man, and is open to the criticism that it only works on the assumption of a determinate meaning to the ironic message, which its speaker knows and the reader does not.

Metalanguage ('beyond language') Language about language, as linguistics may be metalanguage, or as allegory may be. Jakobson discusses the metalinguistic function in language (Jakobson, 1960: 356).

Metaphor (Greek: 'carrying over', 'changing place') The Latin version is *tra (n)slatio*, both 'transform' and 'translate'. The term as used in this book has two senses. It is the trope of resemblance, which describes one thing as though it were another, and is so discussed in Aristotle's *Poetics* chapter 21. I. A. Richards used the terms 'tenor' and 'vehicle' to illuminate the idea that metaphor gives two ideas at once. The tenor is the idea expressed or the subject of the comparison; the vehicle is the image by which this is conveyed. For Richards, if the tenor and vehicle cannot be distinguished, we are dealing with a literal statement; if we can distinguish them, we are dealing with metaphor. The example he uses is Hamlet's question: 'What should such fellows as I do crawling between earth and heaven?', where he argues 'crawling' is metaphoric (Richards, 1936: 95–100, 119–20). The second sense comes from Roman Jakobson's division of language on two axes, horizontal (metonymy) and vertical (metaphor) and considers the metaphorical axis comprising terms linked by 'semantic similarity' (as opposed to metonymy, where terms are linked by positional or syntactic contiguity). In language use, a selective, associative process takes place whereby one term or another similar is selected from this axis, on the basis of likeness. Instead of one term being selected, another is taken from the same paradigm, and this is the basis of metaphorical language, and of allegory, which is seen as extended – developed – metaphor (Jakobson and Halle, 1956: 77).

Metonymy (Greek: 'change of name') In poetic or literary use, when part of an object is used to describe a whole object (though this is more synecdoche, as when 'wheels' substitute for the word 'car') or when something closely associated with an object describes it: 'crown' for 'king' or 'city' when the inhabitants of the city are meant. Like metaphor, it also has a use deriving from Roman Jakobson for the sense of language moving as if on a horizontal axis, between contiguous, sequential terms, where each term will be replaced by its adjacent term. In ordinary language uses, a combinative, syntagmatic process shows itself as each word or term is placed next to another, moving along a horizontal axis. Metonymy gives the sense of terms in language endlessly replacing and displacing each other, and in that sense relates to allegory. For Lacan, the structure of metonymy and metaphor makes all language-speaking simultaneously displacement and condensation: both terms being taken from Freud (Jakobson and Halle, 1956: 81) and linked with metonymy and metaphor.

Pastoral 'A literary work portraying rural life or the life of shepherds, esp. in an idealized or romantic form' (*OED*): term first used in the sixteenth century, and deriving from Theocritus (Greece) and Virgil, and used by Spenser and Milton, amongst others; it also applies to a rural picture.

Personification A specific form of allegory in which an abstract idea is represented by the creation of a fictional figure. **Prosopopoeia** is equivalent: giving a mask to an unseen or absent or abstract or dead quality, so that it appears to have an autonomous identity.

Rhetoric The art of expressive or persuasive speech, first associated with the Greek sophists, such as Protagoras (c.485–411 BCE), Gorgias (485–380 BCE) and Isocrates. They were challenged by Socrates (469–399 BCE) and Plato (427–347 BCE) but Aristotle (384–322 BCE) discussed it (*Rhetoric*) and the study passed over to the Romans, especially Cicero (106–43 BCE), who was credited, wrongly, with the *Rhetoric ad Herennium* (c.90 BCE), influential throughout the medieval period. It pronounced on inventions to make a speech plausible, on organization of the speech, style, on modes of memorizing the speech and of delivery. Quintilian's use of rhetoric follows Cicero. The Renaissance taught classical rhetoric, as with Thomas Wilson in *Arte of Rhetorique* (1553). For an overview of rhetoric in the Middle Ages, see Minnis, Scott and Wallace, 1988. A reaction against rhetoric (including allegory) set in during the seventeenth century, in a preference for plain speech.

Signifier, signified, sign The distinction between 'the signifier' (the material word) and 'the signified' (i.e. its meaning) was made by Ferdinand de Saussure, and it is the basis of structural linguistics and of the semiotic, the study of signs (C. S. Peirce's term), semiology for Saussure. Here, meaning is established by the differences between signifiers as these are put together in a metonymic sequence: there is no necessary link between the individual signifier and the signified. The signifier and signified together make up the sign, which word was for Origen identical to the word 'symbol'. In the medieval period, all signs and symbols related to the universe as a structure of meaning, with hidden correspondences. C. S. Pierce (1839–1914) distinguishes between the conventional sign (the symbol, where the image is not related to the object in any essential way, e.g. a road sign has no relationship to the road), the indexical (where the image and the object are separate but related, as the symptom of a disease is an indexical sign) and the iconic, where there is something shared between the image and the object, or where the image replicates the object, as smoke is a sign of fire, and part of it (Peirce, 1977: 33).

Simile A comparison, where two things are likened to each other for ease of explanation or for poetic effect. Whereas metaphor involves putting two impressions together simultaneously, simile does not; it describes impressions in succession to each other. Homer uses similes, not metaphors.

Symbol From the Greek 'symballein', 'to throw together, to bring together, to collect, to compare'. Fletcher (1964: 13), whose *Allegory* is subtitled *The Theory of a Symbolic Mode*, does not distinguish between allegory and symbolism, but symbolism does not imply so much a metaphysical view of the world, where there is a separation between the natural and the spiritual; rather, one aspect of the natural world is being compared with another. Yet making one thing symbolize another assumes a unity within everything: symbolism's appeal to the Romantics. Coleridge saw the symbol as a manifestation of the immaterial in the material, and the formless in form, 'a Symbol being an essential Part of that, the whole of which it represents' (Coleridge, 2000: V, 698).

Synecdoche (Greek: 'a receiving together') A figure of speech whereby a part is put for a whole: standard examples are 'sail' for 'ship', 'hand' for 'man'.

Totality Hegelian and Marxist term, in the twentieth century associated with Georg Lukács (1885–1971), giving the sense that knowledge can be had in its fullness, and that this will be inclusive in character, including within it everything of 'otherness'.

Trope (Greek: 'tropos', 'a turn') A figure of speech, turning a word or phrase from the sense that is proper to it: familiar in handbooks of rhetoric in the sixteenth century. Use of metonymy, for instance, is a trope: when a metonymy substitutes for another metonymy, so that the 'proper' meaning has been displaced more than once, that double metonymy is **metalepsis**. Another figure relevant here is

syllepsis, or **zeugma**, where a single word in a sentence is used twice, in a proper and figurative sense, serving two purposes, as in the description of Alcmaeon in *Metamorphoses* 9.409 as 'an exile from his wits and from his home' (Hardie, 2002: 230). Fusing two ideas into one is a basic form of allegorizing.

Bibliography and further reading

Adorno, Theodor, 1992. *Mahler, A Musical Physiognomy*. Trans. Edmund Jephcott. Chicago: University of Chicago Press.

Ahmad, Aijaz, 1992. *In Theory: Classes, Nations, Literatures*. London: Verso.

Allen, Don Cameron, 1970. *Mysteriously Meant: The Rediscovery of Pagan Symbolism and Allegorical Interpretation in the Renaissance*. Baltimore: Johns Hopkins University Press.

Allison, David (ed.), 1983. *The New Nietzsche*. Cambridge, MA: MIT Press.

Aristotle, 1965. *Aristotle, Horace, Longinus: Classical Literary Criticism*. Trans. T. S. Dorsch. Harmondsworth: Penguin.

Attridge, Derek, 2004. *J. M. Coetzee and the Ethics of Reading: Literature in the Event*. Chicago: University of Chicago Press.

Auerbach, Erich, 1959. 'Figura' in *Scenes from the Drama of European Literature: Six Essays*. New York: Meridian Books.

——, 1957. *Mimesis*. Princeton: Princeton University Press.

Bahti, Timothy, 1992. *Allegories of History: Literary Historiography after Hegel*. Baltimore: Johns Hopkins University Press.

Baudelaire, Charles, 1982. *Les Fleurs du Mal*. Trans. Richard Howard. London: Picador.

Benjamin, Walter, 1970. *Illuminations*. Trans. Harry Zohn. London: Jonathan Cape.

——, 1973. *Charles Baudelaire: A Lyric Poet in the Era of High Capitalism*. Trans. Harry Zohn. London: New Left Books.

——, 1977. *The Origin of German Tragic Drama*. Trans. John Osborne. London: New Left Books.

——, 1996. *Selected Writings, vol. 1: 1913–1926*. Ed. Marcus Bullock and Michael W. Jennings. Cambridge, MA: Harvard University Press.

——, 1999. *The Arcades Project*. Trans. Howard Eiland and Kevin McLaughlin. Cambridge MA: Harvard University Press.

——, 2003. *Selected Writings, vol. 4: 1938–1940*. Trans. Edmund Jephcott and others. Ed. Howard Eiland and Michael W. Jennings. Cambridge MA: Harvard University Press.

Blake, William, 1966. *Complete Writings*. Ed. Geoffrey Keynes. Oxford: Oxford University Press.

Bloch, R. Howard, 1986. *The Scandal of the Fabliaux*. Chicago: University of Chicago Press.

Blood, Susan, 1997. *Baudelaire and the Aesthetics of Bad Faith*. Stanford: Stanford University Press.

Bloomfield, Morton W., 1952. *The Seven Deadly Sins*. Michigan: State University Press.

Borges, Jorge Luis, 2001. 'From Allegories to Novels' (1949) in *Jorge Luis Borges: Non-Fiction 1922–1986*. Ed. Eliot Weinberger. Harmondsworth: Penguin.

Borris, Kenneth, 2000. *Allegory and Epic in English Renaissance Literature: Heroic Form in Sidney, Spenser, and Milton*. Cambridge: Cambridge University Press.

Brittan, Simon, 2003. *Poetry, Symbol, and Allegory: Interpreting Metaphorical Language from Plato to the Present*. Charlotteville: University of Virginia Press.

Brontë, Charlotte, 1996. *Jane Eyre*. Ed. Michael Mason. Harmondsworth: Penguin.

Brooks, Peter, 1984. *Reading for the Plot: Design and Intention in Narrative*. Oxford: Clarendon Press.

Brown, Jane K., 2007. *The Persistence of Allegory: Drama and Neo-Classicism from Shakespeare to Wagner*. Philadelpha: University of Pennsylvania Press.

Buck-Morss, Susan, 1989. *The Dialectics of Seeing; Walter Benjamin and the Arcades Project*. Cambridge, MA: MIT Press.

Bunyan, John, 1965. *The Pilgrim's Progress*. Ed. Roger Sharrock. Harmondsworth: Penguin.

——, 1966. *Grace Abounding to the Chief of Sinners*. Ed. G. B. Harrison. London: Everyman.

Burlinson, Christopher, 2006. *Allegory, Space and the Material World in the Writings of Edmund Spenser*. Woodbridge: D. S. Brewer.

Burrow, John, 1971. *Ricardian Poetry: Chaucer, Gower, Langland, and the Gawain Poet*. London: Routledge & Kegan Paul.

Camille, Michael, 1986. 'Walter Benjamin and Dürer's's Melencolia I: The Dialectics of Allegory and the Limits of Iconology' in *Ideas and Production* 58–79.

Carlyle, Thomas, 1959. *Sartor Resartus and On Heroes and Hero Worship*. Ed. W. H. Hudson. London: Everyman's Library.

Chambers, Ross, 1993. *The Writing of Melancholy: Modes of Opposition in Early French Modernism*. Trans. Mary Seidman Trouille. Chicago: University of Chicago Press.

Chaucer, Geoffrey, 1990. *The Riverside Chaucer*. Ed. Larry D. Benson. Boston MA: Houghton Mifflin.

Cicero, 1954. *De ratione dicendi*. Trans. H. Caplan. London: Heinemann.

Clark, T. J., 1973. *The Absolute Bourgeois: Artists and Politics in France, 1848–1851*. London: Thames and Hudson.

Coetzee, J. M., 1980. *Waiting for the Barbarians*. Harmondsworth: Penguin

Colebrook, Claire, 2004. *Irony*. London: Routledge.

Coleridge, S. T., 1965. *Biographia Literaria*. Ed. George Watson. London: Everyman.

—— 1969. *Poetical Works*. Ed. Ernest Hartley Coleridge. Oxford: Oxford University Press.

——, 1972. *Lay Sermons*. Ed. R. J. White. Princeton: Princeton University Press.

——, 2000. *Marginalia*. Ed. H. J. Jackson and George Whalley. Princeton: Princeton University Press.

Collinson, Philip, 1981. *Classical Theories of Allegory and Christian Culture*. Pittsburgh: Duquesne University Press.

Conley, Tom, 1992. *Film Hieroglyphs: Ruptures in Classical Cinema*. Minnesota: University of Minnesota Press.

Cuddy, Lois A., 1990. 'The Latin Imprint on Emily Dickinson's Poetry: Theory and Practice' in *On Dickinson: The Best from American Literature*. Eds Edwin H. Cady and Louis J. Budd. Durham, NC: Duke University Press.

Culler, Jonathan, 1981. *The Pursuit of Signs*. London: Routledge.

Curtius, E. R., 1953. *European Literature and the Latin Middle Ages*. Trans. Willard R. Trask. London: Routledge & Kegan Paul.

Dahlberg, Charles, 1988. *The Literature of Unlikeness*. Hanover: University Press of New England.

Damon, S. Foster, 1965. *A Blake Dictionary: The Ideas and Symbols of William Blake*. Providence: Brown University Press.

Dante, 1989. *The Banquet*. Trans. Christopher Ryan. Saratoga CA: Anma Libri.

Deleuze, Gilles, 1986. *Cinema I: The Movement Image*. Trans. Hugh Tomlinson and Barbara Habberjam. Minneapolis: Unversity of Minnesota Press.

——, 1989. *Cinema II: The Time Image*. Trans. Hugh Tomlinson and Barbara Habberjam. Minneapolis: Unversity of Minnesota Press.

Deleuze, Gilles and Guattari, Félix, 1986. *Kafka: Toward a Minor Literature*. Trans. Dana Polan. Minneapolis: University of Minnesota Press.

——, 1988. *A Thousand Plateaux: Capitalism and Schizophrenia*. Trans. Brian Massumi. Minneapolis: University of Minnesota Press.

De Lubac, Henri, 1959. *Exégèse mediévale: 4 Vols*. Paris: Montaigne.

De Lorris, Guillaume and de Meun, Jean, 1983. *The Romance of the Rose*. Trans. Charles Dahlberg. Hanover, NH: University Press of New England.

De Man, Paul, 1979. *Allegories of Reading: Figural Language in Rousseau, Nietzsche, Rilke, and Proust*. New Haven CT: Yale University Press.

——, 1983. *Blindness and Insight: Essays in the Rhetoric of Contemporary Criticism*. Minneapolis: University of Minnesota Press.

——, 1984. *The Rhetoric of Romanticism*. New York: Columbia University Press.

——, 1986. *The Resistance to Theory*. Minneapolis: University of Minnesota Press.

——, 1996. *Aesthetic Ideology*. Ed. Andrzej Warminski. Mineapolis: University of Minnesota Press.

Derrida, Jacques, 1979. *Spurs: Nietzsche's Styles*. Trans. Barbara Harlow. Chicago: University of Chicago Press.

Dickens, Charles, 1965. *Great Expectations*. Ed. Angus Calder. Harmondsworth: Penguin.

——, 1969. *Hard Times*. Ed. David Craig. Harmondsworth: Penguin.

——, 1971. *Bleak House*. Harmondsworth: Penguin.

——, 2004. *David Copperfield*. Ed. Jeremy Tambling. Harmondsworth: Penguin.

Dickinson, Emily, 1970. *The Complete Poems*. Ed. Thomas H. Johnson. London: Faber & Faber.

Dinshaw, Carolyn, 1989. *Chaucer's Sexual Poetics*. Madison: University of Wisconsin Press.

Dodds, E. R., 1951. *The Greeks and the Irrational*. Berkeley: University of California Press.

Donne, John, 1933. *The Poems of John Donne*. Ed. Sir Herbert Grierson. Oxford: Oxford University Press.

Dronke, Peter, 1974. *Fabula: Explorations into the Uses of Myth in Medieval Platonism*. Leiden: E. J. Brill.

Dube, Wolf-Dieter, 1972. *The Expressionists*. London: Thames and Hudson.

Dyke, Carolynn Van, 1985. *The Fiction of Truth: Structures of Meaning in Narrative and Dramatic Allegory*. Ithaca: Cornell University Press.

Eisenstein, Sergei, 1949. *Film Form: Essays in Film Theory*. Ed. Jay Leyda. New York: Harcourt and Brace.

Eliot, T. S., 1969. *The Complete Poems and Plays of T.S. Eliot*. London: Faber & Faber.

Emerson, Ralph Waldo, 1981. *The Portable Emerson*. Eds Carl Bode and Malcolm Cowley. New York: Penguin Books.

Empson, William, 1966. *Seven Types of Ambiguity*. Harmondsworth: Penguin.

Faunce, Sarah and Nochlin, Linda, 1988. *Courbet Reconsidered*. New York: The Brooklyn Museum.

Feeney, D.C., 1991. *The Gods in Epic: Poets and Critics of the Classical Tradition*. Oxford: Clarendon Press.

Ferretti, Silvia, 1989. *Cassirer, Panofsky, and Warburg: Symbol, Art, and History*. Trans. Richard Pierce. New Haven: Yale University Press.

Fielding, Henry. 1999. *Joseph Andrews* and *Shamela* (1742, 1741). Ed. Judith Hawley. Harmondsworth: Penguin.

Fineman, Joel, 1981. 'The Structure of Allegorical Desire' in *Allegory and Representation*. Ed. Stephen Greenblatt. Baltimore: Johns Hopkins University Press.

Fleming, John V., 1969. *The 'Roman de la Rose': A Study in Allegory and Iconography*. Princeton: Princeton University Press.

Fletcher, Angus, 1964. *Allegory: The Theory of a Symbolic Mode*. Ithaca NY: Cornell University Press.

——, 1971. *The Prophetic Moment: An Essay on Spenser*. Chicago: University of Chicago Press.

Foster, Hal, 1983. *The Anti-Aesthetic*. Port Townsend, WA: Bay Press.

Foucault, Michel, 1970. *The Order of Things: An Archaeology of the Human Sciences*. London: Tavistock Publications.

Freccero, John,1986. *Dante: The Poetics of Conversion*. Ed. Rachel Jacoff. Cambridge, MA: Harvard University Press.

Freud, Sigmund, 1957. *Standard Edition of Sigmund Freud vol. 11*. London: Hogarth Press.

——, 1975, *The Psychopathology of Everyday Life: The Penguin Freud vol. 5*. Harmondsworth: Penguin.

——, 1976. *The Interpretation of Dreams: The Penguin Freud vol. 4*. Harmondsworth: Penguin.

——, 1977. *On Metapsychology: The Penguin Freud. vol. 11*. Harmondsworth: Penguin.

——, 1977a. *On Sexuality: The Penguin Freud vol. 7*. Harmondsworth: Penguin.

Fried, Michael, 1990. *Courbet's Realism*. Chicago: University of Chicago Press.

Frye, Northrop, 1957. *Anatomy of Criticism*. Princeton: Princeton University Press.

Furbank, P. N., 1970. *Reflections on the Word 'Image'*. London: Secker and Warburg.

Gadamer, Hans-Georg, 1997. *Truth and Method*. Trans. Joel Weinsheimer and Donald G. Marshall. New York: Continuum.

Gareau, Michel, 1992. *Charles Le Brun: First Painter to King Louis XIV*. New York: Henry N. Abrams.

Gardner, Martin, 1970. *The Annotated Alice*. Harmondsworth: Penguin.

Gissing, George, 1992. *The Nether World*. Oxford: Oxford University Press.

Greenblatt, Stephen, 1980. *Renaissance Self-fashioning: From More to Shakespeare.* Chicago: University of Chicago Press.

Greenfield, Sayre N., 1998. *The Ends of Allegory.* Newark: University of Delaware Press.

Gombrich, E. H., 1972. *Symbolic Images: Studies in the Art of the Renaissance*, Oxford: Phaidon.

Gordon, D.J., 1975. *The Renaissance Imagination: Essays and Lectures by D.J. Gordon.* Ed. Stephen Orgel. Berkeley: University of California Press.

Harbison, Robert, 2000. *Reflections on Baroque.* London: Reaktion.

Hardie, Philip, 2002. *Ovid's Poetics of Illusion.* Cambridge: Cambridge University Press.

Harvey, John, 1970. *Victorian Novelists and their Illustrators.* London: Sidgwick and Jackson.

Hawthorne, Nathaniel, 1970. *The Scarlet Letter and Other Tales.* Harmondsworth: Penguin.

——, 1987. *Young Goodman Brown and Other Tales.* Ed. Brian Harding. Oxford: Oxford University Press.

——, 1997. *The Scarlet Letter.* Cambridge: Cambridge University Press.

Hepburn, Frederick, 1986. *Portraits of the Later Plantagenets.* Woodbridge: D. S. Brewer.

Herbert, George, 1961. *The Poems of George Herbert.* Ed. Helen Gardner. Oxford: Oxford University Press.

Herding, Klaus, 1991. *Courbet: To Venture Independence.* Trans. John William Gabriel. New Haven CT: Yale University Press.

Hobbes, Thomas, 1968. *Leviathan.* Ed. C. B. MacPherson. Harmondsworth: Penguin.

Hogarth, William, 1955. *The Analysis of Beauty.* Ed. Joseph Burke. Oxford: Clarendon Press.

Holland, Eugene, 1993. *Baudelaire and Schizoanalysis.* Cambridge: Cambridge University Press.

Hollander, Robert, 2001. *Dante: A Life in Works.* New Haven CT: Yale University Press.

Holly, Michael Ann, 1984. *Panofsky and the Foundations of Art History.* Ithaca: Cornell University Press.

Hope, Charles, 1982. 'Bronzino's Allegory in the National Gallery' in *Journal of the Warburg and Courtauld Institutes* 45, 239–43.

Honig, Edwin, 1959. *Dark Conceit: The Making of Allegory.* New York: Oxford University Press.

Hourihane, Colum, ed., 2000. *Virtue and Vice: The Personifications in the Index of Christian Art.* Princeton: Princeton University Press.

Irwin, John T., 1980. *American Hieroglyphics: The Symbol of the Egyptian Hieroglyphics in the American Renaissance.* Baltimore: Johns Hopkins University Press.

Jakobson, Roman and Halle, Morris, 1956. *Fundamentals of Language.* The Hague: Mouton.

Jakobson, Roman, 1960. 'Closing Statement: Linguistics and Poetics'. *Style in Language.* Ed. Thomas A. Sebeok. Cambridge, MA: MIT Press.

James, Henry, 1967. *Hawthorne*. Ed. Tony Tanner. London: Macmillan.

——, 1995. *The Portrait of a Lady: An Authoritative Text*. Ed. Robert D. Bamberg. New York: W. W. Norton.

Jameson, Fredric, 1981. *The Political Unconscious: Narrative as a Socially Symbolic Act*. London: Methuen & Co.

——, 1986. 'Third World Literature in the Era of Multinational Capitalism' in *Social Text* 15. 65–88.

JanMohammed, Abdul, 1986. 'The Economy of Manichean Allegory: The Function of Racial Difference in Colonialist Literature' in Henry Louis Gates, JR (ed.), *Race, Writing, and Difference*. Chicago: University of Chicago Press, 78–106.

Jauss, Hans Robert, 1982. *Towards and Aesthetic of Redemption*. Trans. Timothy Bahti. Minneapolis: University of Minnesota Press.

Jencks, Charles, 1991. *The Language of Post-Modern Architecture*. New York: Rizzoli.

Johnson, Barbara, 1987. *A World of Difference*. Baltimore: Johns Hopkins University Press.

Jones, J. W., Jr., 1961. 'Allegorical Interpretation in Servius'. *Classical Journal* 56, 217–26.

Kafka, Franz, 1996. *The Metamorphosis*. Trans. Stanley Corngold. New York: W. W. Norton.

——, 1998. *The Trial*. Trans. Breon Mitchell. New York: Schocken Books.

Keats, John, 1954. *Selected Letters*. Ed. Frederick Page. Oxford: Oxford University Press.

——, 1970. *The Complete Poems*. Ed. Miriam Allott. London: Longman Press.

Kelley, Theresa, 1997. *Reinventing Allegory*. Cambridge: Cambridge University Press.

Kiefer, Frederick, 2003. *Shakespeare's Visual Theatre: Staging the Personified Characters*. Cambridge: Cambridge University Press.

Knapp, Steven, 1985. *Personification and the Sublime: Milton to Coleridge*. Cambridge, MA: Harvard University Press.

Kramer, Lawrence, 1995. *Classical Music and Postmodern Knowledge*. Berkeley: University of California Press.

Lacan, Jacques, 1977. *Ecrits: A Selection*. Trans. Alan Sheridan. London: Tavistock Publications.

Ladner, Gerhart B., 1979. 'Medieval and Modern Understanding of Symbolism: A Comparison'. *Speculum* 54, 223–56.

Langland, William, 1994. *Piers Plowman: The C-text*. Ed. Derek Pearsall. Exeter, Devon: University of Exeter Press.

Lawrence, 1936. *Phoenix*. Ed. Edward D. McDonald. London: Heinemann.

Leer, David van, 1985. 'Hester's Labyrinth: Transcendental Rhetoric in Puritan Boston' in *New Essays on The Scarlet Letter*. Ed. Michael J. Colacurcio. Cambridge: Cambridge University Press.

Lewis, C. S., 1936. *The Allegory of Love*. New York: Oxford University Press.

Lukács, Georg, 1978. *Theory of the Novel*. Trans. Anna Bostock. London: Merlin Press.

Madsen, Deborah L., 1994. *Re-reading Allegory: A Narrative Approach to Genre*. New York: St Martin's Press.

Mâle, Emile,1913. *The Gothic Image: Religious Art in France of the Thirteenth Century*. Trans. Dora Nussey. New York: Harper.

Manning, John, 2002. *The Emblem*. London: Reaktion Books.

Maravall, José Antonio, 1986. *Culture of the Baroque*. Trans. Terry Cochran. Minneapolis: University of Minnesota Press.

Marlowe, Christopher, 1995. *Doctor Faustus and Other Plays*. Ed. David Bevington and Eric Rasmussen. Oxford: Oxford University Press.

Maresca, Thomas, E., 1993. 'Personification vs. Allegory', in Kevin L. Cope (ed.), *Enlightening Allegory*. New York: AMS Press.

Martin, John Rupert, 1971. *Baroque*. Harmondsworth: Penguin.

Marx, Karl, 1976. *Capital*, vol. 1. Ed. Ernest Mandel. Trans. Ben Fowkes. Harmondsworth: Penguin.

Matthiessen, F. O., 1941. *American Renaissance*. London: Oxford University Press.

McQuillan, Martin, 2001. *Paul de Man*. London: Routledge.

Melville, Herman, 1967. *Moby-Dick: An Authoritative Text*. Eds Harrison Hayford and Hershel Parker. New York: W. W. Norton.

Mendelsohn, Leatrice, 1992. 'Saturnian Allusions in Bronzino's Allegory' in *Saturn from Antiquity to the Renaissance*. Eds Massimo Ciavolella and Amilcare A. Iannucci. Toronto: Dovehouse.

Miller, J. Hillis, 1985. *The Linguistic Moment: From Wordsworth to Stevens*. Princeton: Princeton University Press.

——, 1989. '"Reading" Part of a Paragraph in *Allegories of Reading*' in *Reading Paul de Man Reading*. Ed. Lindsay Waters and Wlad Godzich. Minneapolis: University of Minnesota Press.

——, 1990. 'Narrative' in *Critical Terms for Literary Study*. Eds Frank Lentricchia and Thomas McLaughlin. Chicago: University of Chicago Press.

Milton, John, 1930. *Poetical Works*. Ed. H. C. Beeching. Oxford: Oxford University Press.

Minnis, A. J., Scott, A. B. and Wallace, David, 1988. *Medieval Literary Theory and Criticism* Oxford: Clarendon Press.

Mitchell, W. J. T., 1986. *Iconology, Text, Ideology*. Chicago: University of Chicago Press.

Monelle, Raymond, 1992. *Linguistics and Semiotics in Music*. Camberwell: Harwood Academic Publishers.

——, 2000. *The Sense of Music: Semiotic Essays*. Princeton: University of Princeton Press.

Moseley, Charles, 1989. *A Century of Emblems: An Introductory Anthology*. Aldershot: Scolar Press.

Mosley, David L., 1994. 'Gustav Mahler's "Ich Bin der Welt Gekommen" as Song and Symphonic Movement: Abduction, Over-coding and Catachresis' in *Allegory Old and New in Literature, the Fine Arts, Music and Theatre, and its Continuity in Culture*. Eds. Marlies Kronegger and Anna-Teresa Tymieniecka. Dordrecht: Kluwer Academic Publishers.

Murrin, Michael, 1969. *The Veil of Allegory*. Chicago: University of Chicago Press.

Newhauser, Richard, 2000. *The Early History of Greed*. Cambridge: Cambridge University Press.

Nietzsche, Friedrich, 1990. *On the Genealogy of Morals and Ecce Homo*. Trans. Walter Kaufmann. London: Vintage.

Nochlin, Linda, 1971. *Realism*. Harmondsworth: Penguin.

Owens, Craig, 1992. *Beyond Recognition: Representation, Power and Culture*. Berkeley: University of California Press.

Panofsky, Erwin, 1970. *Meaning in the Visual Arts*. Harmondsworth: Penguin.

——, 1972. *Studies in Iconology: Humanistic Themes in the Art of the Renaissance*. New York: Harper & Row.

Parker, Deborah, 2000. *Bronzino: Renaissance Painter as Poet*. Cambridge: Cambridge University Press.

Paxson, James J., 1994. *The Poetics of Personification*. Cambridge: Cambridge University Press.

Peirce, Charles S., 1977. *Semiotic and Significs: The Corrrespondence between Charles S. Peirce and Victoria Lady Welby*. Eds Charles S. Hardwick and James Cook. Bloomington: Indiana University Press.

Penny, Nicholas, 1986. *Reynolds*. London: Royal Academy of Arts.

Pépin, Jean, 1958. *Mythe et Allégorie*. Paris: Aubier.

Plaks, Andrew, 1976. *Archetype and Allegory in The Dream of the Red Chamber*. Princeton: Princeton University Press.

Plato, 1955. *Republic*. Trans. H. Lee. Harmondsworth: Penguin.

Poirion, Daniel, 1999. 'Mask and Allegorical Personification' in *Re-reading Allegory: Essays in Memory of Daniel Poirion*. *Yale French Studies* 95, 13–32.

Proust, Marcel, 2003. *A la recherche de temps perdu*. Paris: Librairie Gallimard, 4 vols.

Quilligan, Maureen, 1979. *The Language of Allegory: Defining the Genre*. Ithaca NY: Cornell University Press.

Rapaport, Herman, 1983. *Milton and the Postmodern*. Lincoln: University of Nebraska Press.

Reynolds, Barbara, 1962. *Dante's Paradiso*. Harmondsworth: Penguin.

Richards, I. A., 1936. *The Philosophy of Rhetoric*. Cambridge: Cambridge University Press.

Riffaterre, Michael, 1985. 'Prosopopoeia' in Peter Brooks, Shoshana Felman and J. Hillis Miller (eds), *The Lesson of Paul de Man* (*Yale French Studies* no. 69). New Haven CT: Yale University Press.

Rivers, Christopher, 1994. *Face Value: Physiognomical Thought and the Legible Body in Marivaux, Lavater, Balzac, Gautier, and Zola*. Madison: University of Wisconsin Press.

Roberts, Julian, 1982. *Walter Benjamin*. London: Macmillan.

Robertson, D. W., 1962. *A Preface to Chaucer*. Princeton: Princeton University Press.

Rosen, Charles, 1988. 'The Ruins of Walter Benjamin' in *On Walter Benjamin: Critical Essays and Recollections*. Ed. Gary Smith. Cambridge, MA: MIT Press.

Ruskin, John, 1904. *The Complete Works of John Ruskin vol. 10*. Eds E. T. Cook and Alexander Wedderburn. London: George Allen.

——, 1906. *The Complete Works of John Ruskin vol. 24*. Eds E. T. Cook and Alexander Wedderburn. London: George Allen.

Russell, J. Stephen, 1988. *Allegoresis: The Craft of Allegory in Medieval Literature*. New York: Garland.

Salter, Elisabeth and Pearsall, Derek, 1967. *Piers Plowman*. London: Edward Arnold.

Samuels, Robert, 1995. *Mahler's Sixth Symphony: A Study in Musical Semiotics.* Cambridge: Cambridge University Press.

Scholem, Gershom, 1988. 'Walter Benjamin and his Angel' in Smith 1988, pp. 51–89.

Schopenhauer, Arthur, 1969. *The World as Will and Representation*. Trans. E. J. Payne. New York: Dover.

Schlegel, Friedrich, 1971. *Friedrich Schlegel's Lucinde and The Fragments*. Trans. Peter Firchow. London: Oxford University Press.

Seznec, Jean, 1953. *The Survival of the Pagan Gods*. Princeton: Princeton University Press.

Shakespeare, William, 1997. *The Norton Shakespeare: Based on the Oxford Edition*. Ed. Stephen Greenblatt. New York: W. W. Norton.

Shelley, Mary, 1985. *Frankenstein*. Ed. Maurice Hindle. Harmondsworth: Penguin.

Shelley, Percy Bysshe, 2002. *Shelley's Poetry and Prose*. Eds. Donald H. Reiman and Neil Fraistat. New York: Norton.

Sheridan, Richard Brinsley, 1979. *The Rivals*. Ed. Elizabeth Duthie. London: Benn.

Simson, Otto von, 1962. *The Gothic Cathedral: Origins of Gothic Architecture and the Medieval Concept of Order*. New York: Bollingen Series.

Sinclair, J. D., 1948a. *Dante's Inferno*. Oxford: Oxford University Press.

——, 1948b. *Dante's Purgatorio*. Oxford: Oxford University Press.

Smith, Gary, 1988. *On Walter Benjamin: Critical Essays and Recollections*. Cambridge, MA: MIT Press.

Socrates, 1955. *Republic*. Trans. H. D. P. Lee. Harmondsworth: Penguin.

Spenser, Edmund, 1978. *The Faerie Queene*. Harmondsworth: Penguin.

Spivak, Gayatri Chakravorty, 1999. *A Critique of Postcolonial Reason: Towards a History of the Vanishing Present*. Cambridge, MA: Harvard University Press.

Tambling, Jeremy, 2003a. 'Monomania of a Whale Hunter: "Moby-Dick"' in *English* 52, 101–23.

——, 2003b. *Wong Kar-wai's Happy Together*. Hong Kong: University of Hong Kong Press.

——, 2004. *Allegory and the Work of Melancholy: The Late Medieval and Shakespeare.* Amsterdam: Rodopi.

——, 2007. *Madmen and Other Survivors: Reading Lu Xun's Fiction*. Hong Kong: University of Hong Kong Press.

——, 2008. *Going Astray: Dickens and London*. London: Longman.

Tasso, Torquato, 1987. *Jerusalem Delivered*. Trans. and ed. Ralph Nash. Detroit: Wayne State University Press.

Teskey, Gordon, 1996. *Allegory and Violence*. Ithaca NY: Cornell University Press.

Touissant, Hélène, 1978. *Gustave Courbet, 1817–1877*. London: The Arts Council.

Tourneur, Cyril, 1978. *The Plays of Cyril Tourneur*. Ed. George Parfitt. Cambridge: Cambridge University Press.

Tuve, Rosamund, 1964. *Allegorical Imagery: Some Mediaeval Books and Their Posterity.* Princeton: Princeton University Press.

Van Reijen, Willem, 1992. 'Labyrinth and Ruin: The Return of the Baroque in Post-modernity' in *Theory, Culture & Society* 9, 1–26.

Virgil, 1999. *Aeneid*. Trans. H. Rushton Fairclough. Cambridge, MA: Loeb Library, Harvard University Press.

Watson, Elizabeth See, 1993. *Achille Bocchi and the Emblem Book as Symbolic Form*. Cambridge: Cambridge University Press.

Webster, John, 1966. *The White Devil*. Ed. Elizabeth M. Brennan. London: Ernest Benn.

Wheeler, Kathleen, ed., 1984. *German Aesthetic and Literary Criticism: The Romantic Ironists and Goethe*. Cambridge: Cambridge University Press.

White, Hayden, 1987. *The Content of the Form: Narrative Discourse and Historical Representation*. Baltimore: Johns Hopkins University Press.

——, 1999. *Figural Realism: Studies in the Mimesis Effect*. Baltimore: Johns Hopkins University Press.

Whitman, Jon, 1987. *Allegory: The Dynamics of an Ancient and Medieval Technique*. Cambridge, MA: Harvard University Press.

——, 2000. *Interpretation and Allegory: Antiquity to the Modern Period*. Leiden: Brill.

Wind, Edgar, 1967. *Pagan Mysteries in the Renaissance*. Harmondsworth: Penguin.

Wohlfarth, Irving, 1988. 'Resentment Begins at Home, Walter Benjamin and the University' in *On Walter Benjamin: Critical Essays and Recollections*. Ed. Gary Smith. Cambridge, MA: MIT Press.

Woodfield, Richard, ed., 2001. *Art History as Cultural History; Warburg's Projects* Amsterdam: G and B Arts.

Woodfield, Richard, and Sedlmayr, Hans, 2001. *Framing Formalism: Riegl's Work/ Commentary*. Amsterdam: G and B Arts International.

Wordsworth, William, 1925. *Literary Criticism*. Ed. Nowell C Smith. Oxford: Oxford University Press.

——, 1936. *Poetical Works*. Ed. Thomas Hutchinson. Rev. Ernest de Selincourt. Oxford: Oxford University Press.

——, 1971. *The Prelude: A Parallel Text*. Ed. J. C. Maxwell. Harmondsworth: Penguin.

Yeats, William Butler, 1961. *Essays and Introductions*. London: Macmillan.

Index